60

A procession of persons associated with Christmas wends its way through the pages of folklore and history. See page 22 for a more complete explanation

1001 𝕮hristmas
Facts and Fancies

By
ALFRED CARL HOTTES

Illustrated by
LINDSAY LOCKERBY FIELD

NEW YORK
A. T. DE LA MARE COMPANY, INC.
1946

Republished by Omnigraphics • Penobscot Building • Detroit • 1990

First Edition
Copyright, October, 1937
Second Printing, November, 1937
Third Printing, November, 1938

Second Edition
Copyright, August, 1944
Second Printing, 1946

A. T. De La Mare Company, Inc.

New York, N. Y.

Library of Congress Cataloging-in-Publication Data

Hottes, Alfred Carl, 1891–1955.
  1001 Christmas facts and fancies / by Alfred Carl Hottes :
illustrated by Lindsay Lockerby Field.
      p.   cm.
  Reprint. Originally published: 2nd ed. New York : A.T. De La Mare,
1946.
  ISBN 1-55888-858-6 (alk. paper)
  1. Christmas.   I. Title.   II. Title: One thousand one Christmas
facts and fancies.   III. Title: One thousand and one Christmas facts
and fancies.
GT4985.H6   1990
394.2'68282—dc20   89-63110
                                                                          CIP

♾

This book is printed on acid-free paper meeting the ANSI Z39.48 Standard. The
infinity symbol that appears above indicates that the paper in this book meets
that standard.

Table of Contents

5

AUTHOR'S FOREWORD

CHRISTMAS—the word itself bespeaks a kindlier feeling toward our fellow men !

It is the author's earnest wish that every one who reads this book may be kindled with some of the joy that was his when he came in contact with some of the people in and from other lands and obtained the fascinating stories concerning each individual group as related in these pages. In addition, the chapters reveal inspiring facts and fancies gathered over a period of years from personal experience and from obscure books—all bound to stir up many thoughts which will make of Christmas an ever-new holiday.

Use the index freely. It contains hundreds of entries one would scarcely believe to be associated with Christmas.

The teacher will find the book helpful as a source of authoritative pageant suggestions. The homemaker will enjoy the new ideas for home fun, decorations and foods. The craftsman can try his hand at the suggested Christmas cards and decorations. The clubwoman will find the book a freshet in planning her part in the Christmas program. Children will enjoy the Christmas tales as retold from these pages.

The writer is indebted to the many friends who willingly contributed information from the store of their Christmas

memories.   Also to Pearl Chase, Chairman Community
Christmas Committee, Santa Barbara, Cal. for many excellent
stories; to the Institute of Immigrant Welfare for
fascinating stories of foreign observance; to Phyllis Hall
Stevens for constant advice and inspiration in the compilation
of the subject matter; to Cora M. Fichtl who has edited
the vast amount of material and condensed it into the allotted
space; and to Lindsay L. Field who caught the spirit of the
text and translated the ideas into splendid scratchboard
sketches.   Mr. Field was with the author during the gathering
of much of the material for this book.

Let's hope for a happier, a more meaningful Christmas
with each succeeding year.

ALFRED CARL HOTTES

▲ ▲ ▲

DEDICATION

I dedicate this book to my literary father—

ALPHEUS THEODORE DE LA MARE

—my friend and guide during the twenty-three years
of my writing life.

ALFRED CARL HOTTES

THE STORY OF CHRISTMAS

I T IS a long road back to the first Christmas. The route is not direct, nor free from obstacles, nor is it clearly marked. Many will stand at the crossroads and beckon us down strange and confusing byways.

Without looking back to the pages of legend and history, we are inclined to make the Christmas story read too simply. If someone were to ask you, "What is Christmas?" would you answer:

"Christmas is the celebration of the birth of Jesus, our Saviour, on December 25. At this time gifts are freely distributed and we tell children that they come from a mythical Santa Claus—a pleasant and harmless old fellow who comes with reindeer from the North Pole and descends the chimney to place Christmas gifts in stockings and on a highly decorated tree."

We give but small thought to the gospel story; we care less that there is controversy over the exact day and year. We shun the idea that all these observances are not of historical Christian origin.

INTERESTING WHETHER FACT OR FANTASY

However, should we care to take some of the byways of thought we would be sure to find facts hidden beneath fiction. We hesitate to say which statements are true and which are not. Let's not make an immediate two-item classification—the true and the false. Let's think of these historical facts and these fancies as traditions of Christmas—a part of our storehouse of culture—interesting whether true or fictitious.

Christmas is, indeed, the celebration of the birth of Jesus, the Holy Babe of Bethlehem, who grew into the Christ, the founder and center of a religion which proclaims one of the foremost philosophies of human conduct; perhaps it is the destined religion for the world.

The roots of Christmas observance, however, go deeply into the folklore of the Druids, Scandinavians, Romans, and Egyptians. What we may read of Christmas in ancient days finds its full flower in the past and present customs of our ancestral homes in Europe. There is not an American home that does not color its Christmas with some European observances—gift-giving, trees, greenery, food, games, or ritual.

Christmas is today's name for the *Yule*, or *Jul* of the northern Europeans, the *Noel* of the French, the *Noche-buena* of the Spanish, the *Weihnachten* of the Germans, and the name given by the Roman Catholic Church to the *Christ Mass*, the feast in honor of the Nativity of Jesus. Sometimes Christmas is written "Xmas" because "X" is the Greek equivalent of "ch," and, therefore, is taken to represent the word "Christ."

BEGINNINGS

Since earliest times many of the inhabitants of the world have observed that there is a period during the year when "the days begin to lengthen and the cold begins to strengthen," and others express it, "when the earth began to waken under the kiss of light, when new hopes rose in frozen hearts." It was the Winter solstice when the sun, parent of fertility, began to rise over the world with renewed vigor and power after having been at the lowest point in the heavens. Some old opinions were that in Winter the sun actually stood still for forty days, based, no doubt, on the presence of the Midnight Sun. The northern people considered the sun as a wheel which alternately threw its glow upon the earth and away from it. This sun wheel was known as *hweol* and, perhaps, from this was derived our word "yule."

FESTIVAL OF LIGHTS

To the Jews this period was the Festival of Lights or Dedication, called *Hanukkah* or *Chanuckah*. Jewish history relates that in 165 B.C. a large force of Maccabees met and vanquished an army of Syrians. Judas Maccabeus entered Jerusalem with his army and found it a place of desolation. Maccabeus began the work of purification and on the 25th day (note the similarity to the 25th of December) of Kislev it was finished and a sacred light was lighted. In their destruction of the temple the sacred oil was practically exhausted, but they did find a jar which they judged would burn for one day. Miraculously, it lasted eight days. Therefore each year the Jews decree that the eight days previous to December 25 be celebrated.

The first night two tapers are lighted. One is known as the torch. The second night a third candle is added and so one for each night until the eighth day. That is why a true Jewish *Hanukkah* candelabrum has nine arms. Even to this day some of the orthodox Jews make their own candles from beeswax, for they dislike the manufactured ones.

Doesn't this impel one to look more deeply into what Judaism really stands for?

WEREWOLVES AND VALKYRIE

In Scandinavian countries great fires were kindled to defy the Frost King. These early peoples gathered around the fires to warm themselves and to quaff great horns of mead, looking forward to the breaking of the ice when their ships might again embark. They spent their time telling strange stories and considered the period as being the time of the longest nights, when men were transformed at will to savage beasts, Werewolves—fierce, ravishing, and thirsty for blood;

also Valkyrie, maidens who searched for souls and conveyed them to Valhalla. These strange spirits were heard in the winds and in the passage of birds. They are familiar to us in the Wagnerian operas of the Nibelungen Ring—*Das Rheingold, Die Walküre, Siegfried*, and *Die Götterdämmerung* (The Twilight of the Gods).

DRUID MYSTERIES

The Druids observed this season in their great roofless temples which are ranked as one of the Wonders of the World. At Stonehenge and Avebury in England, torches blazed and strange ceremonies took place dealing with the cutting of the cabalistic Mistletoe. (See page 149 for a more complete description.) At Carnac another marvelous sanctuary was constructed. Thousands of white columns are grouped in three great avenues open to the sky. We wonder just what was the belief of the Druids who left mute evidence of a stirring religion.

ROMAN SATURNALIA

Two holidays, the Brumalia and Juvenalia, of ancient Rome were merged to form one great celebration in honor of the Italian deity Saturnus,* who taught the arts of agriculture and was dedicated to welcoming the germinating impulse of Nature. It was called Saturnalia and is older than Roman recorded history. These celebrations lasted throughout the years until purified by the Christians.

It was during the reign of Saturnus that peace, happiness, and innocence abounded and was, indeed, the Golden Age of Italy. Gradually things went from bad to worse and many of the original purposes were transformed into unrestrained orgies.

The Saturnalia was not a day but a season of celebration

---

*It is interesting to read in Brand's *Popular Antiquities* that the feast was instituted in honor of Noah, the real Saturnus. The social equalities of the Saturnalia expressed the friendly family relationships of the Ark.

Gayety prevailed as the Romans celebrated the Saturnalia with feasting, songs and processions. The Saturnalia became the forerunner of the Christmas celebrations of Christian days from December 17 to 24; then on January 1 came the Calends of January and both periods were given up to revelry.

In early Roman days a pontiff stood in front of Saturn's temple and exclaimed, "Saturnalia! Io Saturnalia!" The word spread from mouth to ear along the Forum and through the streets. The fetters of convention became loosened. The people gave themselves up to a wild joy. During this period the people and the senate were expected to present New Year's gifts to the emperors. It is related that Augustus had a nocturnal vision requiring that the people annually present money to him. When Caligula came to the throne he appeared on the porch of his palace on the Calends of January and received gifts of all descriptions.

The period was characterized by "processions, singing, lighting candles, adorning the house with Laurel and green trees, giving presents; the men dressed as women or masqueraded in the hides of animals."* Rich and poor were equal and there was no distinction between free man and slave.

The courts were closed and no one was convicted of a crime. Slaves mocked their masters and were allowed to wear a pointed cap as the sign of rank, but today employed as the sign of a fool. The free-born Romans celebrated less boisterously by giving gifts and it is to the merriment and bestowing of favors at the Saturnalia time that we owe our common Christmas practice.

When Augustine and his fellow missionaries landed in Britain 592 A.D. they found December a festive month. By 742, Pope Zacharius had sent out an edict prohibiting the participation of Christians in the heathenish customs of the season.

Egyptian Holiday

Even the early Egyptians celebrated this Midwinter festival. They claimed that Horus, son of Isis, was born at

*Quoted from Parisiis by Alexander Tille, *Yule and Christmas.*

the close of December. See page 155 for notes on the use of
the Palm as a Midwinter symbol.

MITHRAS AND FEAST OF SOL INVICTUS

The followers of Mithras called this period the Feast of *sol
invictus*, representing the time of victory of light over darkness.
Mithras, as a divinity, was worshiped in the centuries immediately preceding and following Christianity so that the idea
of Mithraism fitted nicely to the idea of Christ being the Sun
or Light of the World and the religion and practices soon
merged into the early Christian customs.

WHEN CHRIST WAS BORN

The definite date of the birth of Christ has been fixed
by church councils who gained their knowledge from the
historical records of that period. The people of Christ's
day did not regard Jesus as the Messiah of God from birth
but merely thought of Him as becoming the Christian's God
when He was 30 years old, at the time when the Holy Spirit
descended on Him at the baptism in the Jordan. St. Mark
and St. John both begin with that event as being the first one
of importance in Christ's career. The principal holy days in
the early church were: Christmas (the birth of Christ), the
Epiphany (the coming of the Magi to Bethlehem), Good
Friday (day of crucifixion), Easter (day of resurrection) and
Ascension Day followed by Pentecost (when the Holy
Spirit descended upon the infant church with tongues of fire).

Christendom did not begin to date its years from the
birth of Christ until almost 550 A. D., when the method was
introduced by Dionysius Exiguus, a learned monk of Rome.

In the third century the western countries came to think
of Christ as a God from birth, each of the four gospel nar-
ratives testifying to this. This thought spread through the
Mediterranean regions but never reached the Far East.

To the early church Christmas from the start "bore the
mark of being of Roman creation." Between December 25

and the Roman Calends were twelve days which gradually came to be revered as Twelve Holy Days. Centuries later they were called Twelve Nights. Days were not reckoned by the early Germans but nights were.

St. John Chrysostom, writing in 386, says that Julian made an extensive investigation of the correct birthday of Christ and found that the Western churches all considered December 25 as the Nativity date, although the Eastern churches claimed January 6. There were scattering opinions that the birth of Christ should be observed on April 20, May 20, March 29, and September 29.

St. Chrysostom writes, "They called this December 25, the Birthday of the Invincible One (Mithras); but who was so invincible as the Lord? They call it the Birthday of the Solar Disc; but Christ is the Son of Righteousness."

Julian, basing his opinion on the majority, went ahead and decreed December 25 as the Nativity date for Christ. This was readily accepted by most churches because it had always been a holiday of some sort, as we have shown above —the Winter solstice, the Jewish Feast of Lights, the Roman Saturnalia, and the Scandinavian Yule. Nevertheless, the Armenians did not accept December 25 until after World War I. During these centuries they retained January 6 as the Christmas celebration time.

It is difficult to give definite references for the sources of the preceding account of the history of Christmas, but I am indebted to the following:

Alexander Tille, *Yule and Christmas.*

A splendid story in Munsey's Magazine by Henry J. Markland.

William S. Walsh, *Curiosities of Popular Customs.*

THE GOSPEL STORY

"AND it came to pass in those days, that there went out a decree from Caesar Augustus, that all the world should be taxed. And all went to be taxed, every one into his own city.

"And Joseph also went up from Galilee, out of the city of Nazareth, into Judaea, unto the city of David, which is called Bethlehem, to be taxed with Mary his espoused wife, being great with child. And so it was, that, while they were there, the days were accomplished that she should be delivered. And she brought forth her firstborn son, and wrapped him in swaddling clothes, and laid him in a manger; because there was no room for them in the inn.

"And there were in the same country shepherds abiding in the field, keeping watch over their flock by night. And, lo, the angel of the Lord came upon them, and the glory of the Lord shone round about them; and they were sore afraid. And the angel said unto them, Fear not: for, behold, I bring you good tidings of great joy, which shall be to all people. For unto you is born this day, in the city of David, a Saviour, which is Christ the Lord. And this shall be a sign unto you: Ye shall find the babe wrapped in swaddling clothes, lying in a manger. And suddenly there was with the angel a multitude of the heavenly host, praising God, and saying, Glory to God in the highest, and on earth peace, good will toward men.

"And it came to pass, as the angels were gone away from them into heaven, the shepherds said one to another, Let us now go even unto Bethlehem, and see this thing which is

Ancient woodcut showing the Nativity scene

come to pass, which the Lord hath made known unto us. And they came with haste, and found Mary, and Joseph, and the babe lying in a manger. And when they had seen it they made known abroad the saying which was told them concerning this child. And all they that heard it wondered at those things which were told them by the shepherds.

"But Mary kept all these things, and pondered them in her heart."—*Luke 2:1-19.*

"Now when Jesus was born in Bethlehem of Judaea, in the days of Herod the king, behold, there came wise men from the east to Jerusalem, saying, Where is he that is born King of the Jews ? for we have seen his star in the east, and are come to worship him.

"When Herod the king had heard these things, he was troubled, and all Jerusalem with him. And when he had gathered all the chief priests and scribes of the people together, he demanded of them where Christ should be born. And they said unto him, In Bethlehem of Judaea: for thus it is written by the prophet; And thou Bethlehem, in the land of Juda, art not the least among the princes of Juda: for out of thee shall come a Governor, that shall rule my people Israel.

"Then Herod, when he had privily called the wise men, inquiried of them diligently what time the star appeared. And he sent them to Bethlehem; and said, Go and search diligently for the young child; and when ye have found him, bring me word again, that I may come and worship him also.

"When they had heard the king, they departed: and, lo, the star, which they saw in the east, went before them, till it came and stood over where the young child was. When they saw the star, they rejoiced with exceeding great joy. And when they were come into the house, they saw the young child with Mary his mother, and fell down, and worshipped him: and when they had opened their treasures, they presented unto him gifts; gold, and frankincense, and myrrh.

Albrecht Dürer made this interesting woodcut of the stable showing
the Holy Family, the shepherds, and the Heavenly Host

"And being warned of God in a dream that they should not return to Herod, they departed into their own country another way. And when they were departed, behold, the angel of the Lord appeareth to Joseph in a dream, saying, Arise, and take the young child and his mother, and flee into Egypt, and be thou there until I bring thee word: for Herod will seek the young child, to destroy him. When he arose, he took the young child and his mother by night, and departed into Egypt."—*Matthew 2:1-14.*

THE PALACE AND THE STABLE

"It was the seven hundred fifty-third year since the founding of Rome. Gaius Julius Caesar Octavianus Augustus was living in a palace of the Palatine Hill, busily engaged upon the task of ruling his empire.

"In a little village of distant Syria, Mary the wife of Joseph the Carpenter, was tending her little boy, born in a stable of Bethlehem.

"This is a strange world.

"Before long the palace and the stable were to meet in open combat.

"And the stable was to emerge victorious."—Hendrik Willem Van Loon, *The Story of Mankind.*

PERSONALITIES OF CHRISTMAS

A LONG procession of persons associated with Christmas marches through the pages of folklore and history. They throng upon the scene from all nations of the world. A few of them are shown in our frontispiece where they entwine themselves with the Manger scene as a central climax. Starting from the base of the picture, we see the Arch-Druid, holding aloft a Mistletoe bough, then the Romans celebrating the free-and-easy Saturnalia, leading to the venerable Jew holding his nine-branched candelabrum. The Wise Men, or Magi, kneel at the feet of the Holy Babe hovered by Mary, Joseph and an angel. Two reverential shepherds stand by. At the upper left, the conventional Americanized Santa enters the picture in his sleigh and at his side stands his prototype St. Nicholas, the beloved saint of childhood, maidens, merchants, and the patron of cities too numerous to mention here. Below him we see the ancient Befana, for whom Italian children wait in eagerness on Epiphany. Riding an ass and accompanied by the Father Star, we see Tante Aria, the lesser known of the gift-bearers. Crouching in the corner we see the dreaded werewolf and beneath it, the imp of the Scandinavian attic, Jule-nissen.

Each of these personalities will be discussed in their proper time or place in our book but in the pages which immediately follow you will hear the strange tales of the Wise Men, the pathetic story of Befana, known as Baboushka to those of Russian antecedents; then there is mention of that long series of satellites which have attached themselves to the legends of St. Nicholas. And last, St. Christopher and Tante Aria step briefly into our story.

22

The Wise Men from the East

Who were these Wise Men, these sages, and what wisdom did they have ? From whence in the East did they come and where did they go ? Do we know their names ? To these questions the Bible gives us but scant answers. Legend, however, has clothed their lives with much to stir our fancies.

Before discussing the fascinating tales, let us again read the second chapter of the Gospel according to St. Matthew:

"Now when Jesus was born in Bethlehem of Judaea, in the days of Herod the king, behold, there came wise men from the east to Jerusalem, saying, Where is he that is born King of the Jews ? for we have seen his star in the east, and we

It is usual to consider that there were only three Wise Men, because of the three gifts—gold, frankincense and myrrh

are come to worship him. When Herod the king had heard these things, he was troubled, and all Jerusalem with him. And he sent them to Bethlehem and said, go and search diligently for the child. When they had heard the king they departed; and, lo, the star, which they saw in the east, went before them, till it came and stood over where the child was. And when they were come into the house, they saw the young child with Mary his mother, and fell down, and worshipped him: and when they had opened their treasures, they presented unto him gifts; gold, and frankincense, and myrrh."

This is all we really know about the Wise Men.

Epiphany or Twelfth Night

We believe that they appeared to the Christ Child on January 6, on what is known as the Twelfth Night, or the Epiphany, as designated by the church.

They are called the Magi (pronounced may'-jy), which was a sect of priests among the ancient Medes and Persians, celebrated for their enchantments, their learning as astrologers, and for their great wisdom. It is from the Magi that we have the word "magic" given to the art of enchantment.

Names of the Wise Men

We do not know how many Wise Men there were, nor their names. St. Augustine and St. Chrysostom say there were twelve, but common church tradition names three, no doubt because of the three gifts. Melchior, King of Arabia, 60 years old, brought a casket of gold in the form of a shrine, for he came from a country where the soil is ruddy. Gaspar, or Caspar, King of Tarsus, land of merchants, is often represented as a beardless youth of 20; he is said to have brought myrrh in a gold-mounted horn. Balthasar, King of Ethiopia or Saba, land of spices, 40 years old, reputedly of the black race, brought frankincense in a censer- or thurible-shaped jar. Each of these gifts was considered symbolic or prophetic of what Jesus was to become—gold for a king, frankincense for a high priest, and myrrh for the great physician. In return for their gold they are said to have received the gift of charity and spiritual wealth. For their frankincense they attained perfect faith. For their myrrh they enjoyed perfect truth and meekness. The map on the end papers at the front of this book shows their legendary journey.

Mary presented them a linen band in which the Christ Child was wrapped. On presenting the gifts to the Christ Child they were given a small box.* Inside was a stone which meant that faith should abide in them as firm as a rock. Believing that the stone was of no value they cast it into a well. Whereupon fire from heaven descended into the well. The Wise Men were amazed, feeling that there was some great and holy meaning. So they carried fire back to their countries and placed it in a magnificent church, where it is kept constantly burning and often worshipped by the people.

Journey Predicted

Legend even tells a story of a certain nation near the ocean in the extreme East which possessed a writing ascribed to one with the name Seth, and it would seem that the Star of Bethlehem and the journey of the Wise Men was something which had been in prospect for generations. The quaint account reads as follows:†

"Twelve of the learned men of that country * * * had disposed themselves to watch for that Star; and when any of them died, his son or one of his kindred * * * was appointed in his place. These, therefore, year after year, after the threshing out of the corn, ascended into a certain high mountain, having in it a certain cave, most grateful and pleasant, with fountains, into which, ascending and bathing themselves, they prayed and praised GOD in silence three days. And thus they did, generation after generation, watching ever, lest peradventure that Star of beatitude should arise

*Hackwood, Frederick W. *Christlore* published 1902.
†Sedding, Edmund. *Once a Week*, December 24, 1864.

upon themselves until it should appear descending on the mountain having within itself the form of a man child, and above the similitude of a cross: and it spoke to them, and taught them, and commanded them that they should go to Judaea. And journeying thither for space of 2 years, neither food nor drink failed in their vessels."

Other stories relate that the Wise Men made the journey in twelve days and that they needed neither rest nor refreshment as the journey seemed to be of only one day's length.

When the Kings returned to their own country they decided to distribute their goods to the poor and were baptized. After that they went about in mean attire, preaching the Christ-King, the Prince of Peace. Legend continues that they were martyred in India for their faith.

The Three Kings of Cologne

Three hundred years later their bodies were transferred to Constantinople by Empress Helena, mother of Constantine the Great. After the first crusade their bodies were moved to Milan and finally to the Cologne Cathedral by Emperor Barbarossa. Perhaps you too have visited the magnificent Cologne Cathedral and seen the costly shrine built by the Archbishop of Cologne who adorned the relics with jewels and deposited them in the cathedral, where they still remain. They are now called The Three Kings of Cologne.

Their names for years were engraved on rings used as charms especially against cramps, and anything that touched the skulls of the Three Kings was believed to have the power of preventing accidents so that they became the patron saints of travelers.

In Czechoslovakia the letters C, M, B are written over the doors of the houses at Epiphany, representing Caspar, Melchior, and Balthasar.

In Spain, there is an interesting custom of going to meet the Wise Men, for in that country it is they who bring the presents to children. (See page 277.)

La Befana—The Ageless Wanderer

In a lonely cottage near the great highway on which caravans of camels were constantly passing, there lived an old, old lady called La Befana. Many, many years ago, how many she could not tell, she had journeyed to this spot to forget a child and a husband, both of whom were taken by a plague. Memories are not matters of distance—nor yet of time—and could we have looked into her tiny window we would have seen her frequently kneeling before a chest containing what you and I would hardly have thought worth cherishing.

La Befana always thought that it was best for her to tend to her own problems of life and not interfere with others. She liked to sit long hours and wonder about the sky and the world of Nature. She seldom wondered about people, except about the ruler who she had heard would one day be born to be a king to rule men's hearts rather than to collect taxes for new follies. Daily she watched the horde of strangers pass her door but she never expected to find a friendly face.

On the evening of January sixth, over nineteen hundred years ago, La Befana was busy with her household duties—perhaps gathering wood, or cleaning house, or cooking her supper. At least she was very busy when a group of men stopped in front of her cottage and tried to engage her in conversation. They were foreigners and spoke to her principally in gesticulation. They seemed to be asking her where Bethlehem was. She couldn't remember anyone ever wondering about Bethlehem. In fact, she didn't know whether this was a city or a person.

Her interest was aroused when she saw that three of the men were dressed as kings, wearing magnificent robes and strange crowns. They said something about a baby which had been born in Bethlehem. They spoke of a star which had guided them each night, and she remembered how bright the sky had seemed the night before. She wished that she might go with them. But, was it not as well that she should tend to her own workaday affairs? And yet, was it not better to go? She did not like the idea of traveling at night and already it was becoming dark.

As she watched this long train of travelers disappearing over the horizon she tried to piece together what she thought they meant to tell her.

Soon a shepherd came by and asked her, "Are you not going to Bethlehem? Indeed, you will regret remaining at home without seeing the young King, the Son of God, who comes not as a royal personage but as a babe more humble than you or I. The word has spread through all the country-side that this King was born in a manger near an inn, for his parents are poor. It seems that the city is crowded with those who will pay their taxes and the innkeeper had no room for the Infant's parents—Joseph and Mary. Come with me and let us find the Babe together."

Now, indeed, La Befana was puzzled. Should she go? Or should she remain? She stood long in her doorway and thought. Yes, she would go; but not that night—she'd wait until morning.

When the darkness should have descended she noticed that the sky seemed to quiver with light so that it seemed to be moving. As she looked at the clouds they took form; they seemed like wings and faces. Could it have been a multitude of angels which filled the sky? This was indeed a phenomenal night. It rather frightened her and she considered that she would be far better off inside the house with the shades drawn to shut out this awesome resplendence, but even with her curtains pulled it was as though her eyes were closed but with a light so bright as to penetrate the lids. She could not sleep. No, something momentous had happened.

She rose. She had seen the costly gifts which the Three Kings were bringing to the Infant King and she remembered that the shepherd had regretted that he had so little to give— a bag of wool and a pretty stone which he had polished. She

"As she looked at the clouds they took form. The sky seemed to quiver with light. Could it have been a multitude of angels which filled the sky? This was indeed a phenomenal night"

thought of her treasures and went to the chest in the corner. It contained no gold, nor fragrant oils, it was true—just tiny mementos of her baby. Slowly she extracted from it a doll, made of straw. A tear came into her eye as she thought of parting with it. She looked again at the garment in which it was dressed—a piece of wool that she had worn at her own wedding. Now the doll was quite shabby, for years ago it had been fingered by chubby hands and caressed many times since by her wrinkled fingers. A smile spread over her face as she found once more the large seed which her baby had used as a ball. Should she take that, too? It was so common. Surely a King would have a ball of carved ivory. No, the shepherd had told her that this was a poor child like her own, and she clearly visualized the Infant King now holding the two toys. She wrapped them in some straw and placed them tenderly in a basket—as if they were made of fragile glass. She hastened to add a piece of cloth in which she had woven a border. She was quite proud of the way she had blended several plant dyes to produce a color she called purple. This, at least, would be fitting, for purple was the color of royalty. She also brought a bunch of mixed herbs fearing the Baby's mother would not be so well versed in the lore of the woods.

She could not wait till morning. She blew out her candle, latched her door, and was out on the road. Then she realized that she did not know which way to turn. All that she could remember was that both the Kings and the shepherd had disappeared over the hilltop. She hastened on and on, and strangely enough, the faster she ran, the stronger she felt. In fact, she seemed youthful this night. Now the too-bright star and the tremulous sky seemed less foreboding. "Soon it will be morning and I shall ask someone the way to Bethlehem," she thought.

But when day came, no one knew. On she wandered but that night there was no star to guide her. She knew now she had started too late. Oh, if she had only gone with the Wise Men or the shepherd!

And so La Befana has constantly traveled since that day, searching for the Christ Child, and her story cannot have a proper ending except to say that on Twelfth Night, the night when the Wise Men journeyed to Bethlehem, La Befana goes from house to house, looking into the faces of babies, bringing them gifts, in the hope that at last she will be presenting them to the right child.

La Befana is known to the Italians as the principal gift-bringer. Her name is derived from *Epiphania*, or Epiphany. Some of the Italian grown-ups, not having understood La Befana's true desires, have thought of her as a misshapen old woman and have held her up as a bugbear to frighten naughty children. They even put her image in their windows in the form of an ugly doll.

But the wise Italian children realize that La Befana is a good fairy. Because she was sweeping when the Wise Men passed through, she is always represented as carrying a broom. On Epiphany Eve, the children empty their pockets of all their cherished possessions and hang their clothes in a place where La Befana may find them and fill the pockets with confections, at least one tidbit for each pocket. Inasmuch as all children of Italy are not good, sometimes they find ashes or a birch rod protruding from a pocket, but this is a pleasant warning rather than an angry rebuke.

BABOUSHKA

In Russia, La Befana is known as Baboushka. The Russian version is that she misdirected the Wise Men when they asked the way and that she refused to shelter the Holy Family when they fled into Egypt. Now she journeys through Russia knocking at each door with her staff, entering and holding a candle close to each child's face as he lies sleeping. After slipping a toy under the pillow, she hastens away, still searching for the Babe of Bethlehem, whom she has never found.

The Story of St. Nicholas

Who is St. Nicholas? Is he Santa Claus, the mythical character of childhood? Or is he a real person? To write a biography of St. Nicholas is not like writing a life of the President of the United States. Many persons know for sure whether you are telling the truth about the President. The life of St. Nicholas is surrounded with fiction rather than fact. Nevertheless, it may be interesting to hear some of the tales relating to this great man.*

He was born in Patras, a city of Lycia, in Asia Minor. His father was a very wealthy bishop and his mother an extremely holy woman. At the earliest age, even in infancy, miraculous stories are told of manifestations of his extreme holiness. When most babies were considering food as the only thing of interest in life, Nicholas refused it except once on Wednesday and once on Friday. And as a boy, instead of being interested in the games and follies of childhood, he devoted his interests to the study and understanding of the Scriptures. Because of his remarkable babyhood and childhood he was accepted in later years as the patron saint of children.

Three Dowerless Maidens

Nicholas became very much concerned over the wealth of his parents so, as soon as they died, he decided that he would secretly give away all his money. He heard of a man who had three marriageable daughters, but he was very much worried because he had no dowry for them and so he was sorely tempted to sell them into slavery. Young Nicholas heard of this and one night he stole quietly to the home of the poor father and dropped a bag of gold in the open window. Soon after the eldest daughter was married. Then one night the second daughter also received a mysterious dowry. Therefore,

*The main facts of this story have been derived from an account by Charles Johnston, taken from two Greek manuscripts in the Zion Monastery in Myra.

The traditional appearance of St. Nicholas in Europe is as a bearded saint, riding on a white horse and carrying a basket of gifts for the good children and a bunch of birch rods with which to punish the naughty ones. (Derived from O. von Reinberg-Düringsfeld, *Traditions et Legendes de la Belgique*)

it was possible for her to marry advantageously. Now, only the third and youngest daughter was left. So the father decided to apprehend the giver of such munificent joy to his family. He hid each night near his third daughter's window. One night a figure approached and tossed in a bag of gold. The father seized him and found that he was none other than Nicholas. Nicholas asked the father to keep his secret.

This is only one of the many incidents dealing with his bestowing of dowries upon maidens. Other legends say that maidens need only pray to Nicholas and they will be assured of good husbands in the near future.

A variation of this story relates that when a bag of gold was dropped down the chimney, one of the girls had been expecting it and therefore had placed a stocking in the fireplace in order to receive it.

Sea Tales

Bishop Nicholas, the uncle of the youth, had great faith in the boy and encouraged him in his interest in the church. A trip to the Holy Land by the uncle greatly inspired Nicholas to travel the same route.

When his ship was sailing south and was near Egypt Nicholas proclaimed that he saw a storm demon rushing toward the ship, but the sailors were greatly in doubt for the sea was extremely calm. It was not long before the storm descended and even the sailors were in despair. In the midst of the storm Nicholas offered up prayers and the tempest immediately ceased.

Another incident of this voyage relates that a sailor was mending a sail at the top of one of the masts. He slipped and fell dead on the deck of the ship. Nicholas was immediately called, whereupon he brought the sailor back to life and health.

Arriving in the Holy Land it is said that the doors of the church at Golgotha opened of their own accord at the approach of Nicholas. So impressed was Nicholas with the scenes of the Holy Land that he desired to give up the church and devote his life to prayer in the wilderness. But God commanded him to return to Patras. The ship on which he returned had a captain, a rascal, who had told several of the sailors that he intended to sell Nicholas into slavery. In order to prevent this Nicholas caused a great storm to rage, which drove the ship back to his native town of Patras in spite of the captain's great effort to steer it in an opposite direction.

Chosen Archbishop

Nicholas would gladly have stayed in his uncle's monastery but the voice of God said, "Go on. Live among men, for yours shall not be a life of quietness !" Accordingly, Nicholas, although still a mere youth, traveled toward Myra, the greatest city of Lycia. The Archbishop John had just died on his day of arrival and all the bishops of Lycia were gathered to select a successor. After many ballots, it was decided that the choice should be made, not by men, but by the Lord. As the eldest slept a dream directed that they should watch at the door of the cathedral and he who came to the door first in the morning by the name of Nicholas should be the bishop. The next morning the youthful Nicholas arrived. The assembly arose to greet him and much to his amazement he was consecrated Archbishop of Myra. As Archbishop he was known for his graciousness and his kindness to all.

Miraculous Feeding of Myra

He once saved the people of the Province of Myra when famine descended upon them. The story goes that upon learning the emperor's ships filled with grain were in the harbor, he prevailed upon the shipmasters to aid his people, promising that they would not regret their action. Miraculously the stores within the ships were not depleted, though enough grain was given to save the sufferers.

In those days Diocletian and Maximian jointly ruled the great empire of Rome. Nicholas often opposed their treatment of the populace and because of his courageous preaching and his refusal to worship the statues of the emperors, he was cast into a dungeon.

There are many gruesome stories of how he saved the lives of numerous persons and those who are interested are referred to *St. Nicholas, His Legend and His Role in the Christmas Celebration and Other Popular Customs*, by George McKnight.

St. Nicholas died on December 6, about 343. His death greatly increased his fame as a worker of miracles.

Russia Adopts Nicholas

Six hundred and sixty years after Nicholas's death, Vladimir of Russia came to Constantinople for baptism and carried back with him the tales of Nicholas. Hence Nicholas was made the patron saint of Russia. From Russia his name spread to the Lapps and Samoyeds, the people of the reindeer sleds, among whom his fame is boundless. No doubt the story Santa uses reindeers comes indirectly from these people.

When the Saracens conquered Asia Minor and laid waste to Lycia, the city of Myra was turned into ruins. The people of Bari, on the heel of Italy, were greatly aghast that the good St. Nicholas should be buried among the infidels. They, therefore, in 1087 sent ships and stole his bones and brought them to their city, where a great church was built to contain his remains. Venice also claims to have his bones at present.

Patron Saint of Numerous Places and Professions

Besides being patron saint of Russia, Nicholas also has received that honor from Greece, the Kingdom of Naples, and from many cities, among them Liege, Lucerne and Freibourg, also from the Laplanders, Samoyeds, and Northern Siberians, although they were heathen people. He is highly revered in France, Catholic or southern Germany, Luxembourg, Switzerland, Belgium, Flanders, and Holland. It is said that there are over a hundred churches in Belgium named for St. Nicholas and several writers claim that more churches have been named for Nicholas than any of the apostles of Jesus. There is hardly a seacoast in any Catholic country that does not have a chapel dedicated to him. Many of these chapels are filled with votive pictures representing the dangers of the sea which may be escaped.

St. Nicholas is often represented as holding the three purses of gold which he gave to the three marriageable maidens. The miraculous tales of the seas led merchants to accept St. Nicholas, adopting the three purses as their coat of arms and placing it on their ships. People borrowed from the merchants and in time the three purses or three golden balls became the money lender's or the pawnbroker's insignia.

St. Nicholas is now the patron saint of bankers, pawnbrokers, maidens, children, mariners, and scholars. And, alas, also of thieves!

Transformed to Santa Claus

It was a much changed St. Nicholas which the Dutch settlers brought to the United States. Auld* tells us that in the New World his pale face has become like a rosy apple. The lean ascetic is now a fat, jolly old fellow, more humanist than saint. Laying aside his canonical robes, his miter, and his pastoral staff, he has chosen an ermine-trimmed red cap and suit. He has traded his old gray mare for reindeer and sleigh. Europe has always celebrated St. Nicholas Day as December 6 and this is the day of gift giving. But in the New World St. Nicholas gave up his own day and took over December 25, Christ's birthday.

Protestant countries had long resented the legend that St. Nicholas was the giver of gifts so that in Germany the bestower of presents has always been the Christ Child.

*Auld, William Muir, *Christmas Traditions.*

Nevertheless, the New World idea of Santa Claus, or St. Nicholas, recrossed the ocean and "gained adherents from gloomy Scotland to sunny Australia." His dominion has steadily increased and it appears that he will reign all over Christendom as the King of Christmas.

Acquired Many Satellites

The teachings about St. Nicholas vary so much that the story is much involved, but some conceive that St. Nicholas (Santa Claus, as we call him, as the bestower of gifts) is entirely a virtuous character, giving presents to everyone. Others conceive of him as having a dual role and he is depicted as carrying not only a bag of presents but a bundle of Birch rods. He is expected to reward the virtuous children and punish the bad ones. Among other people, St. Nicholas is accompanied by some servant or spirit from the world of demons variously called Knecht Ruprecht, or Jan, or Pelznickle, and this sinister character is often disguised in a horror-bringing costume. For instance, in Holland, it is common to scare the children to within an inch of their lives before the appearance of the jolly Sint Niklaas. In many parts of Europe the presence of negroes is a great rarity. For that reason St. Nicholas is often accompanied by a negro body servant, called Jan. He is merely Santa Claus's little helper.

Pelznickle to the children of Germany is a terror. He knows all about the children through the Christ Child and is merely the punishing Nemesis. The name is derived from the word *Pelz*, meaning fur, inasmuch as this character is generally robed in a fur coat. The custom of having the Pelznickle come is still observed among the Pennsylvania-Germans (or Pennsylvania Dutch, as they are also called).

To the early Dutch settlers St. Nicholas was a favorite and in New Amsterdam, they named their first church in his honor. Santa Claus became the American form of Santa Nikalaus, or, as they shortened it, to Santa Klaus. At first

Thomas Nast, the originator of the G. O. P. Elephant, the Democratic Donkey and the Tammany Tiger, has also given us our modern conception of Santa Claus (Copied from the original in *Harpers Illustrated Weekly*)

he appeared quite like Father Knickerbocker. Washington Irving in 1809 described him as a tubby little fellow with a jolly manner, who sped through the air in a reindeer sleigh.

In the New York Public Library one may find a scrapbook of pictures taken from *Harper's Illustrated Weekly* containing many of the interesting cartoons drawn by Thomas Nast, who originated the G. O. P. Elephant, the Democratic Donkey, and the Tammany Tiger. It was Nast who apparently gave this white-bearded old gentleman his red, ermine-trimmed coat, so that he is half Father Knickerbocker and half Old King Cole. In 1822 Doctor Clement Moore, taking Washington Irving more or less as an authority for his description of Santa Claus, developed our present-day conception of this jolly saint, in his poem "The Visit of St. Nicholas." And this in itself is an interesting story.

"The Visit of St. Nicholas"

Doctor Clement Clarke Moore was Professor of Divinity in a New York Theological Seminary. On the night of December 23, 1822, he was telling his own children the story of St. Nicholas. A daughter of the Rev. David Butler, Episcopalian rector, was present at the Moore home and heard Doctor Moore read a poem which she hastily copied in her album. She treasured this for the entire year and sent it to the editor of *The Troy Sentinel*, so that it was published December 23, 1823. And the editor explained that, "We know not to whom we are indebted for the description of that unwearied patron of children, but from whomever it may have come, we give thanks for it." The poem brought an immediate response to the editor, who was delighted, but Doctor Moore considered it beneath his dignity as a Professor of Divinity and was greatly chagrined. It was many years before he allowed it to be known that he was the author. However, in 1844 he included it in a volume of his poems. He died in 1863. The poem has been translated into many foreign languages.

THE VISIT OF ST. NICHOLAS

'Twas the night before Christmas when all through the house
Not a creature was stirring, not even a mouse;
The stockings were hung by the chimney with care,
In hopes that Saint Nicholas soon would be there.
The children were nestled all snug in their beds,
While visions of sugarplums danced through their heads.
And Mama in her 'kerchief and I in my cap
Had just settled our brains for a long Winter's nap.
When out on the lawn there arose such a clatter
I sprang from my bed to see what was the matter.
Away to the window I fled like a flash,
Tore open the shutters and threw up the sash.
The moon on the breast of the new fallen snow
Gave the luster of midday to objects below.
When what to my wondering eyes should appear
But a miniature sleigh and eight tiny reindeer.
With a little old driver so lively and quick
I knew in a moment it must be St. Nick.
More rapid than Eagles his coursers they came,
And he whistled and shouted and called them by name.
"Now, Dasher! now, Dancer! now, Prancer! and Vixen!
On Comet! on Cupid! on Donder and Blitzen!
To the top of the porch! to the top of the wall;
Now dash away! dash away! dash away all!"
As dry leaves that before the wild hurricane fly
When they meet with an obstacle mount to the sky,
So up to the housetop the coursers they flew,
With the sleigh full of toys and Saint Nicholas, too.
And then in a twinkling I heard on the roof
The prancing and pawing of each little hoof—
As I drew in my head and was turning around
Down the chimney Saint Nicholas came with a bound.
He was dressed all in furs from his head to his foot,
And his clothes were all tarnished with ashes and soot.
A bundle of toys he had flung on his back
And he looked like a peddler just opening his pack;
His eyes—how they twinkled! His dimples, how merry,
His cheeks were like Roses, his nose like a Cherry!
His droll little mouth was drawn up in a bow,
And the beard on his chin was as white as the snow;
The stump of a pipe he held tight in his teeth,
And the smoke it encircled his head like a wreath;
He had a broad face and a little round belly,
That shook when he laughed like a bowlful of jelly.
He was chubby and plump, a right jolly old elf,
And I laughed when I saw him in spite of myself;
A wink of his eye and a twist of his head
Soon gave me to know I had nothing to dread;
He spoke not a word, but went straight to his work
And filled all the stockings, then turned with a jerk.
And laying his finger aside of his nose
And giving a nod up the chimney he rose.
He sprang to his sleigh, to his team gave a whistle,
And away they all flew like the down of a thistle;
But I heard him exclaim ere he drove out of sight,
"Merry Christmas to all, and to all a good night."
—CLEMENT CLARKE MOORE

In Memoriam

Each year on Christmas Eve the children and friends of Trinity Church at 155th Street, New York, honor Doctor Moore by a pilgrimage to his grave. It was my good fortune to be in New York on the evening of December 24, 1936. In the Chapel of the Intercession a service is held which recalls and portrays the episodes of the gospel narrative of the Nativity of Jesus. At 4 o'clock we assembled. The hushed church was packed to overflowing. The only light in the church came from great rows of candles set upon beams suspended between the pillars under the arches. Soon the narrator began the story of the Nativity and a tableau of angels and shepherds appeared to the accompaniment of singing "Hark, the Herald Angels Sing." Then came a tableau showing the Holy Family and the narrator continued the ever-new story of the shepherds and their visit to the Christ Child. Each shepherd bore with him a simple gift. Soon the Three Kings appeared at the back of the church and as they marched sang "We Three Kings of the Orient Are." Boy sopranos took the part of these Kings and their clear young voices were truly angelic. Then, led by the choir, the worshippers in the church passed the Holy Family in procession and presented their gifts before the Christ Child or placed their money offerings in alms basins held by the angels. While the people knelt the group at the altar sang "Silent Night." The party then filed from the church and was furnished with lanterns, and this procession crossed Broadway's busy artery of life, stopping the flow of commerce while the band of pilgrims entered the churchyard and slowly made its way down the circuitous paths to the grave of Doctor Clement Moore. The pilgrims were furnished with red flares as well as lanterns, and everybody stood in hushed silence while the rector offered a brief prayer. One will not soon forget how the warm glow of the lanterns and the red flares dissipated the chill of early evening as the procession wound its serpentine course homeward.

Tante Aria, the Angels and the Good Star

*Tante Aria** is one of the lesser known gift bearers and may be grouped with the angels and the Good Star, not only as gift bringers but also because of their close association with the Christmas trees in various countries.

In Franche-Comte, *Tante Aria*, the Air or Wind Mother, rides on an ass and bestows Christmas gifts which overflow from the children's shoes and stockings hung from the Christmas tree. Such mother legends are survivals of the Indian mother-goddesses—the tree and cloud-bird.

At the top right in the frontispiece, *Tante Aria* is seen riding with the Father Star above her. *Tante Aria* is the cloud goddess, brought in a car drawn by asses, to wed the moon-god at the Winter solstice, according to the Rig Veda.

In Hungary children devoutly praise the blessed angels as the bringers of their Christmas tree, whereas in Poland the Good Stars from heaven play that important role. The Mother Star is impersonated by a lovely woman in a white robe and veil and is attended by an awe-inspiring Father Star, who dispenses gifts if the children are able to say their prayers and sing their hymns to his satisfaction.

St. Christopher

St. Christopher has been called the Goliath of the Saints. In the *Legenda Aurea, Golden Legends,* as told by Jacopa da Voragine we read that in childhood he was called Reprobatus, a heathen giant who went from one master to another whenever he found a stronger master than his present one. He served the powerful Pharaoh but he noted even this mighty man crossed himself when the Devil was mentioned, indicating that he feared him. Therefore, Reprobatus realized that he must seek service with Satan. He watched and saw that even the Devil was startled by the cross. So he left

*From *Historical Calendars,* a translation from *Les Mois en Franche-Comte,* by Charles Baugnier.

St. Christopher is here shown in what is considered the
world's oldest extant dated woodcut, 1423

the service of the Devil and went in search of Christ. A
hermit ordered him to pray but Reprobatus refused and
he was, therefore, commanded as penance to carry travelers
over the deep river. A virtuous task, at last!

One night a voice called for Reprobatus but he could find
only a little child. He placed the child on his shoulder to
carry him but the weight of this child nearly bowed him to
the earth. "You are, indeed," said he "as heavy as the world."

To this, the child replied, "I created the world, I redeemed the world, and I bear the sins of the world." Reprobatus was no longer a reprobate but became Christofera, the bearer of Christ, or Christopher. To this day, in Catholic countries, he is the patron saint of all travelers and pocket pieces and medals are worn around the necks of the devout to protect them from accident. Christopher always carried a palm stem as his staff which Christ bade him thrust into the soil. Whereupon it blossomed and bore dates.

The interesting woodcut which we are reproducing was used as a Christmas card by my friend Douglas McMurtrie, eminent type designer. In the lower righthand corner one sees the date, 1423, and Mr. McMurtrie considers it the world's earliest extant dated woodcut. St. Christopher is seen with the Christ Child on his shoulder and is using an up-rooted palm tree as a staff. The identity of the mediaeval artist responsible for this composition is unknown. It is interesting to note in the left foreground that a man is driving an ass, loaded with a sack of grain, to the mill driven by an overshot wheel. We see another man carrying a sack of milled grain up the hill. The hermit mentioned in our story is recognized on the right bank by the bell over the entrance to his cell and he holds a lantern to light St. Christopher across the stream. To the left of the date is a crude Latin couplet which may be freely translated:

Each day that thou the likeness of St. Christopher shalt see
That day no frightful form of death shall make an end of thee.

Mr. McMurtrie continues, "The unique copy of the original from which the reproduction is made is preserved in the collection of The John Rylands Library, Manchester, England. It owes its preservation to the fact that it was pasted inside the oak board, covered with an undressed deer skin, as a part of the binding of a Latin manuscript written in the year 1417. It was bound in the Carthusian House, which is one of the oldest convents in Germany.

SYMBOLS OF CHRISTMAS

MANY symbols have become associated in our minds with the Nativity story—the blazing Star of Bethlehem, the quiet, lighted Christmas tree, the awe-inspiring Christmas Cribs adored alike by the peasant and the monarch, the welcoming lights of candles as they beckon us to enjoy their warm glow whether they are placed in a window, among the greenery, or now less often on the tree. We shall speak of bells and the part they have played as they ring through the frosty air. Here we relate the role of the Christmas fire in keeping alive the sacred home and family traditions which are often centered about the hearth. Lastly we shall say a word about the gifts which have become indelibly associated with the holiday season. For another chapter we shall leave the discussion of the Christmas tree and its legends. Then follows the use of greenery in bringing the holiday spirit indoors.

Star of wonder, star of night, star of royal beauty bright,
Westward leading, still proceeding, guide us to thy perfect light

The Star of Bethlehem

The story of the coming of the Magi guided by the Star of Bethlehem has been the subject of much discussion. According to *The Mentor* we may interpret this story in three ways: Through the eyes of the supernaturalist, the rationalist, or those of the historian and astronomer.

"The *supernaturalist* tells us that it is literal history, and that the star was a supernatural phenomenon. He contends that the Creator kindled a light in the heavens for a sign, which, having served its purpose, was extinguished forever.

"Reacting from this extreme, *rationalists* declare the whole story a myth, either supplied intentionally to honor Christ, or transferred to Christ from some older god. Others hint that the story was intended to be symbolic and was not meant to be historic in any sense.

"The modern *historical* view goes to neither extreme. Inclining to the belief that the story is true, it yet sees that it is colored by Oriental imagery. The star is, of course, the main criterion for testing its historicity. Assuming the heavenly apparition to be a natural phenomenon, is there any astronomical evidence for the appearance of any such star?"

Astronomer's View

Four possible hypotheses have evolved out of the astronomical features of the Star of Bethlehem, according to Dr. D. W. Morehouse, president of Drake University, and an astronomer of note. He writes me:

The first possibility is that a very great meteor appeared and that it seemed to fall toward the eastern horizon over the city of Bethlehem. Now we must remember that a meteor is a very transient phenomenon, that under no conditions could it last for more than a few short seconds, that it is quite local in character, and if it were large enough to attract the attention of the ordinary observer over any considerable territory, its place of impact with the earth could still be identified and become an historic shrine. We therefore seem more than justified in dismissing this hypothesis.

The second possibility is that a comet appeared in the eastern sky. This is a much more tenable suggestion. A great comet would attract the attention of all the inhabitants of the eastern world. Comets last for days and have been known to be so bright that they were visible even in daylight. They move through the sky changing their position very slowly and can easily be followed from night to night, but such a comet would certainly be of astronomical record, even in those pre-scientific days. Interestingly enough, the Chinese recorded such a comet in the year 4 B. C. It was visible in the Spring of the year, that is, February to April. While the seasons seem to be at some variance the concurrence of these records cannot be satisfactorily explained as a mere coincidence and the hypothesis remains a very plausible one. We still do not have a star.

We, therefore, turn to the third possibility, that of a new star. The year 1936 gave us a fine example of this extraordinary phenomenon. Such objects have been recorded from time to time during the centuries. Since they are by no means so conspicuous as a comet or even a great meteor, we would scarcely expect to find numerous accounts of them of ancient record. However, tradition credits the great Hipparchus with having noted in the year 134 B. C. a brilliant star where previously no star had been visible. He was so attracted by the unusual phenomenon that he resolved to make a chart of the heavens consisting of all the visible stars. We must now pass over centuries before such another phenomenon is of record—to the year 1572 when Tycho Brahe discovered his famous nova. By ascribing to this object a definite periodicity it has been more frequently identified as The Star of Bethlehem than any other astronomical object. A quarter of a century later in 1604 the great Kepler observed a similar phenomenon. He was then but thirty-three years of age, but this discovery so profoundly impressed him that he turned his entire life to the study of astronomy. His description of the apparition bears this impressive phrase, "In triumphal pomp, like some all powerful monarch." Stimulated by this extraordinary manifestation he wrote three papers on the identification of the year of Christ's birth, which, although forgotten for three centuries, have been recently brought to light. Since this date at least twenty brilliant new stars have appeared and the twentieth century records five of the most brilliant. F. R. Moulton in his *Consider the Heavens* makes this bold statement: "It may well be that the Star of Bethlehem was one of these temporary stars."

The fourth and final hypothesis is that of conjunction or coming together of two or more of the well known planets. Here we enter the realm of astronomical accuracy for we can compute these times of conjunction as far back in history as we desire and project their appearances into the future as far as we are willing to spend time and labor in the computation. The four conspicuous naked-eye planets are Saturn, Jupiter, Mars and Venus. If any three of these should come together it would make an occasion of historic importance. Computation shows that such an event took place in the year 7-6 B.C. At that time Jupiter, Saturn and Mars were in conjunction. This phenomenon recurs with a periodicity of about 800 years. On the 17th of December, 1603, they were again close together with the added attraction of a new star joining this tryst of the worlds. The scientifically minded will recall similar conjunctions of our planets during recent years and we can confidently predict when they will occur in the future. We have not in this conjunction dealt with the planet Venus, which is now most conspicuous in the early evening in the southwest. It would be impossible to include Venus in the aforementioned conjunctions and at the same time be true to the biblical account that the star appeared in the East, for Venus can never be seen in that part of the sky except in the early morning hours. She is most conspicuous in her favorite haunt of the western horizon where she often shines with the brilliancy that attracts even the casual observer. No doubt many will again identify Venus as The

Star of Bethlehem forgetting her location and also the fact that she has appeared in that position about every two years for eons before The Nativity and will continue so to appear until time shall be no more. The fact that during the last decade Venus has been at her greatest brilliancy every two years about the Christmas season has resulted in much confusion and scientific deception.

Modern astronomers are not inclined to give much weight to the foregoing hypotheses. Any astronomical phenomenon would be at such a great distance from the earth that its appearance would be of no value as a local guide. In other words, such a phenomenon would be seen in the same direction from any point on the surface of the earth, and would not, therefore, stand over the place where the young Child lay.

CHRISTMAS CRIB

What the Christmas tree is to northern Europe, the Christmas Crib is to the south of Europe. In France it is called the *Creche* or Cradle. In Italy, the *Praesepe* or Manger. In Germany, the *Krippe* or Crib, in Czechoslovakia, *Jeslicky*. In Spain, the *Nacimiento* or Nativity Scene.

From earliest times it seemed wise, because of lack of books and the inability to read, for the priests and other religious leaders to represent and interpret the Bible to their congregation through literal representation. In this way, mediaeval mystery plays and Christmas Cribs came into being. The true story is interestingly related by Charles Howard,* who writes:

St. Francis of Assisi

St. Bonaventure, in the Thirteenth Century, describes how in the year 1223, St. Francis of Assisi wished to inspire the people with greater religious fervor and received permission from the Pope to set up a *Praesepe* in the little village of Greccio, near Assisi. He caused a sensation by having

*Howard, Charles, *The Christmas Crib*, Apollo, Dec., 1936.

live animals in a stable, complete with a supply of provender. Crowds flocked to the church and St. Francis conducted the service, singing the gospel and giving the sermon. As a result Greccio became famous for its Crib and the animal provender was kept as a miraculous cure for all disease. This presentation served to spread the fashion of Nativity groups more widely than ever.

The Renaissance greatly changed the Crib. Artists became intrigued with the incidentals of the scene. Landscape backgrounds and elaborate groups of quite irrelevant figures were added. Wise Men wore richly woven clothes, figures became more realistic, and the devotional shrine grew into a highly ornate pageant, with central religious figures taking an insignificant place in the great drama.

In the Seventeenth and Eighteenth Centuries the *Praesepe* reached its highest point of development. In some, the religious element had entirely disappeared. Homely episodes were introduced, such as musicians playing, a card table with three men drinking and a gypsy group.

Goethe describes the custom of building Cribs in the open in 1787. "This is the place," says he, "to mention another remarkable fashion of the Neapolitans. That is, the Crib which one sees in every church at Christmas, especially the adoration of the shepherds, angels, and Wise Men, more or less perfect, and elaborately and richly grouped. This presentation among the Neapolitans is built on the flat housetops, a flimsy hut-like erection decked with evergreen trees and shrubs. The Mother of God, the Child, the whole retinue and following is elaborately fitted up, the clothes costing the household a great deal of money. But what makes it all so inimitable is the background dominated by Vesuvius and its surroundings."

W. J. Phillips* tells us that St. Francis was so pleased with his Christmas Crib reception that he stood by the scenes sighing for joy and filled with unspeakable sweetness.

*Phillips, W. J., *Carols*.

Giovanni, a friend of St. Francis, had a vision that a dead child lay in the Manger, but that the child stretched out its arms to St. Francis as he bent over the Crib. St. Francis interpreted this as being not a dead child but the dead Christ, dead in the hearts of careless people, and waking to new life and kindling the whole slumbering universe around him at the touch and breath of supreme love.

We have said above that "St. Francis conducted the service singing the gospel and giving the sermon." So that this simple *Praesepe* was not only the origin of the Christmas mystery plays, the *Praesepe*, but also the Christmas carol, for he sang the service.

Famous Cribs

In various central European countries the Christmas Crib, staged in a box, is carried through the streets by groups of singing children. Also, the Christmas Crib is a feature of every home in southern Europe, although there are many famous Cribs in churches.

The most elaborate Christmas *Praesepe* in Italy is the celebrated shrine of Madonna delle Grazie. After the news of St. Francis' *Praesepe* had spread the Capuchin monks built a grotto 18 feet high, made of Sardinian cork, with galleries giving a perspective of the mountains. They arranged a system by which figures of shepherds, flocks, and the Three Kings moved down to the Manger, the wooden figures carved by the noted artists Gaggini and Maragliano.

The one at Caserta, Italy, includes the most famous Bambino in the world. At Oberammergau the Lang family owns another. Particular mention should be made of the great collection of Cribs in the Bayerisches National Museum in Munich. This is the most important collection in the world.

Construction of the Christmas Cribs

The figures used in most of the Christmas Cribs are made of wood, terra cotta, papier-maché, plaster, cork and faience.

These figures are called *santons* in France and in Marseilles is the home of the cork cutters, who make these figures which are known throughout the world.

When these Christmas Cribs are made life size the clothing is often of the finest material and Charles Howard tells us that queens in religious fervor often stripped off their finery to provide clothing for the dolls. He continues, "In the Victoria and Albert Museum the figures were made as follows: They were modeled in clay and a cast made. The mold was painted flesh color and a liquid wax poured in while the pigment was still damp. The surface of the wax absorbed the color, gaining a pleasant depth of hue. The draperies were made of colored wax, not painted, so that the figures appear to have an inherent quality of color and are exceptionally real."

Without the least irreverence intended Mabel Swan* says these religious figures were sold by crying them out at the races:

"Good bargains, the *Bon Dieu!*
Good bargains, the Virgin Mary!"

and

"One *sou* for the Pope,
Two *sous* for the Virgin Mary,
Three *sous* for the Eternal Father.
Whatever you wish."

Author's Note: Various religious supply houses have simple or elaborate set-ups for Christmas Cribs. The Lutheran Book Concern, Columbus, Ohio, lists plaster, as well as paper, figures. In the Erzgebirge, on the border of Germany and Czechoslovakia, the author found the quaintest carved wood angels and crib figures.

*The author regrets not being able to give the source of this material except that it was written by Mabel Swan and appeared in a magazine clipping found at the Los Angeles Public Library without a definite date or source acknowledged.

The Prayer of the Children of Provence

Before the Christmas Cribs of Provence, France, according to Mabel Swan, the children reverently repeat the following prayer:

> Little Jesus of the Crib,
> Give us the virtues of those who surround you.
> Make us philosophical as the fisherman,
> Carefree as the drummer,
> Merry in exploring the world as the troubadour,
> Eager for work as the bugler,
> Patient as the spinner,
> Kind as the ass,
> Strong as the ox which keeps you warm,
> Give us the sacred leisure of the hunter.
> Give us also the desire of the shepherd for earthly things,
> The pride of the trade of the knife grinder and the weaver,
> The song of the miller,
> Grant us the knowledge of the Magi,
> The cheerfulness of the pigeon,
> The impulsiveness of the cock,
> The discretion of the snail,
> The meekness of the lamb.
> Give us the goodness of bread,
> The tenderness of the wild boar,
> The salt of the haddock,
> The good humor of old wine,
> The ardor of the candle,
> The purity of the star.

CANDLES

The sun, the moon, and the stars have always stood as symbols of the Divine, and in olden times torches, watch fires, beacon lights, and lamps were used to celebrate joyous occasions and festivals. King Alfred measured time by candles, which he inclosed in horn lanterns to prevent the wind from burning them irregularly. Throughout the years they were used by the monks, who notched them or colored

Man has ever longed to prolong the day and scare away the terrors of darkness, so a light has always meant faith and intelligence, and from the earliest ages has been a symbol of Christian joy which ever dispelled the darkness of paganism

them variously to determine the passage of time. The Jewish and Catholic churches have always used an abundance of candles, principally on account of the candle being the symbol of enlightenment, and in the New Testament Jesus is called the Light of the World.

St. Jerome told Vigilantius that candles were used in church not for the purpose of dispelling darkness, but to express Christian joy.

In Norway, Sigrid Tang* tells us that Christmas candles had to be molded very wide and tall, for they must burn through the night without going out, and Christmas night someone had to watch the light, for it was an ill omen and someone in the household would die before next Christmas if the candle went out. Nor must the watcher touch the candle with his fingers.

In Ireland at Christmas no one may snuff the church candles except she whose name is Mary.

It is interesting to see the various types of lights used throughout the periods of history. In Ann Hathaway's cottage at Stratford-on-Avon we may see one of the old rushlight burners. It has a square base and the upright is so arranged with a lever that the weight of a clamp holding a candle holds the rush in place. Rushes from the swamps were soaked in oil and sometimes they were folded so that both ends were burned at once. This is thought to have given rise to the expression of "burning the candle at both ends." Note the rushlight shown on page 55 in the lower left hand corner.

How to Make Bayberry Candles

Growing in the sandy soil from Alaska to Florida is a shrub known as the Bayberry. The branches are thickly beset with gray, wax-giving berries. In early Colonial days animal fats were rather scarce so that the children gathered

*Tang, Sigrid, *American Home*, December, 1932.

the berries for making candles. According to the stern
Puritanical views of the time, *National Geographic Magazine*
tells us that the children could gather berries with more
edification than they could play.

Bayberry candles are more brittle and less greasy than
those made from tallow. They are translucent green, and
when the flame is extinguished, the resulting odor is as sweet
and pungent as incense. From various sources we may learn
how to make these candles.

Cover the berries with water and boil perhaps an hour.
The oil comes to the top but it is often soiled with leaves and
small twigs, so that it should be strained through a cloth.
When this wax becomes cold it will form a cake at the top of
the water. It should be heated again, preparatory to molding the candles. If you have candle molds you will, of course,
use them. If not, you may fasten several wicks to a piece of
wood, which can be dipped into the hot wax, using a tall container of small diameter. Each coat should chill and become
hard before dipping again and the dipping should continue
until the desired diameter is obtained.

A Striped Candle

Ida Childs Field describes how to make attractive Christmas candles from discarded candle stubs. For Christmas,
select red and green, perhaps, or blue and white if such fits
in with your decorations, and melt the colors separately, as
several tints are desirable. Use a bottle of an interesting,
candlelike shape. A catsup bottle may be used. Place a funnel in the top. Suspend a string into the bottle by means of a
stick resting on the rim of the funnel. Pour in your first layer
of wax. Clear the sides of the bottle by heating with a hot
cloth. Then set the bottle in cold water to harden the wax
each time before pouring the next layer. Thus your layers
will be distinct. Cool overnight and the next morning break
the bottle and your candle is now ready to be set in perhaps
a copper or brass bowl.

The Christmas Fire

"When the day had ended and it was too dark and cold to hunt," writes Amy Cryan of Santa Barbara, "the tribe gathered around the fire to feast, and both the fire and the feast have a significance. The fire reminds us of those far-off days when a blazing log at night meant safety, for it scared off wild beasts. A feast also meant security, for when we have broken our bread with a man sitting beside us he will not injure us. This safety from the threatening of man and Nature gave a feeling of very definite happiness that still has its echo in our Christmas fires."

We like to look back and conjecture about the possible source of each of the domestic abilities of man. H. G. Wells in his *The Outline of History* quotes Worthington Smith, who is wondering about the probable origin of fire and its use by man. Some one of our primitive ancestors, no doubt, was squatting one day, fashioning his flint weapons, when he accidentally struck fire on a bit of iron pyrites amidst some dry, dead leaves, and considering this of interest he no doubt tried to keep the blaze going, for the air was bleak and he knew that it would not be easily relit. He no doubt learned early to bank it with ashes. The women and children would need to be continually gathering wood to feed the fire; thereby the tradition of keeping fire would grow up. The young would imitate their elders. Perhaps there would be crude wind shelters of boughs on one side of the encampment, the evolution of a hut. And thus we can see that fire was one of our domesticating influences, for they would have to stay in one place or else move the fire with them. But each night they would all gather closely around the fire and build it up for it was their protection against the wandering beasts of prey.

It is with somewhat this same feeling that you and I gather before our Christmas fireplaces. How snug and warm we feel, how the stories flow! A fireplace is indeed a great inspiration of reminiscence and when all the lights are out, how easy it is for everyone to sing Christmas carols. Let us return to the spirit of Christmas as it is observed in the many lands where the head of the family reads once more the ever-new story from the Bible. Then perhaps follow with Dickens' *Christmas Carol.* I am sure you will be interested in the old story of Hertha:

Hertha, the Hearth Goddess

The early Germans considered the Norse Hertha, or Bertha, the goddess of domesticity and the home.* During the Winter solstice houses were decked with Fir and evergreens to welcome her coming. When the family and the serfs gathered to dine, a great altar of flat stones was erected .and here a fire of Fir boughs was laid. Hertha descended through the smoke, guiding those who were wise in Saga lore to foretell the fortunes of those persons at the feast. Hertha's altar stones became the hearthstones of the home.

Hertha, the goddess of the hearth, appeared to the Anglo-Saxon peoples in the flames of their home fires

We learn from this story of Hertha the reason why Santa Claus comes down the chimney instead of in at the door. It is only a survival of the coming of Hertha in pre-Christian days.

In Germany cakes are baked in the form of a slipper. These are the slippers of Hertha. They are filled with small gifts and they bestow on maidens and children the qualities of virtue,

*Watson, Jeanette Grace, *A Chronicle of Christmas.*

health, and beauty. Incidentally, these slippers of Hertha have given rise, no doubt, to the lucky shoes of Cinderella.

From the *Lincoln Library of Essential Information* we find that Bertha, or Hertha, is the White Lady who guards good German children but is the terror of the bad, who fear her iron nose and big feet. She corresponds to the Italian Befana.

The Yule Log

During the period of the year when the sun returns to the heavens after its long Winter rest and the shortest days have passed, the ancient Teutonic and Celtic races held a festival celebrating the turning of the wheel of time, which was called the *Houl* or the *Hioul*. Some believed that the sun stood still for twelve days at this period of the year. Because this Yule period comes at the same time as Christmas the word is used in most northern countries for the Christmas season. The Druid priests at this period chose a Yule Log which they blest with much ceremony and proclaimed that it should be kept ever burning. Each year a brand was saved to rekindle the new fire. From this early origin arose the present-day custom throughout Europe.

The old books surround the Yule Log with much mystery and superstition. In some places they believe that the Log must be touched or lighted only with clean hands. Others say that if the Log goes out during the night it portends bad luck for the entire year. Three types of people were unwelcome while the Log was burning—a squinting person, one with bare feet, but above all a flat-footed woman.

Alfred Dowling* writes that in the Tyrols a huge block was brought in that had been dried for the occasion. Oak, Pine, Ash, or Olive was used. The Log was highly decorated with paper flowers and bright colored ribbons. The youngest child in the home poured wine on the log and a prayer was offered that the fire might warm the cold, that the hungry might gain food, the weary find rest, and all enjoy heaven's peace.

*Dowling, Alfred, *Flora of Sacred Nativity*.

Placed on a bed of hot ashes previously prepared, the wood blazed and burned throughout the night.

In Franche-Comte* the Yule Log was called *La Tronche* (the tree trunk). This log was put on the fire Christmas Eve and allowed to burn only a few seconds, after which it was removed and covered with a cloth. The children came in armed with sticks. As they beat the Log they shouted, "Come forth!" As nothing was obtained the parents told them to step outside and beg pardon for their faults. During their absence Christmas presents were placed under the cloth. When the children returned they found the presents as the offspring from their beating of the log.

The Yule Log was half burned and then stored in the house as a protection against lightning. It was the old Log which was used to start the fire the next year. The ashes of the Yule Log were buried at the roots of all fruit trees to make them fruitful.

We have discussed some other interesting features of the Yule Log on page 106.

Colored Flames

To have beautifully colored flames in your Christmas fireplace there are a number of different chemicals which may be added to shellac as a carrier. Small pieces of wood may be painted with the mixtures or the chemicals and shellac mixed with sawdust:

Violet color flame	Potassium chlorate
Yellow color flame	Potassium nitrate
Yellow color flame	Sodium chloride (salt)
Orange color flame	Calcium chloride
Red color flame	Strontium nitrate
Apple-green color flame	Barium nitrate
Emerald color flame	Copper nitrate
Green color flame	Borax
Purple color flame	Lithium chloride

Historical Calendars, Westminster Review, January, 1901.

From the deep-toned summoning bell of the church to the tiny bell on a pet bird, bells have always been considered almost living sentient beings. The bells in this picture have been drawn from those in the Metropolitan Museum of Art, New York, and show a wide diversity. In the center of the picture we see a board, covered with bells, designed to stand at the base of the camel's neck. Attached to the net are tiny camel bells which extend from the camel's head to his chest. In early England many bells were made in the form of court ladies wearing hoop skirts. One such bell is shown at the base of our picture. In the lower left are two primitive bells from Africa; the one showing the woman's face is from the Benin district and the strange double bell in the extreme foreground is from Kamerun. The latter is made of two pieces of metal hammered together and the handle is wrapped with leather thongs. Suspended with cords at the top of our picture is an old bell, bearing the date 1599, and it is interesting to see that it bears the name of its owner, Niblich Wolfgang. In the lower left hand corner of the camel board we have an interesting ceremonial bell in which there is a large resounding chamber for the four smaller bells. In such a case the four bells would ring in harmony

BELLS, THE OPERA OF THE STEEPLES

What a world of merriment their melody foretells!
How they tinkle, tinkle, tinkle, in the icy air of night!
While the stars, that oversprinkle
All the heavens, seem to twinkle
With a crystalline delight;
Keeping time, time, time,
In a sort of Runic rhyme,
To the tintinnabulation that so musically wells
From the bells, bells, bells, bells, bells, bells, bells—
From the jingling and the tinkling of the bells.

So many of us have recited this poem of Edgar Allan Poe's in public speaking class that it is surely familiar to all of us and inspires us to know a more complete story of what bells have meant in human history. All medi-aeval people considered bells almost living, sentient beings. They were dedicated before being hung and the dedication was almost like a human baptism. During the ceremony prayers were offered that the sound of the bell might summon the faith-ful, excite devotion, drive away storms, and terrify evil spirits. Auld* writes, "In those dark chambers, high above the turmoil and strife of human life, dwelt the apostles of peace, whose salutations were never so welcome as at the time of the great Winter feasts of Christmas." Victor Hugo says that the ringing of bells is "the opera of the steeples."

Bells are of all forms and have evolved

*Auld, William Muir. *Christian Traditions.*

from the rattle of the savages of Africa into the sweet-toned, silver bells of the church. Church bells are said to have been originated by Bishop Paulinus, of Nola, in Campania, who died in 431. From his town and district we have the Latin names *Campana* and *Nola*, which gave the name *Campanula*, the Latin for *bell*. Some writers doubt this derivation of the word.

The story is told by Walsh* that extremely large bells were in use in ancient days in China, and in one case such a bell was placed over the head of a governor. To it was attached a rope a mile long which extended along the highway leading to the palace, so that the humblest sufferer from injustice seldom hesitated to tug at it. Many of the large Chinese bells lack the clapper, and they are set into vibration by a log suspended by ropes. Such a large bell is found in the Japanese garden at the Huntington estate in Pasadena, California.

Bell Legends†

Two fine bells once hung in a church tower in the town of Lochen, Holland. These bells had not been baptized; so one day the Evil One appeared and suddenly carried them away from the church tower and submerged them in two ponds near the town. This was many years ago but the peasants still believe they hear the bells ringing from these ponds every year on Christmas Eve, precisely at 12 o'clock.

Another legend says that when Christ was born the devil died and for an hour before midnight on Christmas Eve the church bell was rung, just as it would be for some dying person. This was called "the Old Lad's Passing Bell," Old Lad, of course, being a nickname for Satan. At exactly midnight the mournful tolling of this bell changed to a joyful peal.

In a number of places in Europe on Christmas Eve one may hear bells ringing by putting the head to the ground.‡

*Walsh, William S., *Curiosities of Popular Customs.*
†Coleman, Satis. *Bells.*
‡Walsh, *ibid.*

The story goes that these spots were once valleys, in which a service was in preparation and bells were ringing when an earthquake swallowed them up. Since then bells can always be heard on Christmas Eve. One such mysterious valley is reputed to be in Nottinghamshire, England. For years, persons assembled here to hear the Christmas bells.

Where the Gifts Come From

As a part of the good will among men there has always been a desire to share the best things of life with one's neighbor, and the spirit of altruism which most of the good philosophies of the world have fostered leads each man to become his brother's keeper, in a small way at least.

In almost all of the religions and progressive philosophies there has been a period when persons were encouraged to look about them and bestow their abundance upon the less fortunate of the community.

It was a common practice in early Roman days to make presents during the Calends of, or about the first of, January. At this time "men gave honied things that the year of the recipient might be sweeter, lamps that it might be full of light, silver and gold that wealth might attend them."

The custom of giving in England is very interesting. Since the reign of Henry VII Christmas boxes and New Years gifts were a common exactment of royalty from their subjects.* There was a graduated scale for giving and receiving according to the rank of the parties. The amount was as well ascertained as the *quiddam honorarium* of a barrister or a physician.

Queen Elizabeth relied on Christmas gifts to replenish her wardrobe.† Peers and peeresses, bishops, clergy, master cooks, and sergeants of pastry all gave something at the request of the Queen. It is reputed that the Archbishop of Canterbury gave as much as $200, and the Archbishop of

*Sandys, William, *Christmastide.*
†Meller, *Old Times.*

York $150. The loyal, if unwilling, subjects presented rich petticoats, jewels, furs, and one of the ladies of the court presented her with the first silk stockings to be made in Europe. The Queen was so delighted that she declared she would never wear any others. One physician sent her a box of green ginger and another some foreign sweetmeats. The royal dustman sent two bolts of cambric.

Presents are not always given at Christmastime, for in many of the Catholic countries, Christmas Day is a time of solemn religious observance, the giving of gifts being confined to another day in the year.

In Holland and Belgium, December 6, being St. Nicholas Day, is the time when the children receive their gifts from this saint.

In Czechoslovakia (see page 218) an angel who accompanies St. Nicholas is the bearer of the presents.

And in the United States, of course, Santa Claus, a variation of the observance of our early Dutch settlers, presents the gifts Christmas Eve or Christmas Day.

Seldom now do the Germans remember Hertha (see page 59) and bake shoe-shaped cookies as they were accustomed to do in former times. In order to preserve the original purpose of the Christmas celebration they have even put St. Nicholas, or Santa Claus, aside and in his place they think of a messenger coming from the *Christkind*, Christ Child, the Kriss Kringle, who is depicted as a girl child wearing a golden crown, and carrying a small Christmas tree.

In the Sixteenth Century gifts were tied in bundles—something pleasant, something useful, and something for discipline—perhaps candy, pencil, or birch rod.

On Christmas Day in Bulgaria Grandfather Koleda presents gifts to the children and then on New Years the children bestow little remembrances upon their parents (see page 214).

In Denmark, it is an elf, Jule-nissen, who brings the presents (see page 222).

In Greece, St. Basil is the gift-bestowing patron saint (see page 240).

But in many countries the gifts do not come from Santa Claus, nor St. Nicholas, nor the Christ Child. They are connected with the Wise Men. Therefore, this observance of the holiday season is delayed until the Twelfth Night, at which time the Wise Men appear in Poland and Spain, and Befana makes her rounds in Italy (see page 27), and Baboushka in Russia (see page 31).

In Syria the youngest camel which accompanied the Wise Men is called the Camel of Jesus and he presents the gifts (see page 290).

In Switzerland it is St. Lucy and Father Christmas (see page 285) who bestow the presents.

Gifts come from the stars in the heavens in Poland, from the angels in Hungary, and from the *Tante Aria* in Franche-Comte (see page 43).

In Finland, it is *Wainamoinen* and his companion *Ukko* (see page 235), a mythological character depicted as being an elderly gentleman with a long, white mustache.

THE CHRISTMAS TREE

ONCE each year we return to fairyland and if we do not go ourselves, we visit it by proxy through the eyes of each new generation of childhood. Once each year dreams do come true. Once a year we read Dickens' Christmas Carol, we sing hymns, we open our purses to the less fortunate, we trim the Christmas tree—all symbols of Christmas which warm the cockles of our often stony and sophisticated hearts.

Christmas is the children's holiday and when Christmas morning comes, we do indeed descend into fairyland

Are we afraid of sentiment ? Usually yes, but not at Christmas as we look at the glowing tree around which the carols are being sung and from which such peals of innocent laughter ascend.

AN OLD FASHIONED TREE

I like an old fashioned tree best, don't you ? Really now, don't you ? Tell the truth. The more modern tree may look quite like the old fashioned one but it lacks one thing—an important thing, called "associations-with-the-past," or I believe "sentiments" is the better word after all. You know what I mean, but allow me to illustrate; then you may tell your story as you so often have wanted to do.

Sally Volz tells of a four year old girl who watched her parents trimming the Christmas tree and asked if she might not add her little bit. Whereupon she rushed to her room and found one of her tiny shoes with stub toes and runover heels. This she hung on the tree. The family was so pleased by this incident, that although the girl has now graduated from college, each year the tree bears this shoe, besides the many objects which though beautiful, lack the sentiment.

I want the old fashioned Christmas tree to be covered with scores of objects associated with former Christmases and with members of the family. The ideal tree is one for which George, in kindergarten, makes a paper chain, more treasured than any ornament which money can buy. Perhaps Janet, 10, strings popcorn and puts a Cranberry between each ten grains of corn. Margaret, 12, makes a golden star for the top of the tree. Father has been devising a unique setting beneath the tree for some weeks past. At his work bench in the basement he has been putting the finishing touches on the various objects he will use in the Putz, as the Pennsylvania-Germans call the landscape of snow, manger, and shepherds. No one can quite understand where he will hide all the various electrical switches and wires which he plans to use in illuminating the tree and the Christmas scene beneath it. Mother has numerous boxes in the attic and from them she extracts some of the ornaments which she used on the first tree for Margaret. She remembers how happy she was that Margaret was now old enough to enjoy a tree. She had never deprived herself of a tree, for she did not hold the curious philosophy of some friends who said they could not have a tree because there were no children in the family. Oh, yes, mother is sure to find the doll she played with as a child. It had a China head and glossy black China hair. As she looks at the doll now with its faded, prim dress she remembers the struggle she had had in making it. Naturally, she ties this to the tree with her own hands, for nothing must befall it. She remarks about the doll to grandmother. But grandmother is busy with her own contribution. Grandmother came from Germany, and each Christmas she provides a surprise for the family in the form of gilded nuts. She takes English Walnuts and splits them with a knife. Then she writes a little sentiment or a wish for the future on a tiny slip of paper, places it in the nut, and glues the halves together. Oh, the joy of finding your name on one of grandmother's nuts and then being able to read her sentiment. To Margaret, perhaps she writes, "May your new baby doll behave as well as you have." In father's nut one year were these words, "I want to hear you sing, 'Oh, Little Town of Bethlehem' as you did in the boy choir." They well remembered how the upper buttons of his vest strained on the high notes, but he had not dared to let his voice crack, for he had had a most critical audience that night.

Years before, the family had purchased a tree holder which not only revolved the tree but played four lovely Christmas carols.*

Such a tree is more than a decoration for a room. It is a living embodiment of family happiness and we do feel that children prefer a tree loaded with trinkets, secrets, and surprises, whereas grownups often think of the tree in relation to a decorative scheme for the living room. Today evergreens sprayed with silver or white paint are popular, and they may be beautifully decorated with one color lights, particularly blue or golden yellow. Some of the small artificial trees are like little jeweled brooches.

Tin, cellophane, and other fabricated trees are passing fancies, enjoyed for a year or two, and then discarded because they are devoid of the background of sentiment associated with real Christmas trees. However, this is a subject not

*Such a musical tree holder may be obtained from the Lutheran Book Concern, Columbus, Ohio.

open to argument. Our feelings in such matters of sentiment are often more convincing than any amount of logic.

Might it not be interesting, therefore, to turn to the fascinating significance of Christmas greenery and trees ? The Italians have a still different conception and after you have read this chapter, turn to page 248 and read how these people construct something quite as romantic as our time-loved tree, and call it the Ceppo.

CHRISTMAS TREE HISTORY

Since earliest days the bringing of evergreens indoors at Christmastime has been one of the first ways of giving the home a festive air. As Auld* says, "The graceful custom of the use of evergreens has its roots in the profound reverence of the Ancients for all natural phenomena. To their simple and unartificial minds, Nature was everywhere alive. Every fountain had its spirit, every mountain its deity, and every water, grove, and meadow, its supernatural associations. The whisperings of the trees through their leafy boughs was the subtle speech of the god who dwelt within, while the sound of the waves breaking over the pebbly beach was the joyous laughter of the divinities of the sea."

And so, one thing is certain—evergreens were not first used for their decorative value but because of their significance and their ability to bring the world of nature to the indoors.

Perhaps the use of trinkets on the tree dates from the early Roman days when it was common to hang little masks of Bacchus upon trees and vines to impart fertility to every side of the trees to which the wind turned the faces. Virgil refers to these dangling objects as *oscilla* and describes how a pine tree is laden with them.†

The use of evergreens was so closely associated with the garlands of pagan days that in many of the early church

*Auld, William Muir, *Christmas Traditions.*
†*Notes and Queries,* Dec. 16, 1865.

celebrations they were forbidden. For instance, Bishop Martin of Bracae, in 575 forbade the use of all greenery and "other dangerous Calend customs." It was therefore not until the sixteenth century that Christian houses were commonly decorated. In many European countries Fir trees were put up in rooms and adorned with Roses cut from many colored papers, with apples and leafgold and sweets. Perhaps this decoration was reminiscent of the old beliefs that many trees bloomed at Christmastime. (See the Christmas tree legends on page 154.)

Luther and the Christmas Tree

Although Luther was severe in his denunciation of the church which he opposed, and hated the devil who seemed to be lurking near enough him so that he once threw an ink bottle at him, yet he has always been associated with the joys of family life and the love of children. The story of the Nativity had always appealed strongly to Luther. It is related[*] that he wandered through the woods one starry Christmas Eve and became enamoured with the wonder of the night, for the sky was filled with stars. He cut a small, snow-laden Fir tree and when he returned home set this tree up for his children and illuminated it with numerous candles to represent the stars of the heavens, but it was 58 years after his death before we meet with any definite reference to a Christmas tree, so that no doubt it is merely a characteristic story but not an authentic one.

The Strassburg Tree

In Strassburg in 1604 the first Christmas tree appears in literature, although it was not uncommon to bring fruit trees indoors to induce them to bloom in Winter. It is thought that the custom of using Christmas trees in Germany spread from Strassburg and the Christmas tree has always been the center of the German celebration. Writers tell us that as

[*]Auld, William Muir. *Christmas Traditions.*

late as 1860 the German residents of Paris had considerable difficulty in obtaining trees at Christmastime, so that their use is of quite recent date in France.

When Queen Victoria married Prince Albert, he introduced the Christmas tree custom into England.

From the early emigrants of Germany and England we derived our custom of the Christmas trees in America.

CORRECT CUTTING IS A BOON TO FORESTRY

Many well meaning persons have carried on campaigns against the wanton destruction of our forests in order to supply the annual demand for Christmas trees, but eminent forestry authorities tell us that Christmas trees form a very small fraction of the total of forest depletion. Correct cutting of Christmas trees permits sturdier trees to attain greater growth. It is true that our forests are diminishing rapidly, but the solution of the problem is not to prohibit Christmas trees. There would be as much logic in prohibiting the use of lumber for building homes. Life is more than dollars and cents, and may I ask, what better use could be made of a small tree than that it should be chosen to bring as much happiness as does a Christmas tree ? Supposing that our forests are cut to supply them, which is not always the case, for many are being grown especially for sale, yet we are daily destroying more trees for less use than to supply the fireside with an emblem of surprise, joyous homecoming, and the spirit of good will.

The late Charles Lathrop Pack, president of the American Tree Association, said "Conservation is wise use." Those who are interested in growing Christmas trees should send to the Wild Flower Preservation Society, 3740 Oliver Street, Washington, D. C. for Circular No. 35.

KINDS OF TREES COMMONLY USED FOR CHRISTMAS

Depending upon the section of the country in which you live, many different trees are sold at Christmastime for use in the home. The least desirable are the Spruces. You can generally tell the Spruce in two ways; first, the foliage is sharp pointed so that when you grasp it tightly it pricks your hand, and, in the second place, the Spruce is the first Christmas tree to shed its needles. The Fir is the ideal Christmas tree and has been revered for the greatest number of years. It resembles the Spruce except that the needles are not sharp pointed and the tree becomes a golden brown before it sheds its leaves.

The Douglas-fir is commonly used as a Christmas tree. The needles are flat and soft to the touch. The easy way that I have of identifying this tree is to look at the tips of the branches, where there are usually a number of buds which cause the needles to bend aside, changing the regular comblike appearance of the twig. Furthermore, this tree has cones which are furnished with short appendages on each scale.

Hemlock is often sold as a Christmas tree, but this also sheds its foliage when kept in a hot room indoors. A Hemlock is distinguished by having two white lines on the lower side of each of its narrow, needlelike leaves.

Pines have never been favored as Christmas trees, although some of them are interesting if one does not demand conventional, symmetrical trees which resemble the Firs. The Pines are inclined to have an informal habit of growth. They are distinguished by having needlelike leaves which are associated in clusters of three and five.

Redcedars are seldom used as Christmas trees except in certain neighborhoods where they grow wild, but they are not commonly shipped. The foliage in this case is rather prickly but is very tiny and scalelike. It produces berries rather than cones.

What Kind of Christmas Tree Shall I Plant?

There is a growing custom of having living Christmas trees which, after being used in the home, may be set out in the yard to grow more beautiful with the years. Most nurserymen prepare these trees previous to Christmas by digging them carefully and placing them in wooden tubs. If you are located near a nursery it will not be necessary for you to buy tubbed trees for they can be dug with a good ball of earth covered with burlap and then set into any convenient tub in the home, where the tree may be watered without harm to the floor covering.

It is a mistake to buy a living Christmas tree and neglect to water it. We must remember that when the tree has been kept indoors for a long period of time it will be encouraged to grow by the warmth of the home, so that it is wise to set out a living Christmas tree a few days after Christmas.

Those who plant living Christmas trees each year in their home grounds find it is best to chose the spot for the tree late in the Fall before freezing weather arrives. Then the spot where the tree is to be set should be protected with several bushel baskets of leaves or straw, which will serve as insulation for the soil so that it will not freeze. Even though the tree cannot be planted immediately after Christmas because of severe weather, it can be placed outdoors, where it will not be harmed and can be planted as soon as the weather moderates. It is customary to leave the burlap on such a tree, for it will soon rot. However, such trees as are planted in tubs, should be removed from the container before being planted. Even though the soil is frozen, the tree should be copiously watered.

The cheapest living Christmas tree one can buy is the Norway Spruce but on the small home grounds this is not a choice evergreen and the wise gardener chooses a tree which will be of increasing beauty as the years pass, even though the first cost is a little more than for the Norway Spruce.

The Colorado Blue Spruce, the Black Hill Spruce, or the Alcock Spruce are preferable.

Among Firs, the Balsam Fir, sometimes called the Canada Balsam, is the commonest of the desirable Christmas trees when cut and used indoors in our homes. However, these trees grow in the northern forests, where they thrive excellently, but generally make shabby specimens in the usual garden, and for that reason the following Firs should be chosen: Concolor or White Fir, Nordmann Fir, and the Douglas-fir, which is not a true Fir.

Among Pines, the White Pine and Austrian Pine are splendid.

There are many species of Juniper, some of which are known as Redcedar, which are well suited for the foundation plantings of our homes, where the living Christmas trees are seen to best advantage. Most of these do not grow to be extremely tall, but they keep their places near the doorway of our homes. For this purpose we might advise the Common Redcedar or its more beautiful varieties the Cannart, the Schott, and the Silver Redcedar. The Colorado Juniper is extremely hardy and is gray-green in color, as is also the Silver Redcedar mentioned above.

You can make this jolly gnome as a unique Christmas tree decoration (Idea taken from *Der Gute Kamerad*, Germany Vol. 16, 1890

Unique Christmas Tree Ornament

As seen in the sketch on this page, a gnome laughingly holds two candles and balances himself on a branch of the tree. Any number of ingenious figures may be cut from heavy cardboard and colored. Tied to the gnome's feet, an apple holds him in proper balance.

Real candles might be used by gluing blocks of wood to the backs of the arms. On these, the candles could be made to stand.

This is the type of home made decoration which is of greater interest than the ornaments we buy.

Lighting the Tree

Cut trees will shed their needles less readily if placed in water. Some use a tub of moist sand. Others a bucket of water. There are several commercial bases made for Christmas trees which serve as a means of lighting as well. Some are made with a metal cup which holds two quarts of water which does much to keep the tree alive and prevent the needles from shedding. The attractiveness of the base is further increased by the fact that it is provided with sockets for colored lamp bulbs and also an outlet plug for connecting the lights for the tree decorations.

Score Card for Living Christmas Tree

General effect, including color and size.................. 30
Beauty of tree—symmetry, condition, and health....... 20
Propriety of materials used to decorate............... 15
Adequate lighting.................................... 15
Originality and distinction........................... 20

100

Without giving definite points we might judge the tree on its general effect as follows: cheer, originality, and balance.

Famous Christmas Trees

In Wilmington, North Carolina, there grows an extremely large Live Oak tree festooned with Spanish Moss. The spread of the branches of this tree is in excess of 110 feet. Several years ago it was said that 10,000 people attended the celebration beneath this tree. More than 750 multi-colored lights, and over 1000 ornaments were used to decorate this tree. Beneath it, on a brilliantly lighted platform was a cross, illuminated with 12 lights typifying the 12 apostles, and at the left of the platform a Christmas Crib scene was staged.

At Altadena, California, at the foot of the Sierra Madre Mountains, we have a mile-long avenue of Deodar Cedars.

The story of how they happened to be planted is interestingly told by Virginia June, in *Garden and Home Builder*. In 1882 a world traveler, Captain Frederick J. Woodbury, was traveling in India. On the slopes and up to an altitude of 7,000 to 12,000 feet in the Himalaya Mountains, he saw the magnificent Deodar Cedars of India, the older trees of the ancient forests rising to a height of 150 feet. He gathered their seeds and planted them on his ranch in California. Three years later, when the little seedlings were about 2 feet tall, Captain Woodbury's two sons transplanted them on two sides of a spacious private driveway leading to the ranch residence. The ranch is no more, the Captain himself is no more, and the avenue is now a public thoroughfare. These trees are illuminated each year and thousands of visitors come great distances to see this Christmas-tree row.

The Nation's Christmas Tree

At high noon on Christmas Day, 1925, the famous General Grant tree, located in the General Grant National Park, was designated as the Nation's Christmas Tree. This park is due east of Fresno, 64 miles. Quoting from the United States Department of the Interior, the tree is estimated to be 267 feet high and is one of the most celebrated in the United States. It is one of the so-called Bigtrees, *Sequoia gigantea*. Devotional and patriotic services are held beneath the tree each year and are broadcast over nationwide hookups. Snow falls abundantly in these parts, so that sometimes the weather is not favorable. Otherwise, a large number of visitors attend this unique ceremony.

CHRISTMAS GREENERY

Best for Large Wreaths

White Pine. Fine, graceful, gray-green foliage. More graceful than most other Pines.

Fir. According to time used, this will be either gray or almost blackish-green and extremely useful because it does not shed the needles.

Douglas-fir. Blackish green, pliable.

Blue Spruce. According to the variety used, this will offer bluish-or gray-green contrast, but for indoor use it is likely to shed badly.

Boxwood. Useful for making wreaths entirely of this material. It is broad, and does not combine with some other types of fine, needlelike evergreens.

Oregon Hollygrape. A broadleaf evergreen, commonly cultivated and growing wild on Pacific Coast. Foliage, resembling Holly, glistening green, sometimes turning red in Winter.

English Ivy. Dark, blackish-green, making a flat wreath but can be combined with other foliage such as Mountain-laurel and Boxwood.

Glossy Privet. Commonly cultivated in the South. The leaves seem to be made of green wax.

Galax. Heart-shaped leaves, either green or bronze, making a very flat wreath, although they would be very good for use on the cloth in table decorations.

Southern Evergreen Huckleberry. Commonly for sale by florists and has a thick leaf seldom more than ¾ inch long; sold in great sprays of foliage.

Groundpine. In danger of being exterminated from woods, due to the fact that it is the commonest material used for making roping.

Mountain-laurel. Another one of very commonly over-collected material, with thick, glossy, evergreen foliage, and may be ordered from reliable growers.

American Holly. The wild Holly of eastern coast and the South, it has been ruthlessly gathered and in some places almost exterminated.

English Holly. Grown in large quantities in plantations of Northwest. Foliage is glistening green, far more attractive than the American Holly, and generally accompanied by splendid large, red berries.

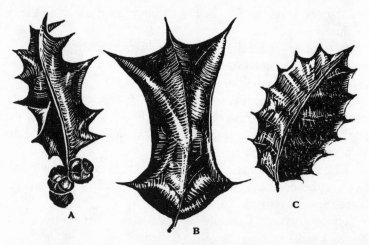

Types of Holly—A shows English Holly, with its deeply notched, spiny toothed, lustrous leaves. B is the Chinese Holly, the leaves of which are almost rectangular. C is the American Holly, so familiar to all at Christmas time

Best for Small Wreaths

Colorado Juniper. Gray-green, very fine, needlelike foliage.
Box. The smaller foliage sort should be chosen.
Arborvitae. Produces flat sprays.
Yew. Generally very dark, almost blackish-green in Winter.

If the evergreens are pruned in the Winter to merely shape them up a little, you can often use the short tips for evergreen arrangements indoors. Pfitzer Juniper generally has some branches which depart from your ideal and can be removed judiciously. Due to the usual great variety in the home planting, a contrast in color is possible.

Not So Good Because Needles Shed

Both Spruces and Hemlocks shed their needles very quickly in the dry atmosphere of our homes but when used outdoors they are satisfactory.

Fruits and Berries to Use

In order to add touches of color to our wreaths almost any of our edible fruits may be used; for example, small apples, such as Jonathans, small oranges, kumquats, cranberries. A number of species of Crab Apples produce attractive yellow and red fruits. Hawthorn fruits may be gathered early in the year and stored in a cool place in the basement for Winter use. Persimmons are useful where they are not too expensive. Many gardeners grow a vast array of small gourds. Small white onions and radishes and green and red peppers are also interesting. Many of these fruits, especially the apples and gourds, may be given a coat of shellac to preserve them as well as to add a shiny luster.

Among the interesting berries of value for Christmas decorations are, first of all, the Winterberry, *Ilex verticillata*, a Holly which sheds its foliage in the Winter. There are many species of Roses, notably the Multiflora, from which our modern Rambler varieties have been derived. Bittersweet and Buffaloberry both contribute an orange color. On the Pacific Coast the Christmasberry, or Photinia, or California-holly, is commonly used but it has never been placed on the eastern market.

Cones

Almost any of the cones of the evergreens may be used, but, of course, some are much more decorative than others. Except for the largest wreaths, the cones of many of the Spruces and Pines are extremely long and poorly adapted for combining in wreaths or evergreen combinations. It is not necessary to give a list of the different species of ever-greens because they vary so much in the different sections of the United States, but the foresighted decorator collects cones throughout the Summer wherever he goes for possible use at Christmastime. Some Firs and the Hemlocks have the smallest cones, and these are particularly desirable for small wreaths and for tiny evergreen arrangements within the home. The Nature lover believes the cones of the Douglas-fir particularly attractive because each scale has a small appendage.

Save Our Woodlands

The excessive use of many of our choice woodland pos-sessions is being prevented by such organizations as the Garden Club of America, National Council of State Garden Clubs, The Wild Flower Preservation Society, also by laws passed in the various states. Holly, Groundpine, and Moun-tain-laurel are the three plants which are most in danger of extermination if the present wasteful destruction goes on.

LET'S DECORATE THE HOME*

TO BE the only one in the neighborhood without some sort of Christmas cheer, even if only a red candle in the window, would be almost like having a "Scrooge and Marley" sign over the front door. And with the wealth of material to work with and the many places to put it—over the doors, from the windows, and across balcony porches—our imagination can start sparking until we see "Christmas" in every available object. First, we think of Christmas greens, and rightly! The use of evergreens in our homes is based on the old belief that the woodland spirits dwelt in them during the Winter, so that when we bring evergreens into our homes we are welcoming perhaps a dryad or a hamadryad.

In the living room our hearts are warmed by the new setting given our Yule Log as it flickers and flares to the chimney. Garlands grace each doorway, and the feast table, of course, is dressed in holiday color, as are all the vantage points throughout the home.

We may have been content with the usual red candle in its green holder until we saw the clever but inexpensive things which one of our hostesses fashioned last season—and with such ordinary objects as cranberries, colored bottles, textile pieces from the scrap box, crepe paper, cotton, nuts, fruits, and cellophane. No, indeed! Christmas decorations are not a matter of money but of ingenuity. I have found it much easier, too, to introduce originality into my Christmas deco-

Suggestions for this chapter contributed by Phyllis Hall Stevens.

rations since I have thought of the adaptability of each available object to my particular home, considering color, texture, and shape, rather than imitate what I have seen.

Christmas Colors

Red and green are the conventional colors of Christmas, no doubt because of the green Holly with its red berries, but there is no historical or legendary reason for these two colors. White is really the true Christmas color if we are to observe the dictates of the church. More and more persons are departing from the conventional green and red, and using dark blue and white or silver, or red gold. Try variations of the usual brilliant and intense red and green, coral and lettuce-green, rust and olive, and wine and blue-green.

FIREPLACE

Inasmuch as the Christmas cheer centers about the fireplace it is interesting to concentrate the attention here, or on the tree. Many times it is quite unnecessary to decorate the mantel elaborately; it merely needs accent. Choose a few luxuriant sprays of evergreens to surround the electric fixtures, and substitute candle bulbs in place of the common globe bulbs, with perhaps a silver or gold star to serve as a sconce.

If, however, the space above the mantel is rather large, it is easy to devise various interesting garlands of evergreen material which drape themselves gracefully from the ceiling or molding, with some evergreens placed on the mantelpiece to form greater unity in the design. Two evergreens are used to flank the opening of the fireplace. See sketch on page 84.

Giant candles* made of wooden frames covered with some translucent material such as cel-o-glass, produce a very attractive appearance when lighted from within by lamps in home-made tin reflectors located at the top and at the bottom. A covering of cellophane may be used to obtain a shiny, frosty appearance, and this, together with a flame-shaped lamp surrounded by a flame-shaped cardboard cutout, makes a decoration suitable for a number of places in the home.

OVER-DOOR DECORATIONS

Rather than the usual garland it will be interesting to make definite treatments for some of the principal doorways indoors or out, as well as windows. In illustration on page 86, for figure A a cardboard was cut to fit over the door and made somewhat like a squat pyramid but resembling the form of a tree. To this cardboard, evergreens were sewed with string, or wired. Small cones or berries may be added

*Christmas Lighting Suggestions, Westinghouse Lamp Company. Contains sketches of this and many other Christmas decoration and lighting ideas. Sent free.

Over-door Decorations. These decorations are fully described in the text on pages 85 and 86

for color. It is suggested that there be a greater mass of color on one side.

For B, a board was used. In this nails were driven from the back so that they were long enough to secure gourds or fruits in position. Various nuts may also be used, in which case they could be glued in place. Pine needles were used as a background.

For C, various cones were wired together in pendant clusters. When finished a few evergreen branches could be added to cover any wires which might show.

For D, three small bells were secured to the door frame with a bow of gay ribbon and a few Pine branches were intriguingly used among them. Sleigh bells, such as were formerly used on the thills of a cutter, would be ideal.

WINDOW ARRANGEMENTS

Let's put a candle, a wreath, or a spray of evergreens in window, each being careful to avoid the garish effects sometimes seen. Read about the community of Beacon Hill, in Boston, page 296, for here the windows of all the homes are filled with beautiful objects.

A Christmas scene cut-out is easily devised by an ingenious person. This may be placed above a door using merely a simple scene cut from cardboard and lighted from the rear. More effective is a multiplane silhouette as shown on this page.* Composition board, wood, and colored lamps (10- to 25-watt) are the materials required.   The planes may be

*How to Light Your Home for the Holidays, General Electric Company, Nela Park, Cleveland, Ohio. This booklet will offer scores of similar Christmas lighting suggestions.

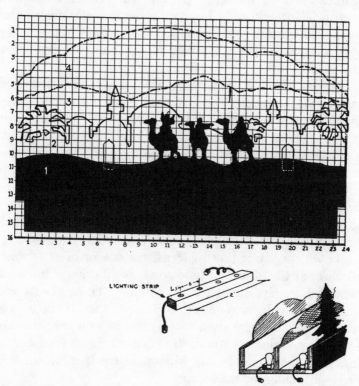

A Christmas silhouette, for use over a door or in a window, which may be easily made by the home craftsman. (See text.)

painted, if desired, to improve the daytime appearance of the display. A suggested color scheme: Plane 1, black; Plane 2, tan, lighted with amber-orange lamps; Plane 3, dark blue or purple, lighted with red and blue lamps; Plane 4, light blue, lighted with blue lamps. The cross-hatching on the diagram enables the builder to enlarge the pattern to any size desired. The model shown is 24 inches wide.

Making Stained Glass Windows*

The curtain rose on a chapel in King Arthur's Court. The walls were hung with a soft gray cyclorama and a huge stained glass window gleamed from back center stage with such brilliant color and beauty that a low murmur rippled over the audience and then there came the thrill of every stage designer's life—a moment of applause for the effective set.

It was my first experience with paper and cardboard stained glass windows and I've used them just as effectively many times since: once for the "Bluebird" production at Nichols School, Evanston, Ill., once for a Christmas pageant, and often for the home. Decorating the home for Christmas is much like dressing the stage and if you haven't tried this economical, yet surprisingly beautiful medium, you'll be delighted with the result. You have only to hold crepe paper to the sun to see the effect these windows will have when brilliantly lighted from the back.

It will be interesting to transform one or more of your windows at Christmastime and create the illusion of having a beautiful, costly, stained glass window. These effects are easily attained by anyone with a little patience. If you have a window which is already distinctive, such as a semi-circular one over your door, this is the best type to choose for decorating, as decorating only one window in the living room will leave an unfinished appearance.

*The writer is indebted to Lindsay Lockerby Field, the illustrator of this book, for the descriptions and designs.

You can easily transform the windows of your home, creating the illusion of beautiful, costly stained glass windows

Key

B	Blue	LB	Light Blue	RV	Red-violet
BG	Blue-green	LR	Light Red (Light Yellow Scarlet)	S	Salmon
BR	Brown			T	Tan
BV	Blue-violet	LY	Light Yellow	V	Violet
C	Coral	O	Orange	Y	Yellow
DB	Dark Blue	P	Purple	YG	Yellow-green
G	Green	R	Scarlet-red	YO	Yellow-orange
Lav.	Lavender	RO	Red-orange		

The most beautiful effect can be attained by the use of crepe paper and black cardboard. The cardboard simulates the lead and the crepe paper the glass, so that the design is traced upon the cardboard, which is then cut to make a stencil of ½ inch width outlining the design. When the stencil has been completed, trace each section on the various colors of crepe paper designated in the sketch. The crepe paper is then cut a trifle larger to allow space for pasting.

It is well to place the paste on the cardboard rather than on the crepe paper. You may produce gradations in the tints of the crepe paper by stretching the paper before you put it on. Sometimes we may use several thicknesses of crepe paper to modify the color, such as yellow over green to produce yellow-green.

Such designs may be cut from heavy black paper and merely hung in the window.

Suggested Patterns

Refer to sketches on page 89.

A, designed for a full window such as is found in the average home. There are six panes of glass at the top and one at the bottom. A large candle running through the three center panes holds the window together and eliminates the half-and-half appearance.

B, designed for a semi-circular window such as you often find in a door. The design is conventionalized Holly, using shades of red and green crepe paper—green for the leaves, and red-violet for the background, with brighter red and orange Holly berries clustered in the center.

C and D are more difficult cutouts, as they involve figures. These could be used effectively as one distinctive pane if you did not wish to cover the whole window.

E and F are extremely simple designs.

G is conceived as a cutout to be placed on a mantel, perhaps lighted from the rear, as shown in illustration on page 87. This can also be used as a cutout, placed directly at the base of one large window pane. It will fit any type of window, as the upper section is left for the clear glass, only the design itself covered with crepe paper.

The Christmas Table

The sound of a bell breaks the long expectancy as we impatiently wait in the living room. Delicious aromas have been assailing our nostrils for ever so long. Of course, there is turkey, mince pie, three kinds of home-made jelly—all these things which we know about but why have we been kept from the dining room ? There must be some surprise.

Eventually, we enter the room. Then we know. Mother has been planning something she thinks we will like— a table decoration. Days before she could start the dinner preparations, she had plenty of time to consider the matter.

At a remnant counter weeks ago, she picked up some dark green curtain material which she has used as a table cloth. Father laughed and wondered how the cloth could be washed if he chanced to spill the turkey gravy on it. Sister begged it, for it was just the color she needed in her room. In fact, everyone had something to say about the table and mother knew her setting was a success.

In the center of the table mother placed a tray (see sketch, page 92). She had purchased a tin one and had given it a coat of silver paint, edged with red. On the tray she set eight or ten candles of various heights, ranging in color from deep scarlet to pure white. Among the candles were sprigs of Holly and some gay Winterberries.

At each plate she set a green nut cup to which she pasted a red paper Poinsettia. Place cards were made from green and red paper cut in the shape of a Holly leaf.

I suppose some folks wouldn't think the table very unusual, but it had a touch of the holiday spirit which all enjoyed because it had been planned and executed by mother with originality and without going to great expense.

Let's make the Christmas table decoration a little different.
The text suggests many ways of doing this

Ideas

This incident is related so that the reader may see that the resourceful Christmas hostess needs only to give the matter a little thought and she can find dozens of new and inexpensive ways of adding originality to the Christmas table. For example:

Try red or blue cellophane over a white table cloth and carry out the accessories in similar or contrasting colors. Cellophane will not discolor the cloth as will some colored papers.

Paste various sized stars to the white cloth. There are scores of other Christmas symbols—Santas, reindeer, Poinsettias, candles, and Holly sprays made of paper.

Use a ribbon of gold or silver paper down the center of the table.

A number of interesting things may be made of paper. Any stationery store can supply Dennison Manufacturing Co. booklets, such as *Gay Decorations for Parties, Dances and Banquets*.

When an uneven number of guests are to be seated at the table, you might confine the evergreen and floral arrangement to one end of the table, father at the other, with the guests seated at the sides.

Imagine the charm added by sewing a few tiny bells along the hem of the cloth so that when the guests move there is a sound of tinkling.

Down the center of the table you might arrange a row of candles of different heights, or the handy man might make the star described on page 101.

Various strange figures may be made from fruits, nuts and gum drops. A large prune stuffed with a marshmallow with a raisin for a head and almonds for feet makes a penguin. Have you seen an orange cut to resemble an elephant? Cut round flaps for ears and long, narrow strips for trunk and tail. Cloves would be used for eyes. Four flaps are cut for legs which cover toothpicks used as supports.

A Santa made from a marshmallow, an apple, three cloves and a bit of cotton

For the table an attractive Santa may be made from an apple. Use a big red apple for the body, a marshmallow for the head, and cloves for eyes and nose. Two skewers can be used for legs, which are covered with cotton batting. Cotton is also used for a belt, whiskers, hair, and for covering short pieces of wire inserted as arms. A little red cap is made from pieces of tissue paper secured to the marshmallow with a pin. A third skewer is inserted at the rear to give Santa a three-point landing.

Amusing gumdrop trees may be made from wire or natural twigs such as Hawthorn. Various colored gumdrops and other candies are secured to the branches.

Read the chapter "The Mediaeval Dinner" (pages 104 to 116). Wouldn't it be fun to stage such a dinner replete with curious old tableware and follow out the manners of another age? For a table spread, you would use a rich but cheap replica of an old tapestry or royal purple material. If you have a theatrical supply house near you, try them as they have gorgeous materials for about sixty cents a yard. You might serve the food in wooden bowls. Gather all the old heirloom silver in the house and put it on the table—goblets, casters, trays, and creamers. Read about the strangely interesting subtleties made of sugar. The clever cook might enjoy making such objects out of cake and sugar frosting. This would be the centerpiece. During the feast, relate the stories of the brawn, the peacock, bringing in the boar's head, Sir Loin—we promise the conversation will not lag.

Read the chapter "Christmas Around the World" (pages 201 to 300). Aren't you inspired with a half dozen unusual Christmas parties that can be planned with appropriate table arrangements representing the various countries?

For instance, there is Sweden. A miniature bird's Christmas tree as the central motif on the table. (See page 257.) A sheaf of wheat and a few birds from the dime store are all that are needed. Paper stores and wallpaper dealers will have unusual materials to be used as a cover; some will have a resemblance to straw or burlap.

Then there are unlimited possibilities in a Mexican Christmas. A gay serape for a cloth, crude earthenware for dishes and a large, highly decorated jar filled with tiny laughable gifts will make a typical *Piñata* for a centerpiece. (See page 254.)

A table planned around the gift bearers would serve as a fascinating outlet for the young aspiring artists of the family. Draw and color pictures of Befana, St. Nicholas, Santa Claus, Christkind, Tante Aria and the Father Star, the Wise Men, the Gentle Camel of Jesus, Jule-nissen—and use these as place cards. A narrow baby ribbon would lead from each figure to an Urn of Fate (see page 248) in the center of the table. A divination would be found at the end of each ribbon—a tiny skillet, a ring, a flat-iron, a coin, and any number of objects which prognosticate the future of the lucky or luckless recipient. Such objects can be obtained from the dime store and are used in wedding cakes.

Rules for Table Decorations

Remember that the expert has rules in all table decoration. The principal ones to observe are:

Let the arrangement be low enough so that the guests may see each other and hold free conversation without dodging the centerpiece.

Let there be plenty of space for good and easy food service.

The receptacles should be subordinated to the material within them.

Have plenty of color but let it be harmonious. Too much green without something else more gay will be monotonous in artificial light.

In judging your Christmas arrangements you will want to think of the points used in flower shows and their relative importance. (See page 100.)

Attractive Wreaths

These descriptions refer to sketches on opposite page.

A. This wreath with its contrasting colors may be made from evergreen foliage for the lower half sprayed white, or from some white foliage such as Artemisia Silver King with red berries of some sort, in this case rose hips, used for contrast. The foliage for the upper half may be fine evergreen foliage or such bolder foliage as Galax or Evergreen Huckleberry, both of which would have a reddish cast. Gray Bayberries would show off to advantage in such a wreath.

B. This wreath is well made upon a manufactured wire frame and is filled with shellacked gourds among evergreens.

C. At a Maryland Evergreen Show, a wreath similar to this was called *Juvenileus Tummyacheus* and won first prize. It is decidedly a children's wreath made of candy. Fill a wire wreath frame with moss and cover the upper half with white paper and cellophane. The lower half should be covered with red cellophane. Wire is bent into the form of hairpins and used to secure candy canes to the moss. White gumdrops are used for color on the red cellophane, and red gumdrops on the white section. A large cluster of candy sticks still wrapped in paper or cellophane is combined with various sorts of Christmas candy to make the mass at the base.

D. A wreath of such fruits as grapes, apples, oranges, kumquats, crabapples, lemons and nuts are used with a background of evergreens. These fruits are best shellacked.

E. Several textures of evergreens are used (Pine and Fir perhaps) and among the branches are tucked a mass of cones.

How to Make a Wreath

Frame. If we desire to make a small wreath, one not over a foot in diameter, a coat hanger can be bent into a circle.

Attractive wreaths (see text on opposite page)

For larger wreaths, wire about the thickness of a coat hanger should be purchased or a soft Willow branch might be bent into circular form.

Florists can supply wire wreath frames which will be useful for large wreaths or for those in which heavy fruits and gourds are used. Such wire frames are wrapped with heavy green paper on the back. Then wet Sphagnum Moss is stuffed tightly into the frame and wrapped round and round with green cord to prevent the moss from falling out. Unless the moss in the wreath is moist, the wires used to attach the fruits will not easily penetrate the moss, so that old wreaths should be soaked before using.

Plant Materials. The evergreens used in the wreath should be cut into sprays about 6 inches long, in which case the tip of each branch is mainly used. If one desires the wreath to be very thick, other material besides the tips may be somewhat worked into the wreath out of sight. If Pine cones are used in the wreath, they should be wired with a thin wire, secured to a few of the basal scales of the cone. Various fruits may be attached with wires by using a loop at one end to prevent them passing through the entire fruit. The wire should pass through so that it strikes the core of an apple, in which case it will be held more securely than when merely pushed through the flesh.

Tying the Evergreens. At the beginning of the making of the wreath it is necessary to decide whether all the evergreens will be tied on in one direction, or whether they will be arranged so that they will face the top or bottom of the wreath. Hold a few evergreens in the left hand and place them on the frame. Then use a fine spool wire, jute cord, or binder twine. Tie this first group of sprays securely and as each successive group of sprays is added they are progressively tied with the wire or cord. One needs to watch the progress of the outline of the wreath, both from the outside as well as the inside. A wreath is more attractive when the opening in the center is large, so that a little less material is con-

stantly added to the inside of the wreath than to the outside.
Minor irregularities may be removed after the wreath is
finished by the use of a shears, but it is impossible to make a
symmetrical wreath out of one that has been irregularly constructed.

We may make a wreath which is beautiful from both
sides, or face the evergreen material in one direction only,
according to the place where the wreath will be used.

In using fruits, berries, or Pine cones, it is well to inter-
sperse them among the evergreens as the wreath progresses.
However, it is always possible to insert additional decorative
material after the wreath is finished.

In using sprays of small fruits such as Rose hips or Cranberries, or yellow Crab Apples, or Kumquats, they should be
wired first so that the stems are long enough to be securely
fastened to the wreath.

How to Make Garlands

In the making of garlands the same process is used as in
the making of a wreath except that a heavy cord is needed
instead of a wire frame. The length of the cord should be
carefully measured by arranging the cord first in the perma-
nent place so that it assumes a graceful festoon effect. It
is then secured with a nail to a wooden table and the pieces
of evergreen are tied to it.

In making large swags for over the mantelpiece, sometimes
a wire framework is used. Ordinary poultry wire or even
window screen is cut to the desired shape. And the evergreen branches are secured to it either by sewing or by short
bits of flexible wire cut hairpin shape.

> We ring the bells and we raise the strain,
> We hang up garlands everywhere
> And bid the tapers twinkle fair,
> And feast and frolic—and then we go
> Back to the same old lives again.
> —Susan Coolidge—Christmas

Score Cards for Christmas Decorations

In judging wreaths, ropes, and other Christmas decorations it is wise to consider the conservation of such plants as Mountain-laurel, Groundpine, and Holly.

Artistic motif and workmanship	30
Appropriateness	30
Originality	20
Economy	10
Conservation idea	10
	100

Evergreen Candlestick

The evergreen candlestick described in the text

A few handfuls of moss, preferably sphagnum moss obtained from a florist, are placed in a coffee can lid or other tin dish. This moss should be packed tightly around the candle and then wrapped round and round with string. Into this, according to the taste of the designer, tiny branches of Boxwood, as well as fine-foliage evergreens and decorative berries, are stuck. In order to make the small fruits stand in the position desired, it may be well to secure each spray to a small wire or toothpick.

A 6-Pointed Lath Star

An interesting variation of a wreath for general decoration for home or church window was seen at the Christmas party of the English Folk Dance Society of New York. Six laths were tacked together to form a six-pointed star, as shown in the illustration, and entwined with a few evergreen branches.

A six-pointed star made from laths, painted half red and half white

A STAR-SHAPED CANDLESTICK

In order to construct the candlestick shown in the illustration, several years ago, I used a star with a radius of 8½ inches, on a base with a radius of 6 inches. Because it is difficult to find a board wide enough so that a star of this size can be cut it is necessary to splice the board. Of course, expert craftsmen would glue this and do a splendid finished job, but for temporary use it is unnecessary to splice the boards permanently, as they can be cut out and merely nailed into position. Five holes about ¾ inch in

A star-shaped candlestick which the handy man will enjoy making for an attractive Christmas centerpiece

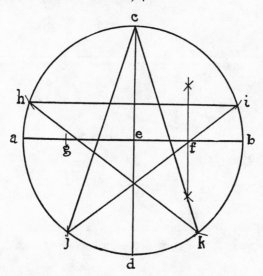

HOW TO DRAW A FIVE-POINTED STAR

Make a four-inch circle and draw the horizontal and vertical diameters, *a-b*, and *c-d*. Mark the point of intersection *e*. Bisect *e-b*, and mark the point of intersection *f*. With *f* as a center, lay off distance from *f* to *c* on *f-a*, marking the point *g*. Now with *c* as the center and *c-g* as a radius lay off *h*, *i*, *j*, and *k*. Then draw the star

diameter were bored, but holes the size of the candles should be used.

This star and base were painted with aluminum paint at the top; the edges of the star painted red, and the edges of the base green. But your color scheme might be different. Careful painting of this star is not very necessary, as evergreens used to decorate the star will hide any poor workmanship.

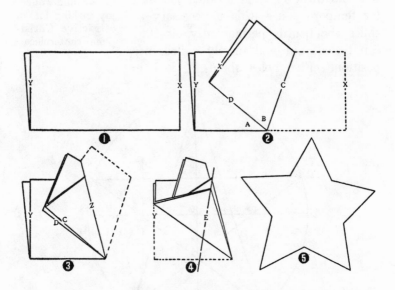

HOW TO FOLD PAPER TO MAKE A FIVE-POINTED STAR

Take a square of paper, size depending on size of star. Fold it as shown in Fig 1. See Fig. 2; then fold at the center so that the angle B is twice that of A. This can be done only by estimating but you will know you are right or wrong when you come to the step shown in Fig. 4. Fold edge C over to the edge of D, with the result shown in Fig. 3. Now fold Y toward Z, with the result shown in Fig. 4. If it does not fit properly you have estimated angles A and B incorrectly so merely unfold and change the angles of A and B. Now cut line E. The more abrupt the angle the more acute are the points of the star. In order to make a star of definite size, larger or smaller, merely draw lines from the points to the center and measure equal distances on each line

Bringing in the Yule Log

THE MEDIAEVAL DINNER

JUST imagine the scene in the kitchen of the old mediaeval castle just before the Christmas dinner. The huge fireplace is big enough to burn the trunks of small trees. An intricate series of spits is ranged up its head-high opening. Huge caldrons are hung upon bracket arms. Each is steaming with some broth or gravy, or meaty viand. Just as in our day, everyone keeps the holiday but the cooks.

CASPAR'S KITCHEN

Witness the busy time of Caspar, the cook, as well as the kitchen men and maids who have been working for days and days. Many have had their ears boxed. The dullards have been told again and again to hold some choice meats closer to the fire so that they will be done as our master, Sir Belvedere, likes them.

"What is the use of my using the finest herbs in the stew if you blockhead maids spoil it in the cooking," scolds Caspar. "I used the whole supply of my best saffron and you have cooked the gravy so long that now it's only a pasty mess. Stand closer to the fire. *You* may roast but you won't broil. And you, too, stir that! Where is the strength in your wrists ? You haven't milked enough cows. Turn the spit slower. You'll have those fowls parched before they are cooked through. Yes, boy, put the wines in the tall ewers. The peacock holds his head too crooked and the feathers of his wings should be spread more. Hurry with the subtleties. Line them up in the order of serving. You have touched St. Joseph with your sooty finger and broken the nose from the angel. Wipe it gently with this cloth dipped in sugar. How will I serve 200 guests with this dull help? The gravy on the neats' tongues is as thin as pea soup. Boil it down quickly. Lady Beatrice will soon be coming in for the peacock. John, you will lead off with the mead as soon as you see the boys enter with the yule log. Peter, you follow with mustard and brawn. It's the best I've served. Sir Belvedere should like it. Then you come, Wilfrid. Be careful with that boar's head. Remember, you always drop things. Your fingers are so slippery. Grasp the platter with both hands, holding the rim. Don't look scared as you carry it. Put on a grin. Pull up your long hose. George, are all the trenchers placed? I've never seen a feast so far from ready for serving as this one. I want the jellies dished, three kinds mixed in each plate."

ROWENA AND THE WASSAIL BOWL

Before the feast, the guests were served the wassail bowl and soon their appetites were awakened and their feet were as light as their heads.

Saxon ancestors quaffed ale from the skulls of their enemies but the story of the origin of the wassail bowl is interesting. Rowena, fair daughter of Hengist presented Prince Vortigern with a bowl of wine and saluted him with, "Lord King, *Wass-heil*," to which he answered, "*Drinc-heile*," and saluted her then after his fashion. He was immediately smitten with her charms and married her soon after.

The Wassail Bowl

"*Wass-heil*" may be rendered into modern English as "What hail" or "Here's to you."

The wassail bowl itself was one of graceful design frequently ornamented with branches of greenery to form a canopy over it. It was generally a mixture of hot ale, sugar, nutmeg or ginger but those who could afford it used rich wine highly spiced and sweetened. Apples floated on the surface and were referred to as lamb's wool, because of its smoothness and softness. Other writers call the whole decoction lamb's wool. By some it was called "old man's beard."

In the reign of Henry VII wassail was introduced with much ceremony, according to Sandys.* Steward, treasurer, comptroller went for a drink, followed by the King's and Queen's servers, with towels around their necks and dishes in hand. Next, came the King's and Queen's carvers, ushers of the chambers, with piles of cups. Gentleman of the chapel stood at one end of the hall. The steward called, "Wassail, wassail, wassail," and the gentleman answered in wassail song or carol.

The Feast

But, let us hasten to the feast. Lords and ladies are seated according to rank. The great candelabra near the fireplace are lighted. Sir Belvedere is concerned lest the candles near the rafters shall not last till the feast is over.

Yule Log

There is a blast of horns without the hall, the sound of gay song is heard. Two men are tugging the yule log. It is a massive log—the base of an ancient apple tree, which has been selected for long burning.

The old story goes that the log is really an old cart horse called Dun who is stuck in the mire. Some of the party try to draw it out but they require assistance. They pull the log along from the forest with songs and merriment and try to drop it on each other's toes.

As they enter the great hall the entire company bursts into the old song, written by Herrick:

*Sandys—*Christmastide.*

Come bring, with a noise,
My merrie, merrie boys
The Christmas Log to the firing;
While my good dame, she
Bids ye all be free,
And drinke to your heart's desiring.

With last yeere's Brand
Light the new Block, and
For good successe in his spending,
On your psalteries play,
That sweet luck may
Come while the log is a treending.

As suggested in the song, a piece of last year's log has been saved and is now kindled so that the new log may soon burst into flames.

Then Sir Belvedere rises and, holding high his cup, he shouts so all can hear, "This yule log burns. It destroys all old hatreds and misunderstandings. Let your envies vanish and let the spirit of good fellowship reign supreme for this season and through all the year."

Not Read by Hungry Men

Agents had been sent to Constantinople, Babylon, Alexandria, Palestine, and Phoenicia to search for new delicacies to inflame a luxurious appetite. Even with all these rare morsels, cooking finesse had not yet developed to the perfection of today and I fear that you and I would consider such a banquet a sorry mess of pottage rather than "a dainty dish to set before the king." Even so, Thomas K. Hervey wrote that the descriptions of the early feasts were so redolent of good things that they cannot be read by hungry men.

The Boar's Head

No article of diet is as often served at Christmas as the boar's head. Its use is based not only on its value as an article of food but it carries symbolism as well. The boar has long been revered as having taught mankind the art of plowing because he roots into the ground with his tusks.

Wilfrid, the bearer of the boar's head, was a lusty, beefy fellow

Some say the custom goes back to pre-Christian days when the Druids killed a boar and offered its head as a sacrifice to the Goddess Freya at the Winter solstice. Henry VI had it served at his coronation feast. As a Christmas dish it was first established by Henry VIII. The eating of suckling pig today is a variation of eating the boar's head.

The boars were slain by men with swords or else they were hunted with hounds. Some old paintings show as many as a hundred dogs attacking the boar.

At our feast the boar's head was brought to the festive table in great state. The Master of the Revels ushered in the bearer of the head and he was followed by choristers and minstrels, singing and playing. Oftentimes a man entered first, accompanied by two pages. He carried the bloody sword with which the boar was slain. Then followed the bearer of the boar's head.

It was a great honor to serve this delicacy, and the lusty, beefy Wilfrid was chosen for the purpose. The head was dressed with a garland of Rosemary and Laurel. As a final touch, a lemon, the symbol of plenty, was placed in its mouth.

Choked the Savage with the Sage

A story says that an Oxford student was studying in Shotover Forest away from the diverting influences of his companions, when suddenly he saw a wild boar rushing at him open-mouthed. The student was reading Aristotle and had presence of mind to cram the book into the jaws of the beast. He exclaimed, *"Graecum est,"* and one writer said that he choked the savage with the sage. Another writes: "The poor student could not waste a good Aristotle by losing it in the neck of a boar, so the head was cut off and the book recovered. But a good boar's head could not be wasted any more than a classic tome, so it was taken to the college and was roasted and eaten. It is still the custom at Queen's College, Oxford, to have elaborate ceremonies at the bringing in of boar's head though it is said that the head is false and contains pieces of brawn.

A TALE OF A MERRY CHRISTMAS CARROLL, SUNG BY WOMEN*

There was sometime an old Knight, who being disposed to make himself merry at Christmas time, sent all his tenants and their families and poor neighbors and bade them sit down to a feast. When they had assembled about the board and were about to set to the food, the Knight rose and said:

"Now, let no Man eat nor drinke until he who is master over his wife shall sing a lusty carroll."

There were many glances about the room to see who would be the musician. After a dry hemme or two, a shy man rose and sang a few words of an olde carroll, but he sat down suddenly through an unseen influence.

Then said the Knight, "Let no Woman eat nor drinke until she who is master over her husband shall sing a lusty carroll."

Whereupon the whole assemblage of Women fell all to such a singing that there was never heard such a catterwalling peece of musicke. Whereat the knight laughed so heartily, that it did him halfe as muche good as a corner of his Christmas pie.

*This has been rendered into more modern English from *Pasquil's Jests*, 1609.

Sir Henry Grey Has a Pie Made

Huge meat pies were made that are unbelievable as to size and content. It is recorded that one gigantic pie was baked for Sir Henry Grey. The recipes of the chroniclers differ but all agree that it was 9 feet in circumference and weighed 165 pounds. It was served from a four-wheel cart built for the purpose. It contained approximately:

2 bushels of flour	6 snipes
20 pounds of butter	4 partridges
4 geese	2 neat's tongues
2 rabbits	2 curlews
4 wild ducks	6 pigeons and
2 woodcocks	7 blackbirds

Lady Beatrice Brings in the Peacock

At our imaginary feast, Caspar has told us that Lady Beatrice has been chosen to bring in the peacock.

The peacock, is indeed, one of the most kingly dishes. It was generally served with all its brilliant plumage and sitting on a great tray. But let us look into the pages of an old manuscript cook book,* written about 1430, and see how to serve it properly. It reads:

"Take a peacock, break its neck, and cut its throat. And flay him, the skin and feathers together, the head still to the skin of the neck. And keep the skin and the feathers whole together. Draw him as a hen, and keep the bone to the neck whole, and roast him, and set the bone to the neck above the broach (spit), as he was wont to sit alive. And when he is roasted enough, take him off and let him cool. And then wind the skin with the feathers and the tail about the body and serve him forth as he were alive, or else pull him dry, and roast him, and serve him as thou dost a hen."

The roasting peacock was often basted with the yolks of

*Austin, Thomas, Editor. *Two Fifteenth Century Cookery Books*, from Harleian Manuscript 279, dated about 1430, published in London, 1888.

Lady Beatrice serves the peacock

eggs. Sometimes the bird was made into a pie; the head appeared from one side of the crust and the tail from the other. The beak was frequently gilded. Often a sponge was saturated with spirits and placed in the beak, then lighted as the bird was being served.

Peacock is a dry meat and is accompanied by much beef gravy.

Serving men never brought in the peacock. It was carried in state by an honored lady of the court. Such was the honor accorded Lady Beatrice who bore the bird with measured tread as she partly balanced it on her shoulder. The tail feathers were beautifully spread, the plumage brilliant.

It was common for knights to take what was known as the Peacock Vow. The knights advanced one by one and laid a right hand on the back of the bird. Then they made their pledge of the year much as we make our New Year's resolutions. One vowed to strike the first blow at his enemy; another swore to defend the virtue of women. Each vied with the next in the bravery or gallantry of his vow.

BRAWN FOR MONKS AND JEWISH ELDERS

Brawn was one essential of such a feast as we are serving today. Large boars were allowed to live in a semi-wild state; then a few weeks before Christmas they were put up to fatten. They were strapped and belted tightly about the carcass so that the flesh might become dense and brawny.

The meat was sold by fishmongers, poulterers, and pastry cooks. It came to market in rolls, two feet long and ten inches in diameter. Served with mustard it was extremely tasty but rather indigestible, so it was served with wine.

The story* is told that when the monks of Calais tasted it one day, they looked slyly at each other and exclaimed:

"Ha, ha, that's capital fish. We'll place it on our fast day list."

A committee of experienced Jewish elders decided that it was impossible to consider it a form of pork, derived from impure swine, so they included it in their menu of clean animals.

TABLE MANNERS

Perhaps it is bad manners for us to point out the etiquette of these early Britains. At first they lacked knives and forks,

*Sandys, William. *Christmastide.*

and fingers were used. Great trenchers, or trays, of two-day-old bread were placed for each two persons to use as a sop for food. Seldom was each person given an individual serving. Huge bowls of food were so placed that all could reach. Instead of napkins, the diners dried their hands by waving them in the air—or, alack-a-day, wiped them on their gorgeous garments. Even such personages as Queen Elizabeth and her illustrious father tossed the meat bones over their shoulders to the hungry dogs which surrounded all festive boards. To be perfectly fair, we'll admit that basins of water were sometimes passed into which the hands could be dipped.

CHARLES II AND SIR LOIN

Huge salt cellars were often found on the table. They were sometimes three feet tall and made of solid gold. In London may be seen the great salt cellars of Charles II. You recall it was he who almost sold England to Louis XIV, of France, and after whom North and South Carolina were named.

The story is told that one evening Charles II was at his dinner surrounded by his admirers. In a felicitous mood he was speaking to them of their loyalty. Finally, he paused and, looking down at the table, he remarked:

"Fond as I am of all of you, yet I have a still greater favorite—the loin of a good beef." He reached for his sword and touching the great roast before him continued:

"Therefore, good beef roast, I knight thee, Sir Loin, and I proclaim that a double loin be known as a Baron."

Thus we have our choice beef today known as sirloin but, although the baron of beef is known in England, it is not a term used in America.

It was the same Charles whose wax effigy, dressed in his old finery, now stands in the Chapel of Abbot Islip in Westminister Abbey. On the glass cabinet where it was placed someone has scratched, with a diamond ring, these words:

"Here lies our sovereign lord, the King
Whose word no man relies on,
Who never said an honest thing
And never did a wise one."

WATER EWERS

Water ewers were frequently made in the form of beasts, the unicorn being a favorite. The mane formed a handle. The horn did not serve as spout but the water flowed from a spigot in the chest.

SUBTLETIES

After each course, interesting sugar statues were placed on the table. They were known as Subtleties and depicted biblical scenes, such as the Wise Men and the Holy Family. They were generally ushered in with ceremony and song.

NINE HOURS OF FEASTING

And so, the feast goes on often from three in the afternoon until midnight.

"The most eloquent tribute to the appetite of our forefathers is that after 'getting away' with the dinner, it was customary to have wheeled into the drawing room about midnight, a barrel of oysters with pheasants on the side, the whole of which formed an accompaniment to several big bowls of steaming hot punch."*

THE LORD OF MISRULE

There was an effort to have the guests take part in having a good time so a Lord of Misrule was appointed. Sometimes he was called Abbot of Misrule or Master of Merry Disports.

A variation and revival of the Roman Saturnalia, this officer was appointed by many kings in England and the noblemen followed their examples and had their masters of

*Harper's Weekly, December 31, 1910.

revels. In 1348 Edward III furnished his guests at Guildford with eighty tunics of buckram of varied colors, a large number of masks, mantles with embroidered dragons, and tunics with the heads and wings of peacocks. From the eve of October 31, All-Hallows Eve, to February 3, Day of Purification, this Lord of Misrule led the masques, sports, dances, and games. He looked upon all infringements of his authority as being worthy of ridiculous punishments.

The Lord of Misrule is indeed the master of merry disports

Some call such a functionary a King of the Bean. This name is derived from the Parthians. At the feast of Mithras, the king descended from the throne and mingled with his people. Another ruled in his stead. Because this new king was chosen by bean ballots he became known as the King of the Bean.

HOT-COCKLES

There was a typical Christmas game known as Hot-cockles. One person kneels or lies face downward in the center of the room, and is blindfolded. The others take turns tapping him on the shoulder, while he guesses their names. When he has guessed correctly, that person takes his place and the game continues.

Quoted from the *Spectator* for December 28, 1711 is this amusing letter:

"Mr. Spectator, I am a Footman in a great Family and am in Love with the House-maid. We were all at Hot-cockles last Night in the Hall these Holidays; when I lay down and was blinded, she pull'd off her Shoe, and hit me with the Heel such a Rap, as almost broke my Head to Pieces. Pray, Sir, was this Love or Spite？   T."

Hot-cockles was also the name of a small shellfish but there seems no connection with the game.

SNAPDRAGON

Another favorite pastime at Christmas was to snatch objects out of burning brandy and pop them into the mouth. Generally, raisins were the fruits used. Snapdragon* was the name given to the game and the word is thought to be derived from *Schnapps*, liquor, and *Drache*, dragon.

---

*Walsh, William. *Curiosities of Popular Customs.*

CAROLS AND HYMNS OF CHRISTMAS

"**B**ECAUSE of song, man alone can rightly praise the Lord," an Esthonian legend* states. It tells how the God of Song descended on the sacred wood of Domberg, and there he played and sang until all Nature was aquiver in harmony. Around him stood all the woodland creatures. Each had learned its part of the celestial strains. The trees discovered how to rustle their leaves. The brooks murmured among the rocks. The birds became a veritable orchestra of wind music—trilling, zooming, echoing, and re-echoing through the tree tops. And the tall reeds were the batons keeping the whole chorus of Nature in time. Yet, man only of them all was able to synchronize all the musics of Nature until they produced what possibly Sir Arthur Sullivan would have called "The Lost Chord." And, therefore, man alone can rightly praise the Lord.

*This legend is based on facts found in Duffield's *English Hymns*.

As the waits go from house to house in England their cheery voices are heard through the frosty air

117

THE HEAVENLY HOST

Perhaps the first of all the Christmas carols was that sung in the heavens by the angels, "Glory to God in the highest, and on earth peace, good will toward men"—the *"Gloria in Excelsis."*

We are not sure why many of our Christmas songs are called carols, but it's pleasant to think of the word as coming from the Latin which meant "to dance in a ring," and it is very true that some of our first songs of this sort were accompanied by exceeding happiness, attendant upon dancing. Others like to think of the word "carol" as having the same derivation as the word "chorus."

ST. FRANCIS OF ASSISI SINGS WITH JOY

Historically, many say that St. Francis of Assisi was the first to make the carol popular. In our story about Cribs (see page 50) we have told how he staged one of the first Christmas mangers, using real people and real animals to surround the manger, and every account of this event tells how joyous St. Francis was and that he burst into happy song. Some say that "carols are the layman's most beautiful contribution to his religion." Most of the oldest carols have no known history and are merely the spontaneous outbursts of some forgotten man's joyousness.

Some musical writers say that the ballad type of carol is the only true Christmas carol, for these are songs which have been handed down from generation to generation and are truly the creation and evolution of the people. They like to think of the other Christmas songs as hymns—those which have definite composers and which are more elaborate musically. Some of the old carols were most convivial and many of them had but little religious atmosphere, for they proclaimed that Christmas is a time of mirth and feasting.

PURITANS FORBADE CAROL SINGING

From the Santa Barbara Community Christmas Committee, through the courtesy of Miss Pearl Chase, I copy these notes:

Musically the fifteenth century, which saw the real beginning of carols as such, was beginning to break away from the monotonous church chants and experiment with melodies of different modal and intervallic relationships. Folk songs and minstrelsy, both ministered to the new art. And it was fostered and kept alive in little villages and towns all over Europe, especially in England. The custom of carol singing (not alone for Christmas but for all important festivals) continued until the Seventeenth Century Puritanism came in with its severe repression, substituting fasts for feasts and a long visage for a joyful look. But, however much Puritanism forbade public performance of carols, they were by this time so deeply entrenched in the hearts of the people that they traveled "underground" by word of mouth tradition. But "broad sheets" were printed annually and kept the texts alive with more or less accuracy.

Carols Re-discovered in Nineteenth Century

After the Restoration carols were too democratic, not to say plebeian, for Eighteenth Century sophistication. However, in the Nineteenth Century, some truly musical hearts re-discovered this type of folk music still circulating in the country districts. Enlightened churchmen and laymen united in an effort to discover and preserve ancient texts. Now there is a real carol literature, so let us learn more each year and incorporate into our hearts many of these quaint and delightful gems of musical and verbal literature.*

The Waits

"Like that first great Christmas carol sung amid the stars above the plain of Judaea, some of its sweetest echoes on earth have sung in the open air," so writes Harold Vincent Milligan.† Strolling bands of minstrels and troups of little chil-

*If you are interested in the carols of all nations send to the Old Orchard Book Shoppe, Webster Groves, Missouri, for *Carols, Customs and Costumes Around the World*, by Herbert H. Wernecke, 50 cents.

†Milligan, Harold Vincent. *Garden and Home Builder*, December, 1926.

dren, going from door to door, in the streets and highways of Old England, scattered these songs throughout the land and from the high tide of their popularity the days of Richard Cœur de Lion till the Reformation, down to the present day, songs and singers have voiced the joy of the holiday season.

Community Carol Singing

The singing of carols at Christmastide is being observed more each year in the cities throughout the United States and could we tell all the stories of the joy brought to those who are confined to their homes, to the strangers away from home, to the revival of memories, even then we would be doing small justice to the custom.

According to the last survey of the National Bureau for Advancement of Music there were only 30 cities which conducted community carol singing in 1918, whereas in 1928 there were 2025. In Santa Barbara it is the custom each year for bands of singers to dress in flowing red capes and peaked hoods and go about the streets reviving the Old English folk custom and contribute a strong flavor of mediaevalism, cheering the lonely and friendless, and serenading their neighbors and friends.

"Silent Night"

The organ of the little church of Arnsdorf near Salzburg, Austria, had in the last days before Christmas become unfit for further use. Mice had eaten at the bellows, and this seriously troubled the parish priest, Father Josef Mohr. He went to his organist and school master Franz Gruber and expressed his disappointment, saying, "We must have something special for midnight mass."

On the day before Christmas Eve the Father was called to administer the last rites to a dying woman. It was late when he returned. Pausing on a height overlooking the town he fell to musing. The snowy mountains loomed above him and below in the valley the dark outline of the village could

"It must have been something like this—that silent holy night in
Bethlehem"

be discerned. Here and there a faint light glimmered in the dark, and over all was that vast stillness so peculiar to the wide open spaces of Nature. Suddenly, the good man murmured, "It must have been something like this—that silent, holy night in Bethlehem."

Powerfully affected, he hastened home, sat at his desk and wrote. Late at night he paused, read over what he had written, then read it again:

1

Stille Nacht, heilige Nacht,
Alles schläft, einsam wacht,
Nur das traute, hochheilige Paar,
Holder Knabe im lokkigen Haar,
Schlaf in himmlischer Ruh,
Schlaf in himmlischer Ruh.

1

Silent night, Holy night,
All is dark, save the light,
Yonder where they sweet vigils keep,
O'er the Babe, who in silent sleep,
Rests in heavenly peace,
Rests in heavenly peace.

2

Stille Nacht, heilige Nacht,
Hirten erst, kund gemacht,
Durch der Engel Halleluja,
Tönt es laut von fern und nah,
Christ, der Retter ist da,
Christ, der Retter ist da.

2

Silent night, peaceful night,
Darkness flies, all is light;
Shepherds hear the angels sing,
Alleluia! Hail the King,
Christ the Saviour is born,
Christ the Saviour is born.

3

Stille Nacht, heilige Nacht,
Gottes Sohn, O wie lacht,
Lieb aus deinem göttlichen Mund,
Da uns schlägt die rettende Stund'
Christ in deiner Geburt.
Christ in deiner Geburt.

3

Silent night, Holy night,
Child of Heaven, O how bright,
Was Thy smile, when Thou wast born,
Blest indeed that happy morn,
Full of heavenly joy,
Full of heavenly joy.

—It pleased him and he thereupon retired to bed. Arising next morning, he took up his manuscript, reread it, hastened to his friend Franz Gruber, and read it to him. As soon as Franz Gruber read the lovely words, inner voices seemed to fill his humble quarters with an angelic chorus. Indeed, he caught the true spirit of the hymn. He sang it to his wife, and in the hushed silence that followed, she said, "We will die—you and I—but this song will live."

At Christmas Eve midnight the organ did not sound in the church at Arnsdorf. The congregation indeed felt a lack of it—until with Father Josef Mohr singing and Franz Gruber playing his guitar, the hallowed strains of "Silent Night" fell upon their ears, and the echo of the first rendition of this holy hymn has not died away in the world, even now, at the conclusion of over a hundred years. The congregation sat enthralled; no organ, no—but a special gift has been given to the Christ Child on His birthday.

This story was related by Father Richard, of the Old Santa Barbara Mission.

On Christmas Eve in 1936 many listeners at the radio were charmed to hear virtually this same story coming over the air from far-away Hallein, a village to the south of Salzburg.

Felix Gruber, using his great grandfather's original guitar, sang "Silent Night" fervently. Listeners were deeply moved to hear this song coming from near its original birthplace.

We inquired about Franz Gruber as we rested in an inn at Hallein, last summer. The *Wirtin* led us to another room where four generations of Grubers, in large photographs, adorn the walls. "All have been singing masters here," she remarked. "Even now, Felix, the great grandson, comes once each month to direct."

There is another interesting observation. For many years "Silent Night" was considered merely as a folk song and Michael Haydn was given credit for being the composer. The song did not appear in print, however, until 1840. Those who listened on the radio noted that Felix Gruber sang it a little differently than we in America had heard it.

In an article in *Better Homes and Gardens*, December, 1932, by Hazel Gertrude Kinscella, we read, "that the reason the song received so wide an acceptance is due to two things —its simplicity, and, astonishing as it may sound, the broken organ in the little church. The organ builder from the Zillertal, who happened to be repairing the organ in St. Nicholas' Parish Church that Christmas Eve, was struck with the beauty of the air and carried the melody home with him. Four sisters from the Zillertal—Strasser by name—famous for their beautiful singing of native mountain songs heard the organ builder's version of 'Silent Night' and immediately carried it with them on their concert tours. So it circulated from this little valley to the great towns of the earth, from where it traveled on its way about the world."

But we in America will remember "Silent Night" most vividly through the marvelous voice of Mother Schumann-Heinck who for years sang it each Christmas Eve over the radio, and in the days when our phonographs were more popular, small indeed was the collection of records which did not include a recording of this incomparable song by this most sympathetic of voices.

"HARK, THE HERALD ANGELS SING"

Charles Wesley, younger brother of John Wesley, who founded the Methodist denomination, was the author of 6000 poems. Among the best known are "Christ the Lord Is Risen Today," "Jesus Lover of My Soul," "Love Divine All Love Excelling," but perhaps the most popular of all is his Christmas hymn "Hark, the Herald Angels Sing" written in 1730.

Originally the first two lines read,

"Hark! how all the welkin rings,
Glory to the King of kings!"

He was inspired to write this lovely hymn while listening to the peeling of the bells as he walked to church one Christmas morning. The poem was not completed in 1739 but was altered by Martin Madan in 1760, by Conyers in 1774, and by De Courcy in 1775.*

The musical setting is taken from Mendelssohn-Bartholdy's "*Festgesang* for Male Chorus and Orchestra," composed for and first performed at the festival held at Leipzig in June, 1840 to celebrate the anniversary of the invention of printing. Dr. W. H. Commings was the organist at Waltham Abbey and copied parts from Mendelssohn and had it sung

*Bennett, J. Lionel, *Famous Hymns, Their Writers and Times.*

by the choir. Finding that it was received with favor he published it in 1856.

In writing a description of his music, Mendelssohn said, "I am sure that piece will be liked very much by the singers and hearers but it will *never* do to sacred words. There must be a national or merry subject found out, something to which the soldier-like and buxom motion of the piece has some relation, and the words must express something gay and popular, as the music tries to do it."*

LUTHER'S CRADLE HYMN

It is interesting to know that this hymn is not familiar to Germans inasmuch as Luther did not write it. It is said that Luther did sing his child to sleep and some writer has imagined this song to be the type he would have sung.

> Away in a manger, no crib for His bed,
> The little Lord Jesus laid down His sweet head;
> The stars in the sky looked down where He lay,
> The little Lord Jesus, asleep in the hay.
>
> The cattle are lowing, the poor Baby wakes,
> But the little Lord Jesus no crying He makes;
> I love Thee, Lord Jesus, look down from the sky,
> And stay by my cradle to watch lullaby.

"O COME ALL YE FAITHFUL"

Few Christmas hymns have stirred the multitudes as much as "O Come All Ye Faithful" translated from the Latin "*Adeste Fideles.*" The origin of this hymn is somewhat controversial. The words were translated into English by Tractarian Frederick Oakeley, in 1841, under the title of "Hymn for Christmas Day." Some say it was written by Bonaventura, Bishop of Albano, born in 1221 in Tuscany. But Samuel Duffield in "English Hymns" says that it is a *graduale* of the Cistercians.

The music is usually called the Portuguese Hymn and it is variously credited to Vincent Novello and Marco Portogallo, the chapel master for the King of Portugal.

*Dearmer, Percy. *Songs of Praise Discussed.*

"Good King Wenceslaus looked out
On the feast of Stephen, when the snow lay round about,
    Deep, and crisp, and even."
(The carol refers to the martyred King Wenceslaus of
Bohemia, who commenced his reign in 1361 but who was
killed by a friend of his heathen brother. It was written
            by Rev. Dr. John Mason Neale)

Others credit the air to John Reading, organist of Westminster College, about 1680.

Perhaps the true solution is that this hymn has been
gradually changed by various musical writers. Translated
from the Latin, its English lines do not rhyme yet few persons
have realized this.

It is said to have been the favorite of the late President Theodore Roosevelt.

"It is one of the hymns of the ages which apparently is to live for centuries, a hymn which has stirred religious loyalty in the hearts of countless numbers of happy folks, which have gone on before us and thousands of generations to come," so writes Harold Gregson, director of the Santa Barbara Christmas Chorus.

"O LITTLE TOWN OF BETHLEHEM"

Bishop Phillips Brooks while rector of the Church of the Holy Trinity in Philadelphia was asked by his Sunday School children to write a Christmas song, so in 1868 he wrote this lovely hymn. Three years previous he had visited the Holy Land and worshipped in the Church of the Nativity. After writing the hymn he went to his church organist, Sunday School superintendent, and teacher of one of his classes, Lewis H. Redner, and asked him to furnish a tune for the new hymn. Mr. Redner says that the melody came to him in a dream on Christmas Eve and the harmonies were completed for the service next day.*

> O little town of Bethlehem,
>   How still we see thee lie!
> Above thy deep and dreamless sleep
>   The silent stars go by;
> Yet in thy dark streets shineth
>   The everlasting light;
> The hopes and fears of all the years
>   Are met in thee to-night.
>
> For Christ is born of Mary;
>   And, gather'd all above,
> While mortals sleep, the angels keep
>   Their watch of wond'ring love.
> O morning stars, together
>   Proclaim the holy birth!
> And praises sing to God, the King,
>   And peace to men on earth.

*Benson, Louis F. *Studies of Familiar Hymns*. First series. This book gives an interesting biography of Bishop Brooks.

CHRISTMAS CARDS

O F COURSE, it would be difficult to say definitely when the first Christmas card was sent, for in our literature we find that it was a common practice for children, even in the reign of Queen Anne, to write Christmas pieces—specimens of handwriting laboriously produced to show the progress from the preceding year. Some of these specimen sheets had engraved borders which were supposed to represent some of the important events which took place during the year—battles, earthquakes, coronations. Some were of scriptural subjects. Many of the sheets had colored borders and others

One of the first Christmas cards was made for Sir Henry Cole by John Calcott Horsley

had outline sketches which the children colored. These
Christmas pieces sold in the shops up until 1840.

THE FIRST CHRISTMAS CARD

It is reputed that the first Christmas card, as we now
think of it, was dispatched in 1845 by W. C. Dobson, one
of Queen Victoria's favorite painters. He sent lithograph
copies to his friends.

The following year John Calcott Horsley, Royal Aca-
demician, was asked to design a card for Sir Henry Cole. It
seemed that Sir Henry, finding himself very busy, and not
able to write a vast quantity of Christmas letters to his
friends, asked Horsley to produce a card which he might send
out in lieu of correspondence. Copies of this card are in
existence, and herewith Mr. Field has drawn it in pen and
ink, although the original card was lithographed and then
colored by hand.

I am indebted to Clementine Paddleford in *The American
Home*, December, 1935, for some interesting facts about this
card, and the reader who would like to know more about the
history of Christmas cards, would do well to refer to this
article.

In Horsley's card we see a merry family, three generations,
leaning back comfortably, kindly disposed toward the fruit
of the vine, and celebrating their annual deed of kindness to
the poor. There was "brimming cheer" for everyone, from
grandma to little Nell. Mr. Horsley's drawing was severely
criticized by the zealous friends of temperance, declaring the
design was an out-and-out promoter of drunkenness. There
was such an unwarranted to do over the point that by the
time Christmas, 1847 rolled around a number of people who
might never have known about the Cole card were getting
out one of their own. At each side of the happy family group,
in smaller panels, were shown acts of charity: "Feeding the
Hungry" and "Clothing the Naked."

The name of Louis Prang is an outstanding one in the

history of Christmas cards. Mr. Prang was an exile following the German revolution of 1848 and the founder of L. Prang and Company, who introduced the art idea to public schools in the form of the Prang Method of Education, which was the first to develop the creative impulse in students and train them in good taste. Prang started to print cards in 1874, in Roxbury, Mass., using and perfecting a lithographic process which sometimes employed as many as 20 colors. At this period it was common to offer prizes for the best design submitted. One, Dora Wheeler, received a prize of $2,000.

We shall not linger long over the interesting change which has taken place in Christmas cards during the years.* Some years they were extremely sentimental. Other years tiny animals were popular. Then the card design was switched to the ridiculous.

The Japanese New Years cards are interesting. Merchants send them to their customers. They generally bear the symbol of a stork, which is supposed to live a thousand years, or a turtle, which lives 10,000 years. These include a message wishing the recipient a long life. They often have the pictures of the Seven Gods of Good Fortune—Ebesu, happiness; Daikoku, prosperity; Benten, music; Gero, long life; Fukuroku, good luck; and Bishamon, protection against evil. The Pine tree, which is the symbol of good fortune, is also used in the design.

Making Your Own Cards

There is true economy and lots of fun in making your own Christmas cards, and then, too, how much more you appreciate the home-made Christmas card, over the one of standard design of which you are likely to receive two or three of a kind during one season. Some little bit of handiwork from a friend, even though it be somewhat crude, is a true token of friendly remembrance.

Why not try some of the following Christmas cards?

*Chase, Ernest Dudley. *Romance of Greeting Cards.*

Photograph

Use a photograph of your home, your family, your fireplace, your front door, or some intimate feature of home life which your friends associate with you. Your photographer will be able to suggest many attractive ways of using your snapshots as your personal greetings on a good grade of stiff, photographic paper.

Pen Sketch

If you are handy with your pen you can make interesting sketches of any of the home objects mentioned above, and the most popular type of card is one which caricatures the members of your family or has a semi-humorous note. These pen sketches, then, would be taken to your printer, who would make zinc etchings, from which any number of cards could be printed.

Blue Print

If a sketch is made on tracing paper or tracing cloth, it can be used like a photographic negative to make blueprints, or photostatic copies. Blue prints are merely exposed to the light and placed in water for a half hour.

Garden Objects

Garden lovers enjoy sending each other a packet of favorite seeds, an evergreen branch, a spray of Holly, or some other attractive nature object which can be ingeniously attached to a Christmas card.

Poems

Some of the most delightful cards received each Christmas are those which poetize the family gossip of the year.

Scratchboard

One of the most fascinating and successful home-made types of cards is to execute the design in scratchboard. This is the method used so freely throughout this book, and is described in detail starting at foot of this page.

Spatter Prints

Spatter prints are illustrated and described on page 141.

Linoleum Blocks

It is fun to try your hand at linoleum block printing if you have not done so in the past. This is more or less a variation of wood engraving, and effects similar to Japanese prints may be attained after some little experimentation. This is described on page 135.

Paper to Use

In all this matter of making Christmas cards, experiment with the different types of paper available. Go to some foreign sections of your city and here you can often obtain interesting rice paper, wallpaper, even face-cleansing tissues, as well as a delightful array of textiles varying in color and finish.

If you desire to economize, the ordinary government penny postals may be used for some of the processes described above.

Also for economy it is best to make your cards to fit a standard size envelope. Or else, purchase both paper and envelope before designing your card. Otherwise, you may have great difficulty in getting them to match in color and shape.

When you find difficulty in getting envelopes to match, merely make your paper or cards large and fold them so that they may be sealed with a sticker or sealing wax, thereby eliminating the necessity of an envelope.

SCRATCHBOARD

What It Is

Scratchboard is a cardboard coated with a chalky surface, which when covered with ink may be scratched off to produce a wood-block effect. After the original drawing is made, zinc etchings can be made of it and used for reproducing the prints. Most of the illustrations in this book are made in scratchboard. In scratchboard one combines a pen-and-ink and wood-block technique.

Materials Needed

Figure 1, page 134, shows the supplies necessary.

Ross Extra Heavy Scratchboard (the kind we have found satisfactory) obtained at art stores. Those coated with too thin a layer of chalky material do not allow for reworking the sketch.

Waterproof India ink.

A set of scratchboard tools sold by all art stores in the larger cities for less than a half dollar. A stiff bristle brush. Speedball pen about C-4 size. Ruler with steel edge. Several sheets of white paper.

Process

First draw your design on a sheet of ordinary white paper, being sure that the design is carefully worked out and studied for areas which are to be black and which are to be white in the finished scratchboard sketch. Determine the size of the drawing and trace the outline but not the details of the drawing on the scratchboard. Instead of using commercial carbon paper for transferring the design, we would suggest that you use a sheet of ordinary white paper, blackening it on the back with a pencil. Carbon paper has a waxy surface and its markings are difficult to cover with ink.

Figure 2. With a stiff bristle brush fill in the entire area with black India ink, taking care not to go back over the blackened area nor to leave large pools of ink. Allow this to dry thoroughly.

You are now ready for tracing the details of the design. Trace the design with a medium hard pencil, using the home-made carbon paper under the original design. See Figure 3.

Fig. 1—The materials, showing the scratchboard, pen, brushes, tools, pencil, ink, ruler and design

How to Make Scratchboard Christmas Cards

Fig. 2—The scratchboard is covered with India ink, using a stiff bristle brush

Fig. 4—The design is executed using one of the three tools shown at the top of the cut, each of which has a different function

Fig. 3—The design is traced on scratchboard

Fig. 5—When the design is finished it is outlined with a ball-pointed pen

Scratch. The three tools shown above the drawing in Figure 4 indicate the technique possible with each tool. The upper tool is useful for outlines, the middle tool for dots and heavier lines, and the broad tool for scraping surfaces white or for running across a number of parallel lines made with either of the other tools, to give a high light. This tool was used in the general high lighting in Figures 1, 2, 3, and 4.

In Figure 4 we have merely indicated the transferred design on the scratchboard black surface, but had to show it in white, as it would be only a glossy pencil line. The tool will produce best results by pulling it to the right or toward the body. The tools must be kept sharp at all times and their original cutting edges maintained. An oil stone is necessary, for it is very important that the cutting edge be free from any irregularities or nicks; otherwise, double lines will result.

It may be desirable to outline the entire drawing after it is finished, in which case the Speedball pen is used (see Figure 5). Any irregularities which extend beyond this black line may be removed with the broad-bladed tool. It is always possible to fill in with black the areas which have been scraped away, but it is difficult to remove the black more than once, as the chalky surface is generally destroyed. Any mistakes then made must be filled in with Chinese white paint. Whenever an eraser is used it should be art gum or else the original pencil lines may be scratched out with one of the tools.

Scratchboard is fun and you can't help but get pleasing results.

LINOLEUM BLOCK PRINTS

In making linoleum block prints the main advantage is that the design is carved in linoleum and can be reproduced directly from the block. Its limitations are that it is not easy to get any fine lines, and also because the plate is made in reverse, it is difficult to judge the results. However, its boldness and simplicity are sometimes its greatest charm. It is possible to reproduce as many as 100,000 prints from a linoleum block on a monotype press without showing appreciable wear on the block.*

Materials

Battleship linoleum is generally used. It may be purchased in art shops, mounted on blocks which are type high, but this will be more expensive than obtaining the linoleum from a linoleum dealer or department store, at which place one may often pick up small scraps which will be very serviceable for ordinary use. Any art store can furnish an assortment of inexpensive tools, including a gouge, 2 veiners, and a knife with a handle. The more expensive wood-carving tools will, of course, hold their edges better.

Special block printing, water-soluble ink is also sold in the same stores, or printer's ink may be used, but then a supply of benzine is necessary for cleaning purposes. It will be desirable to have two brayers, or rollers, although only one

In this linoleum block print, the glass, the roller, the ink, as well as the three types of tools used are shown

This cut shows the use of the tool in carving. The linoleum block is held in place by two strips of wood

*Frankenfield, Henry. *Block Printing with Linoleum.* C. Howard Hunt Pen Company, Camden, New Jersey.

is really necessary. These are used for inking the block and making the print. A piece of glass or marble is needed, upon which the ink may be spread.

A block printing press or letter press would be convenient if available for printing.

It will be the easiest to make the prints on any absorbent paper. The new face-cleaning tissues work splendidly, or unprinted newspaper may be used.

Process

In the selection of a design for a linoleum block print it must be extremely simple and when drawn on a piece of white paper it is well to blacken all areas you intend to be black in the final print, for it is a little confusing to work in reverse (see illustration, page 138). Fine, black lines are very difficult to make, but fine, white lines may be removed with a veiner.

In drawing the original design it is well to draw it on thin paper such as tracing paper; then the drawing can be reversed and you are ready for transferring it, for everything on a linoleum block print must be carved in reverse—even the letters.

In order to hold the piece of linoleum while you are working on it, tack two strips of wood to a drawing board, forming a right angle in which you can anchor your block, as shown on opposite page. This prevents the tool from slipping.

Transfer the design, using a good piece of carbon paper, as it is wise to have the marks on the linoleum as clear as possible. The prepared blocks purchased in the art shops are coated white so that the marks of the transfer are plainly visible. The white coated surface also is smoother than the usual commercial battleship linoleum. White paint may be used but it is likely to flake.

Each tool supplied in the set has a definite use. A fine veiner is necessary for the finest lines. The coarse gouge can be used for removing large areas of linoleum readily. The knife makes distinct corners and points. In using the tools,

In making a linoleum block print such as this one of the writer's home, it is possible to reproduce directly from your homemade block

it is necessary to hold them quite upright, but it is not necessary to make the cuts deep, particularly if they are narrow. And it is very unwise to undercut the linoleum by gouging beneath the design as this portion of the print will soon break down and will not print well. As the design progresses one can easily visualize the final result by filling in the spaces with flour, scraping off the excess.

Remember, you can always take out more linoleum but you cannot put any back. Warm linoleum cuts easier than cold.

Printing

In printing the linoleum block it is necessary that it be thoroughly inked and this can be done properly only when the ink is very evenly spread upon a pane of glass or slab of marble. Every fleck of dust or irregularity in the ink roller is inclined to show up on the block print, so that this inking process must be carried on where no dust is flying. The more black areas you have in your print, the more difficult it will be to make a good reproduction, so that the black areas are commonly broken up with either lines or dots, such as the background in illustration on page opposite.

We have designed an alphabet for linoleum block printing which is simplified so as to require a minimum of difficult carving

A simple and well executed linoleum block Christmas card. Used by courtesy of C. Howard Hunt Pen Co.

Linoleum blocks may be printed by the use of a special block press, or by an ordinary letter press such as was formerly used in most offices; or they may be put through a clothes wringer, and if the paper is thin enough it may be rolled with a brayer or a photographic print roller. Some use a spoon. It is possible even to print them with your feet. Place a drawing board on the floor, then your paper, with the linoleum block on top of this. By stepping carefully on this linoleum block good prints may be made.

Color Adds Life

Don't be afraid to try colored inks and colored paper. A deeper-toned ink than paper, or contrasting colors are often effective. Try blue on silver paper, purple on coral, green on yellow, red on gray, yellow on gray. Mix red and violet inks for a red-violet on gold or copper. One of the most effective I have seen was a simple star printed in black on silver paper, mounted twice on two papers, both values of blue-green.

As I look over a group of Christmas cards, one linoleum block was printed in a dark, almost blackish, gray-green on white paper. The design is a spray of Pine needles out of which rises a lighted candle from the lower half of the picture. A third color has been added by painting the candle flame red.

Another interesting card is printed in milk-blue, on white paper, to which a little silver was added with a brush.

SPATTER PRINTS

Refer to Figure 1 on page 142, in which we have made a spatter print. This is particularly adapted for soft tones in the background. In combination with a dash of color it is effective. The scene on this card was originally designed with the roof and tower of the church painted red.

Materials

All that is needed is a bottle of India ink (any color), Gypsy dye (or showcard color), stencil paper, common pins, a single-edge razor blade (or sharp knife), a rubber finger stall, a toothbrush (or a fixative spray or a small "Flytox" spray).

Design

A design should be chosen which lends itself to very simple treatment without too great complication so that the

The Evolution of a Spatter Print

Fig. 1—A spatter print can easily be made by the amateur. The evolution of this picture is shown in the next four illustrations, all of which have been executed by this method and illustrate the variety of effects which may be obtained by one who likes experimentation

Fig. 2—The part of the design to be spattered is cut away from the stencil

Fig. 3—The stencil is pinned to your paper. In the hand you see a light spray on a dark background

Fig. 4—Spraying the design with a fixative sprayer

Fig. 5—After the ink is dry the stencil can be pulled off

white areas are connected. This will be easily understood when we describe the process.

Process

All the areas that are to be white in the final picture should be traced on the stencil and the part to be sprayed is cut away. See Figure 2. As soon as the stencil is ready, it is placed on a piece of paper and secured with pins at intervals so that the parts of the design will not curl when moistened by the spray. See Figure 3.

In spraying the picture you may use a toothbrush and rubber finger stall, in which the ink is placed on the toothbrush, and with the bristles down; the finger is then pulled across the brush, causing a fine spray of ink to spatter on the uncovered portion of your print. By holding the brush in one position the ink will be concentrated at this point and tint out lighter. A fixative sprayer (see Figure 4) or "Flytox" sprayer may be used instead of the toothbrush.

After spraying, allow the ink to dry, remove the pins, and carefully pull off the stencil. See Figure 5.

In making the diagrams to illustrate the process of spraying, of course more than one stencil was used on some of the pictures. In Figure 2 and 4, several stencils were used in making the hands shown to get a variety of tones. In Figure 3 I have demonstrated in the hand how a darker paper may be sprayed with lighter ink. In this case, several stencils were used also.

Silver paint is particularly effective when sprayed on any darker paper, such as green, red, or blue, because it catches the light.

Any number of prints can be produced from one stencil by following the process described, but for a large quantity, it might be well to choose your best print and have a zinc etching made of it, which could then be put in the hands of your printer. Spraying is particularly effective in producing the sky effects and for round objects.

PLANT LEGENDS

LEGENDS OF THE CHRISTMAS-ROSE

The Magic Garden*

THERE are two stories that tell of the mystery of the Forest of Göinge in Sweden. They are related by Selma Lagerlöf, the eminent writer.

In one tale we learn that years ago there was a Christmas Eve when all the flowers, fruits, trees, and birds awakened. For a few hours everything grew and sang and became near perfect until the forest was indeed a Magic Garden. There was a sound of bells mysteriously borne on the night air, then came the *Gloria in Excelsis* sung by the multitude of the heavenly host. On this night there came Abbot Hans accompanied by a doubting monk. Even after witnessing these wonders, the monk decided that it was the work of Satan. Because of the doubts, the Magic Forest vanished and to this day no flowers, save one, are to be seen at Christmastime. Typifying the beauty, strength, and purity of the One born on Christmas Day, the Christmas-rose has persisted to remind us of this Magic Garden.

Another Story of the Forest of Göinge*

In the second tale we may read how a group of poverty stricken peasants were driven farther and farther into the forest where, being not only poor but far from home, they could make no Christmas preparations for their children. When the night fell, the whole silent forest became suffused

*The first story is from *The Girl from the March Croft*, the second from the *Legends of Christ* as related by Ellen Geyer in Pittsburgh Radio Series No. 33.

with a whitish glow. The next morning the earth was found to be covered with Christmas-roses.

The Gift of Madelon

It is said that when the Wise Men were journeying toward Bethlehem they came upon Madelon, a young girl who was tending her sheep. Madelon gazed upon the magnificent gifts which they were bearing to the Christ Child and tears came to her eyes for she had no gift to offer. She sank to the ground and wept bitterly. Soon she caught the fragrance of a Lily and looked up to see an angel standing before her, who asked, "Why do you weep?" And she answered, "The Wise Men have so much to give to the Holy Babe, even the shepherds had a white dove, some fruits and honey, while I— I have not even a simple flower, for it is Winter."

The angel waved her wand of Lilies, whereupon the entire pathway to Bethlehem was flowered with glistening white Christmas-roses. Gathering her arms full of blossoms, Madelon hastened to follow the Wise Men. From the distance she watched them present their gold, and frankincense, and myrrh. Finally Mary saw her and said, "We have been waiting for you. Come, bring your precious gift." The Holy Child turned with a smile toward Madelon as she offered the flowers, and when the fingers of Jesus touched the white flowers they became suffused with pink.

The Glastonbury Thorn

Legend states that before the crucifixion, Christ was resting in a woods. The magpies realizing his danger, shielded Him from His enemies by covering him with Hawthorn fruits. As soon as the soldiers had passed, the swallows, which are called the Fowls of God, removed this Hawthorn screen and in honor of the Hawthorn, Joseph of Arimathea chose a thorn staff when he started on his journey.*

*Adapted from Charles M. Skinner, *Myths and Legends of Flowers, Trees, Fruits and Plants.*

Another legend states that after Christ's death Joseph of Arimathea came to England, terminating his long pilgrimage in Glastonbury. As soon as he arrived at his new home he stuck his walking stick into the soil. It put forth leaves and shortly it acquired the habit of producing flowers each Christmas Eve.

In 1753, there was a controversy about the change in the calendar, making September 2 into September 14. This would also throw Christmas twelve days late. When Christmas Day approached, the caretaker of the ruined Abbey of Glastonbury was much perturbed at the profanity of changing the dates. He wrote a letter to King George, gravely warning him that the change was against Nature. When Christmas Day, new style, arrived, 2000 persons assembled to see if the Glastonbury or Holy Thorn was in bloom, and not finding even a bud on it, they agreed that it was not the right Christmas Day. They therefore refused to go to church or to treat their friends to any of the usual Christmas courtesies. When on January 5, which was Christmas Day, old style, it blossomed, it proved without shadow of a doubt the evil of the new calendar. So that, finally, the neighboring ministers to appease the people gave notice that the old Christmas Day would be observed.*

Mr. Eyston in Hearne's *History and Antiquities of Glastonbury* published in 1722, gave the first account in print of this Thorn. Mr. Eyston says that he came to the conclusion that "Whether it sprang from St. Joseph of Arimathea's dry staff, I cannot find, but *beyond all dispute it sprang up miraculously!*"

Previous to Charles I a branch of this Thorn was carried in the procession on Christmas Day and during the Civil War the Puritans tried to hew down all the Thorns, believing that they savored of Popery. The story goes that one tree growing on Weary-all-Hill had a double trunk and at the first blow the ax glanced the bark and cut off the leg of one of the men and a chip flew to his head, putting out one of his eyes. One

*Tille, Alex. *Yule and Christmas.*

trunk remained and flourished for 30 years, when it was stolen. The branches were badly mutilated. The old trunk was carved with initials, and flowers were sent to all parts of the world. Finally this trunk was also cut down by a "military saint," as someone called the culprit. Fortunately, many cions were taken from the old trees and many others were growing near Glastonbury.

In spite of all the legends connected with this tree, there is actually a species of Hawthorn which resembles the ordinary English Hawthorn and which the botanists call *Crataegus monogyna*, variety *praecox*, and it is true that it blooms near Christmas each year.

Pilgrimages were made to the Holy Thorns each Christmas, for it was thought that to touch them would take away all evil of disease in mind or body.

The Glastonbury Thorn in America

Stanley Austin, owner of the ruins of Glastonbury Abbey, in 1900, gave a cutting of the Glastonbury Thorn to the late Right Reverend Henry Gates Satterlee, first bishop of Washington. The Bishop planted it near St. Albans School. It grew, and December, 1918 it blossomed at Christmas for the first time. It has blossomed each year since. At the present time the tree is flourishing, and I would judge that it is 20 feet high and 27 feet across. Each Christmas thousands visit this tree at Mount Saint Albans.

It is said that in mediaeval times whenever English royalty visited Glastonbury a bit of the bloom was plucked, placed in a silver box, and presented to a member of the royal family. In 1919 the Prince of Wales visited Washington Cathedral. Although it was November the tree produced two or three blossoms. They were plucked, placed in a silver box, and presented to him by the Bishop of Washington on the day of his visit.*

*Little, Blanch. *The Miracle Tree.* Also, I have derived some interesting facts by corresponding directly with Edwin N. Lewis, of Mount Saint Albans, Washington, D. C.

Holly

Some persons believe that the word "Holly" is a form of the word "holy" because of the association of these evergreens with Christmas. This is not the true derivation, however. Holly is merely a variation of Holin, Hollin, or Holm, which are the names given it by the early writers such as Dodoens (1578). The name Holme is now used for a kind of Oak. Various kinds of Holly are shown on page 80.

It was admired by the Druids who believed that its evergreen leaves attested to the fact that the sun never deserted it and it was therefore sacred.

A Christmas carol of the fifteenth century tells of the contest between the Holly and the Ivy for the place of honor in the hall. They have an argument which is a duet, each setting forth his or her claims to superiority. It is finally decided that the Holly with its red berries shall have the place of honor, instead of the Ivy whose berries are black. Moreover, the birds are attracted to the Holly, but only owls love Ivy !

Legends relate that the Crown of Thorns was plaited from the Holly. Before the Crucifixion the berries were white but turned crimson like drops of blood.

Holly is hateful to witches and is therefore, placed on doors and windows to keep out evil spirits.

Whoever brings the Christmas Holly into the house first, either husband or wife, is the one who will rule the ensuing year.

Mistletoe—Gift of the Gods

Some say that the word "Mistletoe" comes from the missel thrush, a messenger of the gods who brought the plant to the earth. Actually the bird is very fond of the berries and is responsible for the wide distribution of Mistletoe. Growing as it does, on trees as a semi-parasite, it is at once showy because of its huge masses of dense light green growth. For this reason there is another, and more plausible, explanation

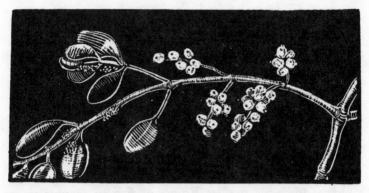

A spray of Mistletoe with its oval pale green leaves and pearly white berries

of its name. It comes from Mistletan—different twig. Its Latin names, *Phoradendron* (tree-thief) and *Viscum* (European M.).

Readers of Virgil remember the Mistletoe as the Golden Bough, by the plucking of which Aeneas was enabled to descend to the underworld and came back safely.

The Druid Rites

In ancient Britain it was the sacred plant of the Druids. The Arch-Druid and his fellow priests performed their rites at the Winter solstice with elaborate ceremonies centering about the Mistletoe.

The chief Nature festival of these forest worshippers was held five days after the new moon. Men, women, and children went to the forest. They moved toward the Oak tree that had the most Mistletoe on it. First came the bards, then a herald. As they came in sight of the tree they hailed it with loud shouts of delight and reverence. In the midst of this group one figure towers—the Arch-Druid.

A golden chain was about his neck; gold bands were around his arms. He was clad in flowing white robes.

He ascended the tree to the lowest bough on which the sacred Mistletoe was growing. With a golden sickle he cropped the branch and allowed it to fall in a fold of his ample robes. This plant was so sacred that it must never touch the earth. The priest then broke the branch in many pieces and gave a twig to each of his followers with a prayer that each one who received a branch should find divine favor and a blessing from Nature.

Kissing Under the Mistletoe

In the language of flowers, Mistletoe means "give me a kiss." This has its basis in a Scandinavian myth.

Balder (the Scandinavian counterpart for Apollo) received a charm from his mother Frigga or Freyja (equivalent to Venus) against all injury from everything which sprang from the four elements—fire, water, air, and earth. Loki, an evil spirit, having an enmity against Balder, formed an arrow from Mistletoe which did not grow from any of these elements. The arrow was placed in the hands of the blind Helder, whom Loki directed was to launch at the seemingly invulnerable Balder. The Mistletoe dart struck Balder to the ground. The tears of Frigga became the white berries of the Mistletoe. Through the concerted efforts of the gods, Balder was restored to life and Frigga decreed that the plant must never again serve as an instrument of mischief.

Frigga, being the goddess of love and beauty, grateful for the return of her son, is said to bestow a kiss upon anyone who shall pass under the Mistletoe.

From this old tale we derive our custom of kissing under the Mistletoe. As it hangs upon the chandelier or in the doorway each lad may claim a kiss from the maid who chances beneath it with this provision: that the lad remove a berry to give to the maid until, at last, when no berries are left, the bough loses its spell and no more kisses are then available.

Crippen tells us that the maiden who receives no kisses under the Mistletoe will not marry that year. Others claim that the kiss under the Mistletoe is a survival of some ancient marriage rite.

A lad must remove a berry each time he kisses a maid
beneath the Mistletoe bough

So dear is this plant to Scandinavian antiquity that if
enemies met by chance beneath it in a forest, they laid down
their arms and maintained a truce until the next day. From
this may have arisen the custom of hanging the branch over a
door, entering which was a pledge of peace and friendship to
be sealed by a kiss.

Church and Mistletoe

The church never sanctioned the use of Mistletoe in the
decoration of a religious edifice because of its heathen origin.
No restriction was strong enough to banish it from the home
where it will always be used by those who desire to preserve
our old and interesting customs.

Medicinal Use

Amulets were worn about the neck in France to prevent
sickness and for the same reason, rings of Mistletoe were worn

in Sweden. Monkish herbalists did not refer to its connection with paganism but named it *Lignum Sanctae Crucis*, the Wood of the Sacred Cross. They declared that the cross of Calvary was made of it. We can imagine that when Shakespeare wrote of it as the "baleful Mistletoe" he had in mind its association with the Cross. The herbalists prescribed its use inwardly as an antidote for every poison, as a remedy for falling sickness and epilepsy. They recommended that pieces be hung about the neck to ward off diseases.

EVEN THE HUMBLEST GIFT WITH LOVE*

It was Christmas Eve in Monterrey. The great night had come. Music resounded along the narrow streets. Maria was a little girl with big, solemn, dark eyes. Last Christmas her world had been bright and beautiful. Then her mother and father were still with her and together they had mingled with their friends in celebration of Los Pastores. Now she minded babies and ran errands for centavos with which to buy bread. But tonight the relatives and friends were all playing with their own babies so that Maria had no centavos for bread.

She passed the great Plaza de Hidalgo with its gay music, and it seemed like fairyland. From every direction people were hurrying with their gifts. Many were going to the church for the chimes were beginning to ring clear and sweet. Someone called and there she saw Anita carrying a basket filled with gay paper flowers, and Dolores with a crimson candle.

"Are you not going to the cathedral, Maria ?" they asked. Answered Maria sadly, "I have no gift." "If you think hard," insisted Dolores, "you will remember something that will please the Christ Child. Hurry and look and we will wait for you." She hastened to her little hut and there she saw a pottery cup, brilliantly painted in rose and blue.

"I could take that" she said happily. "It's so beautiful."

*Excerpt from "Bright Shawl" of Junior League.

But as she hastened from the hut to rejoin her friends she stumbled and the cup flew out of her hands, and was broken into many pieces. "Go to the cathedral without me for I cannot join you," she said sadly.

"Do come with us," they entreated "for we will surely find something on the way."

Maria brushed the tears from her eyes as the girls pointed out a plant by the wayside.

"Take this," they said, "Remember that even the humblest gift with love is beautiful in His sight."

"But," cried Maria, "I can't take a weed."

Nevertheless, she bent down and gathered some, a choking sob in her throat and her tears falling fast and mingling with the dewdrops on the weeds.

As she climbed the steep path the shining cross and lighted dome kept urging her on. When she came to the splendid entrance, her heart failed her, but the girls urged her on. She passed down the aisle forgetting her modest gift as she marvelled at the stained glass windows that cast a radiant glow over the interior. Arriving at the altar she caught her breath at the dazzling sight. Golden lights of many candles shown upon the Nacimiento—the crib of our Lord.

"Oh," cried Maria, "There is the Infant Jesus that I have so wanted to see, and there is His Mother bending over Him, and there are the Kings with the crowns on their heads kneeling at His feet with their gifts, and there is St. Joseph and the shepherds." Kneeling she laid her gift on the altar, murmuring: "With all my love, dear Christ Child."

As she turned to go, she stopped in wide-eyed amazement. The dry, brown stalks were turning green. The upper leaves of the weed changed to a beautiful scarlet flower. Reverently the great crowd of people knelt when they perceived the miracle of the flower. The humble offering that was given by a little child had been transformed into the Flor de la Nochebuena as it is called in Mexico, or Flower of the Nativity—the Poinsettia.

CHRISTMAS TREE LEGENDS

Fir Is Tree of Life

A LEGEND states that the Fir is the tree of life, which once bloomed and fruited freely but that Eve plucked its fruits, whereupon its foliage became shrunken into tiny needlelike leaves. But on the night that Christ was born it began to bloom again.

Alexander Tille* writes that Albrecht Adam, of Nordlingen, born 1786, tells us that months before Christmas a Cherry tree was put in a big pot so that at Christmas it stood in full bloom and reached the ceiling. Families competed with each other for the best trees. This, of course, is merely a practice derived from the legend.

The Viking Tree

When Ansgarius preached the White Christ to the Vikings of the North, Jacob A. Riis† tells us, that the Lord sent his three messengers, Faith, Hope, and Love to light the first tree. They sought a tree that would be as high as hope, as wide as love, and that bore the sign of the cross on every bough, and chose the Balsam Fir, which, best of all trees, met this requirement.

A Tree from Eden

In some old almanacs we find that every day has the name or names of saints, and on the 24th of December appears the

*Tille, Alexander. *Yule and Christmas.*
†Riis, Jacob A. *Century Magazine*, December, 1908.

name of Adam and Eve.   J. F. Lageman, in a Columbus Horticultural Society Annual Report, tells us that when Adam left the Garden of Eden he brought a twig of The Tree of the Forbidden Fruit.   It was this same tree which became the Christmas tree, and afterwards the wood for the Holy Cross of our Saviour.

A Scandinavian Version

The Scandinavians relate the story of a Service-tree which sprang from the blood-drenched soil where two lovers had died.   On certain nights of the Christmas season mysterious lights were seen from its branches—lights that no wind could extinguish, so here again is a legend dealing with our present light-bedecked tree which has become the symbol of Christmas.

An Egyptian Version

"The palm tree is known to put forth a shoot each month so that a spray of the tree with twelve shoots on it was used as a symbol of the year completed."   So writes Hazlitt in *The Dictionary of Faith and Folklore*.   Therefore, this story infers that the Christmas tree originated in Egypt because it was used in connection with the festival of the goddess Isis.

St. Wilfred or Wilfrid

A far more familiar origin of the Christmas tree is the story of Wilfred.

One day he was standing in the midst of a crowd of his converts, and in order to indicate that they had severed all connection with the Druids and such heathen practices, he hewed down a giant Oak, which, of course, was one of the principal objects of Druidic worship.   As it fell to the earth with a thunderous noise it split into four pieces and from its very center there grew a young Fir tree, pointing a green spire toward the sky.   The converts gazed in amazement.

Wilfred let his ax drop and turned to speak, "This little tree, a young child of the forest, shall be your Holy tree

"I saw the tree was covered with candles, some hanging down and others standing upright. What seemed to be a star at the top of the tree was really a vision of a child with a pale amber halo about its lovely head"

tonight. It is the wood of peace, for your houses are built of the Fir. It is the sign of an endless life, for its leaves are evergreen. See how it points toward the heaven. Let this be called the tree of the Christ Child; gather about it, not in the wildwood, but in your own homes. There it will shelter no deeds of blood but shall be surrounded with loving gifts and rites of kindness."

Tale of Bonchevalier*

The word spread rapidly through the valley that Bonchevalier had seen a vision, dreamed a dream, or experienced a real phenomenon. It was Christmas Eve and he was going through the deep forest, when, it was said, he saw from afar a tall evergreen tree. Even in the distance it seemed aglow with lights and a star appeared to rest among its topmost branches.

"How can I tell what I saw ?" said Bonchevalier. "Truly it was unbelievable. As I came nearer, I saw the tree was covered with candles; some were hanging down and others stood upright. What seemed to be the star at the top of the tree was really a vision of a child with a pale amber halo about its lovely head. I cannot interpret this strange vision, if vision it was."

This was what he told the wise men of his community but they shook their heads. He went to his mother but she was not puzzled.

"My son," she said, "your fortunate journey through the forest has revealed to you the Tree of Humanity. The candles were people. The good persons were represented by the upright candles; alas, the bad ones were inverted. And the Child at the top was the Infant Jesus. He watches over all the world of humanity. All France is, indeed, blessed by your vision."

*This story is also related by Shimrock in *Der Handbuch der Deutschen Mythologie* and is found in various versions relating to the French as well as the Germans. In Shimrock's story the knight bears the name of Durmars.

OTHER LEGENDS OF CHRISTMAS

The Little Stranger

IN A small cottage on the border of a great forest lived a poor wood cutter with his wife and two children. Rising early each morning, Valentine and Mary assisted their mother with the chores. It would seem that the harder the poor wood cutter worked the less money he was able to make for his devoted wife and his ever cheerful children.

One Midwinter night they all sat about their fire eating their supper, if such we could call such meager fare. A storm was raging outside and one was not sure whether it was only the storm or a rapping at the door, but the good wife felt sure she heard a knock and sent the wood cutter to see. Opening the door they heard a small voice say, "I am a poor child. Please let me in, for I have nothing to eat and no place to go."

"Come in, dear child," said the wood cutter's wife. "We do not have much food to share but you may sleep in the children's warm bed." The child eagerly entered and soon after eating a few morsels was sound asleep on the cozy cot, while the children hovered together on a bench near the fireplace, and uttered a prayer to God, thanking Him for their snug house, saying that whereas the little stranger had only heaven for its roof and the cold earth for a bed, they had loving parents and a warm home. Soon they fell asleep with thankful hearts.

In the middle of the night Mary suddenly was awakened, for she seemed to hear beautiful songs. She looked out of the

To all parts of the world the Christkind travels each Christmas,
bringing all good children a gift to make them even more happy
than they are the rest of the year

window and saw the child standing out in the snow with a vast throng of angels singing a most delightful chorus. The stranger child was no longer in poor rags but was dressed in gleaming radiance. Noting the surprise of the family, the child exclaimed, "I am the Christkind, bringing happiness to good children. I shall bring you a blessing. This little Fir outside the window shall be my emblem." They looked at their familiar Fir but it was covered now with silver nuts, lights, apples, and threads of gold.

To all parts of the world the representative of the Christkind travels each Christmas, bringing all good children a gift to make them even more happy than they are the rest of the year. In one form or another this story is familiar to all German children, and typifies the Biblical injunction, "Inasmuch as ye have done it unto one of the least of these my brethren, ye have done it unto me."

WHEN YOUR CANARY SINGS

A fierce Winter storm was raging through the Harz Mountains one Christmas Eve. Each blast was filled with sleet and snow, so heavy that massive trees were split and went crashing down the mountainsides. Only the Fir trees, with their gnarled roots, were able to withstand the cruel onslaught of the terrific gale. In each brief lull could be heard the distressing cry of the wind-tossed golden canaries. The great old Fir trees heard it. As the wind blew through their needles, the Fir's call was carried to the birds: "Come into our branches. We will protect you as our family has protected many of the earth's living things."

The poor little spent canaries, hearing the call, used their last bit of strength to fly into the protecting arms of the Firs to stay until the storm was over. "We will make our homes with you and we will forever sing our praises to you as the sacred home of birds all over the earth," they sang.

Now when your canary is singing his sweetest, you know that he is singing about Christmas Eve in the Fir trees that

"Come into our branches," said the Firs. "We will protect you."

protected the canaries in the Harz Mountains so many years ago.

The Silver Cones

Another delightful legend of the Harz Mountain Firs tells of a poor miner family. The father became ill, leaving his wife and children without food or fuel. Each morning the wife would climb one of these mountains to pick up cones to sell as fuel for another day's living. As she entered the woods near Christmastide a little old imp jumped out from a Fir tree and said to her, "Take only the cones under this tree, for they are the best."

The woman thanked him, and as she started to pick up the cones there was such a downfall of them that she was frightened. Her basket was soon full. As she started home it became heavier and heavier, until she could scarcely reach her door. When she emptied the cones upon her table, every one of them was made of pure silver. Even now Fir cones are gathered and covered with a silver-like sulphur paint and placed in bags to burn and crackle gayly in our Christmas fires.*

The Old Pine Is Blessed†

The edict of the evil King Herod found Joseph, Mary and the Christ Child fleeing from the soldiers. Too weary to proceed, they came to a forest. A huge Pine tree, aged and hollow, bade them rest inside its cool trunk. It lowered its arching branches and concealed the Holy Family until the soldiers of Herod had passed. When morning came the Christ Child raised His arms and blessed the aged Pine. Some say that if we cut a small Pine cone lengthwise we may still see the imprint of His hand.

*These two delightful stories of the Canaries and the Silver Cones are told by Fae Huttenlocher in *Better Homes and Gardens*, December, 1933.

†Adapted from Charles M. Skinner. *Myths and Legends of Flowers, Trees, Fruits, and Plants*.

The Spoons Were Moved*

The Tyrols were resplendent with moonlight and unnumbered stars scintillated in their cold serenity.   Inside the home of Andreas, the storekeeper, preparations were being made for midnight mass for it was Christmas Eve.

"May I put my spoon in first?" asked Josef, "I am the oldest."

"You must wait till grandmother places hers as she is the most honored by years," cautioned mother.   "After her, we will each place our spoons."

A large bowl of milk had been set on the little carved table. A treasured picture of the Holy Family rested against the wall so that the beam of a candle played full upon it.

Now each member of the family chose his spoon to place around the rim of the bowl of milk. First grandmother, then mother and father, for they were the same age; then Josef, and Gertrud, and Lizbet, and Hermann; lastly, mother chose a tiny spoon for baby Barbara but it had to be stilted up on a small box.

"We are all ready. Let us get into our warm clothes so that we may go to the church and thank our loving Father for sending the Christ Child to earth—even as each one of us was brought from another world of hopefulness," said mother, and continued, "Whose spoon will be moved tonight? Only waiting will tell."

As the family knelt in the pew of the St. Nikolaus Kirche, Josef's eyes often rested on the painting of the Holy Family which hung upon the wall above the high gilded altar. Josef thought he could see a bowl of milk and a row of spoons but it was only the books and the chalice of the holy priest. He could hardly wait till mass was over so that he might rush home faster than the others to see whether his spoon had been moved. He knew that the milk had been placed as a welcome to the Holy Family. He knew that Mother Mary might feed

*The legend on which this story is based was related by Louis Golding in *Country Life*, December, 1928.

"Josef rushed on ahead of the family. What did he see
when he looked in the window ?"

the Holy Infant, and if so, the spoon she used would be moved. The one whose spoon was used would have great luck for the year. Josef desired that it would be his.

As the strains of the organ dismissed the group of pious mountaineers, Josef rushed on ahead of the family. What did he see when he looked in the window of his home? Baby Barbara's spoon was not there now. And the grandmother's spoon was in the milk with the handle resting on the rim of the bowl. Who can say how the spoons became changed?

THE ANIMALS IN THE STABLE

The Horse, the Ox, the Mule, and the Goat stood near the manger in which Mary laid her Babe. She gathered the hay from the far corners of the stable to make a comfortable bed for the Infant Jesus.

When the selfish Horse saw his food being used for bedding he was greatly displeased. As soon as Mary deposited her handfuls of hay, he ate them until at last the Christ Child was almost lying on the bare boards. Finally, Mary said, "You never-satisfied Horse, you and all your progeny will always be hungry and you will forevermore serve and help mankind as he goes about his daily tasks."

The Ox heard Mary's words and picked up huge mouthfuls of hay which he deposited in the manger and blew his warm breath upon the Christ Child. He leaned his big head toward Mary and whispered that the Cow had expected to come but she asked to be excused as she also had become a mother that day and desired to present the Calf to the Babe in due time. Mary blessed the good creature and said, "You, the patient Ox, and she, the willing Cow, for your unselfishness, shall forevermore enjoy your food so much that you will chew it again and again, and—," she added, "Tell the Cow she will have a Calf each year."

The Mule laughed loud over the words of Mary and she asked, "Why are you laughing?" The Mule answered "I was amused that the Cow was to calf each year." To which Mary said, "Because you ridiculed the Cow and her baby Calf, you shall never, never know the joy of having young of your own."

One would have thought that the Goat would have learned a good lesson but no—the Goat bleated in the Christ Child's ears and gave Him no chance to sleep. Finally he gave such a shrill cry that he frightened the Mother and Child. "From this hour," Mary calmly said, "your tremulous, pitiful laugh will always be irritating to people. Your milk will be insipid and men can use it only for making cheese."

So this explains why the Horse is a servant of Man, why the Cow chews her cud, why the Mule is sterile, and why the Goat's voice is so hideous.

—*Freely translated from a Slavic legend in Walter Schmidkunz's "Christusmaerchen."*

THE MAN IN THE MOON

One Christmas Eve a peasant felt a great desire to eat cabbage and, having none himself, he slipped into a neighbor's garden to cut some.* Just as he had filled his basket, the Christ Child rode past on a white horse, and said, "Because thou hast stolen on the Holy Night, thou shalt immediately sit in the moon with thy basket of cabbage." And so. we are told, the culprit was immediately wafted up to the moon and there he can still be seen as the Man in the Moon.

Other legends state that the peasant instead of stealing cabbage was gathering wood on the Holy Night.

Another story† says that a man was hoping to find an isle on which there was no death. He found, at last, the moon, and there he lived a hundred years. Here Death called for him one Christmas Eve. A fierce struggle ensued but the man was victorious and today we may find him in the moon.

*Chamberlain, Alexander. F. *Book of Christmas*, edited by Hamilton Wright Mabie.

†*Harper's Weekly*, Vol. 502, 1906.

CHRISTMAS TOASTS

SINCE early days it was common to float warm substances in a bowl of liquor such as snapdragon (see page 116), roasted crabs, or a piece of bread toast.

An old story relates that one day a favorite court lady fell into a pool whereupon the gallants who stood around proposed that all take a drink of the water in the pool. A wag quickly remarked that "he preferred the toast to the liquor," and jumped in the pool, pressing a delicious kiss upon the maiden's lips. Hence the origin of the toast.

It is an old British custom to drink to an absent person after dinner and such a person was known as a *toast*. Gradually the meaning was changed to signify anything that was commemorated, as "The King," "The Land We Live In," "The Sweetest Girl in the World," or "A Merry Christmas and as Happy a New Year as You Can Stand."

Almost any popular Christmas poem will suggest a few lines to suit the Christmas holiday occasions but here are just a few:

> At Christmas play and make good cheer,
> For Christmas comes but once a year.
> —THOMAS TUSSER (1523–1580) in *A Farmer's Daily Diet*

*   *   *   *   *

> Now Christmas is come,
> Let's beat up the drum,
> And call all our neighbors together,
> And when they appear,
> Let us make them such cheer
> As will keep out the wind and the weather.
> —WASHINGTON IRVING

At Christmas be merry and thankful withal.
—WASHINGTON IRVING

* * * * *

Ye who have loved each other,
Sister and friend and brother,
  In this fast fading year;
Mother and sire and child,
Young man and maiden mild,
  Come gather here.

Let sinned against, and sinning
Forget their strife's beginning,
  And join in friendship now:
Be links no longer broken,
Be sweet forgiveness spoken,
  Under the Holly bough.
—CHARLES MACKAY

* * * * *

From our snug fireside this Christmas-tide
  We'll keep old Winter out.
—THOMAS NOEL

* * * * *

What sweeter music can we bring
Than carol for to sing?
—HERRICK

* * * * *

Heap on more wood !—the wind is chill;
But let it whistle as it will,
We'll keep our Christmas merry still.
—SIR WALTER SCOTT

* * * *

I heard the bells on Christmas Day
  Their old, familiar carols play
    And wild and sweet
    The word repeat
Of peace on earth, good-will to men!
—H. W. LONGFELLOW

* * * * *

Everywhere – everywhere, Christmas tonight!
Christmas in lands of the Fir tree and Pine,
Christmas in lands of the Palm tree and vine,
Christmas where snow peaks stand solemn and white,
Christmas where corn fields lie sunny and bright,
Everywhere, everywhere, Christmas tonight.
—PHILLIPS BROOKS

OLD WIVES' TALES

MAN gropes for knowledge. The primitive people living, perhaps, a little closer to Nature than we, had to contend with hurricanes, tempests, earthquakes, the behavior of their crops, and as soon as they began to think about these things they tried to interpret. Until science had developed to the stage of asking "why ?" and proving the answer, superstitions reigned and these, of course, were the forerunners of true, classified, exact knowledge which since the time of Sir Francis Bacon has been true science. It is only normal that primitive people should try to make some explanation of the natural phenomena beyond their control. This was especially true of those dependent upon the weather for their material gains, their crop successes, and their safety on the sea.

SUPERSTITIONS—OMENS—DIVINATIONS

Superstition may be defined as a belief founded on irrational feelings, especially of fear, and marked by the ability to believe the improbable or impossible. Included with superstitions are *omens*, which are phenomena or incidents which have a prophetic significance. They are an indication of something that will come to pass, which happens, as it were, by accident, without seeking for it. *Divination*, on the other hand, is a conscious effort on our part to find out or foretell by assumed supernatural aid. To illustrate, we consider it a bad omen for someone to enter our home with an open umbrella, but by divination we find out whether our lover is true by plucking the florets from a Daisy.

169

Some say that ever 'gainst that season comes,
Wherein our Saviour's birth is celebrated,
The bird of dawning singeth all night long;
And then, they say, no spirit can walk abroad;
The nights are wholesome; then no planets strike,
No fairy takes, nor witch hath power to charm;
So hallow'd and so gracious is the time.

HAMLET, Act I, Scene 1

As long as the church and state step in to infuse people with a spirit of reverence and obedience, instead of inquiry, superstitions continue to be prominent in the thinking. As soon as science attempts to give us the correct explanation, superstition fades and dies.

It is not necessary, nor possible, to believe all the various religions of the world, but it is a part of our culture to know some of the main tenets of these "Two-and-Seventy Jarring Sects" so that we may derive from each its essence of philosophy and pleasure.

Many interesting divinations may be played at the Christmas party. The Russians find it great fun to determine their fate by dropping melted wax into cold water. See page 273

Art and Superstition

In those countries where literature and art, both dependent on imagination, thrive best we can expect superstitions
to be rife. As we look through the folklore of the Italian and
Scandinavian peninsulas, we find that there is much fanciful
belief and also the greatest artists, poets, and writers.

Old Ideas Come Up Unnoticed

T. Ribot observes that each man carries in his mind the
ideas of his ancestors, usually unconsciously and dimly recognized. Some external stimulus occurs and these tendencies
blaze up. This explains superstition. We try to escape the
ideas but they come up unnoticed.

Everyone likes to think he is not superstitious. But it is
strange, isn't it, that so many remember that they have
started certain work on Friday, or that they have walked
under a ladder without any ill fate befalling them. We say
we are not superstitious yet we recall these incidents.

Old wives' tales are repeated from year to year and there
is always evidence for each superstition. For when a superstition is substantiated, we remember it, and when it does
not come to pass there are always extenuating circumstances
to explain that, too. Therefore, in reading the following
superstitions as related to Christmas let us not think of them
in the light of belief or unbelief. Let us consider the poetry,
perhaps even the pathos, of those who have ordered their
lives by these precepts in the past. And let us thank science
that now we have more nearly correct explanations for
the behavior of weather and crops—and even lovers.

Born Lucky

There is a Scottish belief that to be born on Christmas
is to have the power to see spirits and even to command them.
Sir Walter Scott says that the Spaniards imputed the hag-
gard and downcast looks of Philip II to the terrible visions

he was able to see because he was born on Christmas.—Crippen.

The French peasants believe that babies born on Christmas have the gift of prophecy. In the Vosges a baby born on Christmas Eve possesses the "gift of gab," whereas the Christmas Day baby has less tongue and better logic. Daughters born on December 25 will be wise, witty, and virtuous.

In Silesia a baby born on Christmas will become either a lawyer or a thief.

In middle Europe it is said that a baby born at sermon time Christmas Eve portends that someone in the house will die within the year.

English mothers used to take sick babies to the door Christmas Eve midnight. Mary was expected to pass with the Christ Child. If the baby recovered, it is the sign that it has been touched by the Christ with healing fingers, and if it died the Christ Child had called the baby to be His playmate in heaven.

A variation of this belief, according to Crippen, states that there is a certain group of Christmas angels sent to earth commissioned to awaken a new-born infant from its first sleep and carry it to heaven. There it was honored by being placed in the choir of the Christ Child.

"But Love Can Hope Where Reason Would Despair"

In the ancient Duchy of Swabia girls went to the woodpile Christmas Eve to draw sticks. If they drew a long one their future husband would be tall; if a thick one, he would be stout, and if crooked he would be deformed. His business could be determined by dropping melted lead into a pan of cold water. The lead would resemble the insignia of his occupation: shoe-shape, a cobbler; hammer-shape, a carpenter; rod-shape, a schoolmaster; and as every piece of lead resembled some occupation to the wise old wives, this was a popular Christmas Eve diversion. To determine who would be married first, girls formed a circle and let loose a blind-folded goose among them. The girl to whom it went first would be the first bride.

In Bohemia the girls would go into the night and stand-ing in the garden they would take a branch of Elder and cry loudly, "Sweet Elder, I shake, I shake! Tell me ye dogs that wake, where is my lover tonight?" They would wait for the sound of the bark and a lover would be expected to come from that direction.

On Christmas Eve a maiden would set a bowl of water outside a window to freeze. The form which the ice took would determine her future husband's occupation.— Daniels and Stevans.

According to the *Irish Monthly* the maidens would take four onions, placing one in each corner of her room. Each one was given the name of a man of her acquaintance. The one that first threw out a shoot before January 6 would be her future husband.

In northern England girls placed Holly under their pil-lows and repeated:

> Good St. Thomas serve me right
> And send me my true love tonight,
> That I may gaze upon his face,
> Then him in my fond arms embrace.

In Old England a spray of Holly was placed on the hive to wish the bees a Merry Christmas

Some make an indigestible cake of flour, water, and salt. They eat this on Christmas Eve and it makes them dream of their future husband.

To accept a bunch of Edelweiss at Christmas in Switzerland is to also accept the man who proffers it.

BEES AND BEASTS

One of the most current legends of Christmastime is the story that in honor of the Christ Child bees hum a carol, and in England they place a spray of Holly on the hive to wish them a Merry Christmas. The bees are also told of births and deaths.

In the German Alps it is believed that on Christmas Eve all animals can speak, but of course no one should put this superstition to the test. A servant is reputed to have hidden himself in the barn. Just before midnight he heard two horses speak. Said one, "The servant is heavy." "Yes," said the other, "it is very steep up to the churchyard." The servant was buried that week.

In Spain everyone is admonished to treat cows very kindly because it is believed that cattle breathed upon the Christ Child to keep Him warm.

In Bohemia a horse is driven into the river at Christmas and made to walk against the current. The rider throws an apple into the stream and if it hits the horse it will be stronger during the coming year.—Daniels and Stevans.

If you remember Dickens *Cricket on the Hearth* you will recall the delightful story of how a chirping cricket brought good luck and had a singing match with the kettle in Dot Peerybingle's kitchen.

To dream of a black cat on Christmas Eve is the sign of an alarming illness.

A dog which howls on Christmas Eve will go mad within the year.

A wash cloth used on Christmas day to groom the horses will cause them to grow fat.—Southern Cross.

At the conclusion of midnight mass in the Tyrols, the congregation often breaks into song, some whistling like birds, so that God's choristers may not be forgotten.—Dowling.

To Insure Crop Success

Tie wet bands of straw around fruit trees to make them fruitful, or tie a stone to a branch, or beat the trunks with a whip.

If you steal hay on Christmas Eve and feed the cattle they thrive and you will not be caught in future thefts.

On St. Barbara's Day, December 4, in southern France, two plates of grain are chosen. The percentage that grows determines the harvest for the year. It is used as a Christmas table decoration.

In the Netherlands it is thought that nothing sown on Christmas Eve will perish, even though the seed be sown in the snow.—Daniels and Stevans.

Take an onion on Christmas Eve and cut it through to form twelve cups. Put salt on each and place in a row, giving each the name of a month. The months in which the salt is found wet on the following morning will be wet, and the contrary.—Thorpe.

FEEDING SUPERSTITIONS

Eat a raw egg before eating anything else on Christmas morning and you will be able to carry heavy weights.

To pick apples or nuts from the ground on Christmas will bring sores to you.

When a Bohemian wife burns a Christmas cake she believes she will die within a year.—Daniels and Stevans.

Tyrolean peasants listen to the bake ovens. If they hear music it means an early wedding, but if they hear bells it means the speedy death of the listener.

In Denmark some of the bread baked at Christmas is kept until sowing time, then crumbled and mixed with the seed to insure an abundant harvest.

In Germany the crumbs from the Christmas table when shaken on the soil cause a little plant known as the Crumb-wort to spring up. This little plant is said to have great healing powers.

In England it is said that bread baked on Christmas will never become moldy.—Clemens.

Some say that he whose appetite gives out first at Christmas dies first.

GENERAL ADMONITIONS

In the Netherlands they tell you to take a Fir stick, thrust it into the fire and let it burn partially and put it under the bed. This serves as lightning insurance.—Daniels and Stevans

In Ireland it is believed that the gates of Paradise are always open on Christmas Eve. Dying then one would not enter Purgatory.—Crippen.

In middle Europe if your light goes out on Christmas morning you will see spirits and if you burn Elder on Christmas Eve all witches will be revealed to you.

In Scandinavia some families place all their shoes together, as this will cause them to live in harmony throughout the year.—Daniels and Stevans.

In many places it is believed that nothing made of leather at Christmas will be durable, and in Hertfordshire wearing new shoes on Christmas is very unlucky.

In Lancashire, Worcestershire, and Gloucestershire no one will give matches, fire, or light to be taken from the house on Christmas Day, believing trouble would arise.—Clemens.

In Shropshire and other sections of Europe ashes must never be thrown out on Christmas Day for fear they will be thrown into the Saviour's face.—Miles.

There is a story current in Poland that Jacob's ladder is brought back to earth on Christmas Eve and that the angels ascend and descend bringing peace and goodwill to the earth. Only saints have claimed to be able to see this ladder.—Walsh.

Never launder a Christmas present before presenting it, as this takes out the good luck.—Daniels and Stevans.

These superstitions have been derived from the following sources: Thorpe, Benjamin, *Northern Mythology*.

Daniels, Cora Linn and Stevans, C. M. *Encyclopaedia of Superstitions, Folklore and Occult Sciences of the World*.

Crippen, T. G., *Christmas and Christmas Lore*.

Dowling, Alfred, *Flora of Sacred Nativity*.

Clemens, Will, *Holy-days and Holidays*.

STORY OF CHRISTMAS SEALS*

BESIDES the United States, more than forty different countries throughout the world now have, or have had, Christmas seals or stamps that are sold wholly or partially for tuberculosis work. Little did Einar Holboell realize,

This is the first Christmas seal, sent out by Denmark

when he conceived that first Danish Christmas seal, launched in 1904, that his simple idea would in a generation circumnavigate the globe.

In many countries the Christmas seals are sold through the post office largely. For instance, in Luxemburg, in Belgium and the Netherlands, one may buy Christmas seals at the post office paying, let us say, a penny extra over and above the face value of the usual postage stamp.

THE DENMARK PLATES

Those who visited the San Diego Exposition in 1936 were very much interested in the series of 30 Copenhagen porcelain plates which were used to decorate the Danish house along the Avenue of Nations. Upon inquiry I found an interesting story back of these plates. It seemed that a certain tubercular man designed the first one and proposed selling a small number to aid the fight against tuberculosis. Since that year new plates have been added until now, instead of Christmas seals, these exquisite works of art bring in a large sum of money.

*Jacobs, Philip P., *Christmas Seals Around the World, Journal of Outdoor Life*, September, 1934.

"MERRY CHRISTMAS" AS OTHERS SAY IT

Afrikander......................Een Plesierige Kerfees
Bohemian..............................:Vesele Vanoce
Bulgarian...............................Chestita Koleda
Croatian..................................Sretan Bozic
Danish.....................................Glaedelig Jul
Dutch...............................Vroolijk Kerfeest
Esperanto.......................Gajan Kristnaskon
Esthonian.......................Roomsaid Joulu Puhi
Finnish...................................Iloista Joulua
French......................................Joyeux Noel
German.......................Froehliche Weihnachten
Hungarian................Kellemes karacsonyi unnepeket
Irish...........................Nodlaig mhaith chugnat
Italian...........................Buone Feste Natalizie
Jugoslav................................Cestitamo Bozic
Lettish.........................Priecigus Ziemassvetkus
Lithuanian...........................Linksmu Kaledu
Norwegian...................................Gledelig Jul
Polish......................................Weselych Swiat
Portuguese.................................Boas Festas
Rumanian............................Sarbatori vesele
Serbian.....................................Hristos se rodi
Slovakian................Sretan Bozic or Vesele vianoce
Spanish.................................Feliz Navidad
Swedish..Glad Yul
Ukranian.....................Srozhdestvom Kristovym
Welsh....................................Nadolig Llawen

IMPORTANT HISTORICAL EVENTS ON CHRISTMAS DAY

1065................Westminster Abbey consecrated
1066....................William the Conqueor crowned
1492............."Santa Maria," Columbus' ship, wrecked
1642...........................Sir Isaac Newton born
1745..Peace of Dresden concluded between Austria, Prussia, and Saxony
1776..............Washington crossed the Delaware River
1777.......Christmas Island discovered by Captain Cook
1780......................Nashville, Tennessee, founded
1786......................Shay's Rebellion broke out
1821..............................Clara Barton born
1837...........Battle of Okeechobee with Seminole Indians
1840............Birthday of Peter Ilyitch Tschaikovsky
1842...........................Battle of Mier in Mexico
1849...............................San Francisco fire
1875..........First penny newspaper printed in Chicago

IMPORTANT HISTORICAL EVENTS ON NEW YEAR'S DAY

1735.............................Birth of Paul Revere
1801....Importation of slaves prohibited in United States
1863........Emancipation Proclamation issued by Lincoln
1877..............Victoria proclaimed Empress of India
1898....................Greater New York established
1901.............Commonwealth of Australia proclaimed

CHRISTMAS

The earth has grown old with its burden of care
  But at Christmas it always is young,
The heart of the jewel burns lustrous and fair
And its soul full of music breaks forth on the air,
  When the song of the angels is sung.

The feet of the humblest may walk in the field
  Where the feet of the holiest have trod,
This, this is the marvel to mortals revealed
When the silvery trumpets of Christmas have pealed,
  That mankind are children of God.

—Phillips Brooks

FOODS AROUND THE WORLD

ARGENTINA—See page 202

ARMENIA

In Armenia, seven is considered a lucky number on New Years Day. They serve seven kinds of fruit, seven kinds of nuts, seven dishes, and bring water at dawn from seven different fountains (see page 202)—Miss Zabelle Tahmizian.

AUSTRIA

Characteristic foods of Christmas are: *Fruchtbrod,* made of raisins, currants, chopped figs and dates and made into a cake which is served hot; chopped and baked carp; beef, vegetables and beer.—*Harper's Weekly*, December 31, 1910.

BULGARIA

Goose is baked on a bed of sauerkraut which takes away the strong goose flavor.

On New Years Eve a great supper is prepared which often includes rice, nuts and prune sauce. A loaf of unleavened bread contains a penny for luck, a ring to portend a wedding, a thimble for an old maid.

COSTA RICA

Crede Calhoun says that he was served a roast *Tepis-quintle.* The host told him it was the Indian name for a *paca,* a cross between a wild hog and a glorified rat.—*Panama Times*, December 26, 1925.

Czechoslovakia

In Czechoslovakia baked carp with a spicy dark sauce is the chief Christmas Eve dish, and in thousands of Czechoslovakian homes in the United States this delectable dish will grace the table. The carp, according to custom, must be caught and kept alive until the time to clean and cook it has arrived. Its preparation is elaborate and of great interest, and is usually watched or participated in by every member of the family.—*Folk-News.*

A sweet roll filled with raisins and almonds is often baked. It is called *Vanocka.*

*Moravian Cookies**

Don't forget that the dough for Moravian cookies must be mixed a couple of weeks before they are baked. You can roll this hard, cold dough almost paper thin, and then cut it in animal shapes which will delight the children:

- 1⅞ cupfuls pastry flour
- ¼ cupful melted butter
- ½ cupful molasses, heated
- ¼ cupful brown sugar
- ⅛ teaspoonful ginger
- ⅛ teaspoonful cloves
- ⅛ teaspoonful cinnamon
- ⅛ teaspoonful nutmeg
- ⅛ teaspoonful allspice
- Dash of salt
- ⅛ teaspoonful soda

Combine butter and molasses, add sugar, spices, salt, and soda. Add flour gradually, mixing well. Let stand about ten days in a cold place. When ready to bake, roll dough paper thin and cut in fancy shapes. Bake at 375 deg. F. for 6 minutes. This recipe makes about 100 cookies.

For Czechoslovakian meals see also page 219.

Denmark

Goose is the usual Christmas meat. Eva Le Gallienne,† the actress, tells of a dinner in Denmark as follows:

Christmas dinner was to be at Uncle Kai's on Christmas

*Mullen, Doris L. *Christmas Cookies, The American Home,* December, 1935.

†Le Gallienne, Eva. From *At 33,* quoted in the *Christian Science Monitor,* December 24, 1936.

Eve at 6 o'clock, immediately followed by the tree and presents; in Denmark it is the custom to celebrate on *Juleaften* (Christmas Eve) rather than on the twenty-fifth itself . . . It was a real Danish family dinner: Uncle Kai and his wife Anna, Mogens and his little sister Gerda, Bet, Mother and I. Danish people as a rule are gay, lively, warm, and emotional, and the little party was animated and noisy with expressions of happiness, affection and goodwill.

The dinner was an important business. First there was the excitement of who should find the almond in the *Risengrod* (a sort of rice porridge with which the meal began). The lucky one received an extra present, and I am sure that my little grandmother always saw to it that the coveted almond always turned up on my plate. The prize was, as I well knew, a large pear of *marzipan*, a candy which I particularly doted on. After the *Risengrod* came many other marvelous dishes, until the roast goose was carried on amidst loud applause, decked with tiny Danish flags and stuffed with prunes and apples. Then there were delicious Danish cakes, candies, and fruit in plenty.

The merry repast came to an end, and in old Danish fashion each one went up to the head of the house and said *"Tak for Mal"* (Thanks for the meal), to which Uncle Kai smilingly answered *"Velbekomme !"* (May good come of it!). He then opened the big double doors leading into the drawing-room, where the tree stood glistening with tinsel, stars, flags, and candy. Also see page 221 for Danish menus.

ENGLAND

Christmas is so much a time of feasting in England that it is difficult to know where to begin and end a discussion of the good things served at this season. Nevertheless, there are a few old stories about foods which will be of great interest.

Also see page 225 for English stories of meals and menus. A mediaeval feast is described on page 104.

Yule Dough

From earliest times, even in Roman days, it was common to bake the Yule Dough. It was generally a flat cake in the shape of a baby, which bakers presented to their customers in the same manner that chandlers presented Christmas candles.—*Westminster Review*, 1905.

Plum Pudding

"One indispensable old-time Christmas dish which is never heard of today was furmety, or frumenty, which, according to the oldest recipe now extant was 'wheat boiled till the grains burst, and when cool strained and boiled again with broth or milk and yolks of eggs.'" So writes Beatrice Plumb and Clementine Paddleford. They continue: "And that is all furmety was in the first place—the correct accompaniment of fat venison or fresh mutton. That boiled wheat mixture must have

The plum pudding has evolved from a sorry mess of watery gruel pottage

been pretty awful, for every Christmas we find somebody trying to do something about it, by adding an egg or two, a dash of mace, a slice of ginger cake, or a handful of raisins, currants or prunes. Then the whole decoction was boiled up into a pulp—but still served in a soup tureen!

"Later lumps of good English suet were added, until 1670, the old pottage, after centuries of culinary evolution, had sweetened and stiffened into plum pudding much as we now eat it."

In the Book of Common Prayer of the Church of England the Collect or Prayer for the Last Sunday before Advent began with the words, "Stir up." And this the good people of Peterborough, England, took to be a reminder that they should start their plum pudding on the last Sunday before Advent, and it was stirred each week, each person in the house giving it a stir now and then until it was finally cooked.

According to Chamber's *The Book of Days* Mrs. Fraser in a cookbook published in 1791 was the first person to mention "Plum Pudding" under that name.

Here is the recipe for a modern plum pudding which Edith Barber* advises:

English Plum Pudding

½ pound of chopped seeded raisins
½ pound of Sultana raisins
¼ pound of candied peels of citron, orange and lemon, shaved fine ·
¼ pound of chopped figs
½ pound of chopped beef suet
4 cupfuls of fine dried bread crumbs
½ cupful of flour

½ teaspoonful of cinnamon
¼ teaspoonful of cloves
½ teaspoonful of salt
½ cupful of brown sugar
1 cupful of cider or fruit juice
Sherry flavoring (non-alcoholic)
6 eggs

Mix the fruits together and add the suet, crumbs, and flour with which the spices and salt have been sifted. Add the sugar, fruit juice, flavoring, and beaten eggs. Fill the pudding mold two-thirds full and tie oiled paper tightly over the top. Steam 5 or 6 hours.

Christmas Pudding Sauce

2 egg yolks
1 cupful of confectioners' sugar

½ cupful of whipping cream
Flavoring

Beat the egg yolks, add the sugar, and beat until smooth. Fold in the whipped cream, and flavor with sherry or rum flavoring or with vanilla or nutmeg.

Mince Pie

Mince pie has always represented a compound of the choicest productions of the East, and symbolizes the gifts of the Wise Men to the Child Jesus. As early as 1596 mince pies were popular under the name of mutton pies; later neats' tongues were substituted. At first these Christmas pies were called shrid pye, that is, shredded pie, or minced pie.

*Barber, Edith. *Christmas Comes But Once a Year, Better Homes and Gardens,* December, 1930.

"Our hardy ancestors thought of the good things in life in terms of eating and had valiant confidence in their digestive powers," says Miss Pearl Chase, "for there was an old saying that you would have as many happy months in a year as mince pies you tasted at Christmastime."

Mince pies were first baked in the form of the manger, and the old books always called the upper crust of the pie its coffin. Sometimes the pie was not covered by a coffin but was cross latticed and this represented the hayrack of a stable.

In some way or another, these mince pies began to be associated with the church and Rome. Many of the old writers of religious tracts called mince pie an "idolatrie in crust," and one old writer who did not like to mince his words wrote, "Such pye is an hodge-podge of superstition, Popery, the devil, and all its works."

Mince pies or Christmas pies were watched on the night before Christmas so that thieves would not steal them. Herrick has this poem:

> Come guard the Christmas pie
> That the thief, though ne'er so shy,
> With his flesh-hooks don't come nigh,
>   To catch it.

Although mincemeat is decidedly British, the recipe we would like to present is from Edith Barber,* the heritage from her Pennsylvania grandmother.

Mincemeat

4 pounds of chopped lean beef	3 pounds of currants
2 pounds of chopped beef suet	½ pound of finely cut citron
6 quarts of chopped apples	1 quart of fruit juice
3 pounds of sugar	1 tablespoonful of cinnamon
2 cupfuls of molasses	1 tablespoonful of powdered cloves
2 quarts of cider	2 grated nutmegs
4 pounds of raisins, seeded and cut in pieces	1 teaspoonful of pepper
	Salt to taste

Cover the meat and suet with boiling water and cook until tender. Cool in the meat stock, so the suet will rise

*Barber, Edith. *Christmas Comes But Once a Year*, *Better Homes and Gardens*, December, 1930.

within the memory of living men. Besides the blacksmith, the writer has met with only one other person who can remember seeing a turnspit dog employed in its peculiar vocation; but no better authority can be cited than that of Mr Jesse, the well-known writer on rural subjects, who thus relates his experiences:—

'How well do I recollect in the days of my youth watching the operations of a turnspit at the house of a worthy old Welsh clergyman in Worcestershire, who taught me to read! He was a good man, wore a bushy wig, black worsted stockings, and large plated buckles in his shoes. As he had several boarders as well as day scholars, his two turnspits had plenty to do. They were long-bodied, crook-legged, and ugly dogs, with a suspicious, unhappy look about them, as if they were weary of the task they had to do, and expected every moment to be seized upon to perform it. Cooks in those days, as they are said to be at present, were very cross; and if the poor animal, wearied with having a larger joint than usual to turn, stopped for a moment, the voice of the cook might be heard, rating him in no very gentle terms. When we consider that a large solid piece of beef would take at least three hours before it was properly roasted, we

may form some idea of the task a dog had to perform in turning a wheel during that time. A pointer has pleasure in finding game, the terrier worries rats with eagerness and delight, and the bull-dog even attacks bulls with the greatest energy, while the poor turnspit performs his task with compulsion, like a culprit on a tread-wheel, subject to scolding or beating if he stops a moment to rest his weary limbs, and is then kicked about the kitchen when the task is over.'

The services of the turnspit date from an early period. Doctor Caius, founder of the college at Cambridge which bears his name, and the first English writer on dogs, says,—'There is comprehended under the curs of the coarsest kind a certain dog in kitchen service excellent. For when any meat is to be roasted, they go into a wheel, which they turning about with the weight of their bodies, so diligently look to their business, that no drudge nor scullion can do the feat more cunningly, whom the popular sort hereupon term turnspits.'

The annexed illustration, taken from *Remarks on a Tour to North and South Wales*, published in 1800, clearly exhibits how the dog was enabled to perform his curious and uncongenial task. The letterpress in reference to it says:—'Now-

A TURNSPIT AT WORK.

castle, near Carmarthen, is a pleasant village; at a decent inn here a dog is employed as turnspit; great care is taken that this animal does not observe the cook approach the larder; if he does, he immediately hides himself for the remainder of the day, and the guest must be contented with more humble fare than intended.'

One dog being insufficient to do all the roasting

490

for a large establishment, two or more were kept, working alternately; and each animal well knowing and noting its regular turn of duty, great difficulty was experienced in compelling it to work out of the recognised system of rotation. Buffon relates that two turnspits were employed in the kitchen of the Duc de Lianfort at Paris, taking their turns every other day to go into the

In *The Book of Days* we find this picture of the hard-worked turnspit dog, as he assists the cook in the preparation of the Christmas joint

to the top, forming a cake of fat which may easily be removed and chopped with the meat. Add the chopped meat and suet to the finely chopped apples. Then add the sugar, molasses, cider, raisins, currants, and stock in which the meat and suet were cooked, reduced to 1½ cupfuls. Heat gradually, stir occasionally, and cook slowly for 2 hours; then add the fruit juice and spices and cook for 30 minutes. Pack into jars and seal. Juices saved from canned fruits, particularly peaches, are delicious in mincemeat.

The Turnspit Dog

In early England it was common to harness a dog to the turnspit used for roasting the meats. When we know that it often took three hours to roast a solid piece of beef we may judge the task a dog had in running constantly for that long a time. The cooks were often cross and the poor dogs were urged on by cuffs.

As Chambers, in *"The Book of Days,"* writes: "A pointer has pleasure in finding game, the terrier worries rats with eagerness and delight, and the bull dog even attacks bulls with the greatest energy, while the poor turnspit dog performs his tasks with compulsion, and is then kicked about the kitchen when his task is done."

The illustration from *Remarks on a Tour to North and South Wales*, published in 1800, shows how the dog accomplishes his uncongenial task. The description that accompanies the picture reads:

"At a decent inn here (Newcastle) a dog is employed as a turnspit; great care is taken that the dog does not see the cook approach the larder; if he does, he immediately hides himself for the remainder of the day, and the guest must be contented with more humble fare than intended."

Two dogs are needed in some of the larger establishments— one to work one day, the other the next. The story is told of a dog which in a fit of laziness hid so that the other was forced to turn the wheel instead. When the roast was finished, the dog barked for the kitchen scullions to follow him. They went upstairs to find the lazy dog hiding beneath the bed, whereupon the dog attacked and killed its shirking fellow-worker.

FINLAND

Finns have as a first course none other than the well known dried codfish that has been soaked in a special solution for weeks ahead and boiled. It is snowy-white and fluffy as down. It is served with boiled potato and cream sauce, and sprinkled with allspice for seasoning.

Then the Finns place roast suckling pig or fresh ham on the table that is always accompanied by Lingenberry relish something like jam. The vegetables are usually mashed potatoes, baked mashed turnips, and several others usually *en casserole*, as baked macaroni, carrots, and rice.

For dessert there is rice boiled in milk and served with cream topped with sugar and cinnamon. An almond is put into the large dish of rice and the one who is lucky enough to get this almond will be especially favored for the coming year. Then there is the coffee with *torttu* pastry tarts filled with apples or prunes, small cookies, and coffee cake.—Lyyli Aalto, *Folk-News*.

Interesting notes on foods are also found on page 233.

FRANCE

Characteristic foods are: Truffled turkey, black pudding, Strasbourg pie made of truffles, and the livers of fattened geese; boar's head jelly stuffed with pistachios, oysters, lobster, crayfish, snails, and frog's legs.—*"What the Different Nationalities Eat at Christmas," Harper's Weekly*, December 31, 1910.

A dark brown gingerbread is baked, called *pain d'epice.*

French foods are also described on page 235, and on page 236 the interesting story of the China Bean and the *Fete des Rois* is described.

GERMANY

"Tonight Santa is baking," so the word goes through the German household a whole month before Christmas. The large family is assembled in the kitchen for there is something for everyone to do. There is Pfeffernüsse, and Sprengerle, and Lebkuchen to be baked. Everyone must stir the dough for any one person's arms would be tired stirring the large batch which is needed for the home, the absent members

German Christmas cakes

of the family and for the numerous friends.

Perhaps you would like to remain in the kitchen with them and observe the process. Let's watch them make Pfeffernüsse (pronounced fef'-er-nis-ee and translated Gingerbread Nuts). Mother gets a large bowl and puts in:

1 pound of sifted flour	1 tablespoonful cinnamon
1 pound of sifted sugar	Peel of 1 lemon
4 large eggs	1 teaspoonful nutmeg
3 ounces citron	Baking powder
1 teaspoonful ground cloves	White pepper

She mixes this all together, then she counts noses and finds that there are Gretchen and the three boys. Father doesn't count; he claims to have rheumatism tonight, and Grossmutter doesn't count either as she has measured all the spices and has another and most important task to perform later.

"That's four to help stir," she proclaims. "One hour at least, fifteen minutes for each—at least fifteen minutes each. Now Grossmutter, you may put in the hartshorn. You are the only one who knows exactly how much—or how little— for I'd be afraid to spoil the Pfeffernüsse." Her thoughts are that perhaps this will be Grossmutter's last time to help with the Christmas baking. Hartshorn is a form of ammonia used as an ingredient of smelling salts and advised by all true bakers.

Everyone stirs and tells how his arms ache but mother merely tells them to keep up the motion and not talk so much. "Sing some songs, Kinder, and the time will pass rapidly," she adds.

Gretchen has found the three-section cutter and rolls out the dough so that she is soon placing the tiny cakes in pans where they will be allowed to dry overnight.

Mother tells Gretchen not to make such big holes in the tops. "Just use your little finger and touch them ever so lightly—just a dimple is all that's needed," she adds.

Early in the morning the cakes are individually turned so that the now moist bottom is on top. Soon they are in the oven and a spicy, indescribable odor fills the house.

Oh, Santa baking is such fun for there is Sprengerle to make on the next night—and Lebkuchen—and so many other good cookies each night.*

German Christmas Cakes

The recipes marked with [1] are from *Better Homes and Gardens*, December, 1929; those marked [2] are from the same publication, in an article by Edith Barber, December, 1930; those marked [3] are from *Practical Cook Book* by Henriette Davidis.

Almond Macaroon Cakes[1]

½ cupful of butter	¼ cupful of grated or chopped almonds
½ cupful of granulated sugar	2 cupfuls of sifted pastry flour
1 egg	

Cream the butter, sugar, and egg (without separating) until very light. Add the nuts and the flour. Put the dough on a well floured board and knead a little, using only enough

*The facts for the story are mainly derived from Albert J. Klinck, *House Beautiful*, December, 1912. The recipe is from Henriette Davidis, *Practical Cook Book*, standard authority in Germany and has gone through 35 editions. Published in America by C. N. Caspar Co., Milwaukee, Wisconsin.

flour to keep the dough from sticking. Roll rather thin, then cut with a small round cutter. Lay on a cooky sheet covered with wax paper, and prepare the

Macaroon Frosting

1 egg	1 cupful of chopped almonds
1 cupful of granulated sugar	4 chopped bitter almonds
1 tablespoonful of lemon juice	

Beat the egg (without separating) with the sugar for 10 minutes. Add the lemon juice and the grated nuts and beat well. Place a small mound of this mixture on top of each cake. Bake in a moderate oven (350 degrees) until the dough is nicely baked and the frosting is crinkly and done throughout. For variety, place small bits of candied cherry, citron, or angelica in the center of the macaroon frosting.— A. W., Wisconsin.

Christmas Cookies[2]

2 eggs	1 teaspoonful of nutmeg
Juice of 1 lemon	1 teaspoonful of cinnamon
2 cupfuls of honey	1 cupful of brown sugar
4 cupfuls of flour	½ teaspoonful of salt
1 teaspoonful of soda	¼ pound of sliced candied citron
1 teaspoonful of cloves	¼ pound of almonds

Add the beaten eggs and lemon juice to the honey. Sift the flour with the soda, cloves nutmeg, cinnamon, sugar, and salt. Add the citron and almonds. Combine the two mixtures and add more flour if necessary to make a very stiff dough. Roll and cut into fancy shapes and decorate with blanched almonds. Bake in a hot oven (425 degrees) for 15 minutes. Store in a tightly covered box.

Cringele[1]

½ pound of butter	1 teaspoonful of vanilla
½ cupful of sugar	¾ to 1 pound of flour
2 eggs	

Let the butter just begin to melt, then stir it into a cream with the sugar. Separate the eggs and add the yolks, then add the vanilla. Stir well, and add just enough flour so that the dough can be rolled into shape without sticking to the fingers. With the hands, roll a little of the dough at a time, on the board, into round ropes. Curl these ropes into rings and cross the ends. Dip one side of each ring into the egg whites, unbeaten, and sprinkle the dipped side heavily with a mixture of cinnamon and sugar. Lay the rings far apart on a cooky sheet, and bake in a moderate oven (350 to 375 degrees) until a light brown.—Mrs. F. H., Iowa.

Eier Kringel[1]

1 egg	½ cupful of butter
3 hard cooked egg yolks (put through a ricer)	2 cupfuls of sifted cake flour
	½ teaspoonful of powdered cardamon
½ cupful of sugar	Small amount of grated lemon rind

Separate the egg and beat the yolk with the riced egg yolks, the sugar, and the butter, until the whole is well mixed and smooth. Add the flour, the cardamon, and the lemon rind and knead well. Then roll out about ⅛ inch in thickness, using flour sparingly. Cut with a doughnut cutter, and dip in egg white, then in granulated sugar mixed with coarsely chopped blanched almonds, and bake in tins, lined with wax paper, until a delicate gold. Bake in a moderate oven (305 to 375 degrees) and watch carefully, for they scorch easily.

Holly wreaths can be made of these by brushing each unbaked ring with egg white. Then cover with finely chopped pistachio nuts and place a group of three tiny red candies to represent berries on one side, and a single one or two here and there.—A. W., Wisconsin.

Gingerbread Men[2]

¼ cupful of boiling water	1 teaspoonful of soda
½ cupful of fat	1 teaspoonful of salt
¼ cupful of brown sugar	½ tablespoonful of ginger
½ cupful of molasses	½ teaspoonful of grated nutmeg
3 cupfuls of flour	⅛ teaspoonful of cloves

Pour the water over the fat, then add the sugar and molasses. Add the flour, soda, salt, and spices mixed and sifted together. Chill thoroughly and roll thin. Cut into shapes with a cutter (or use a paper pattern) and bake for 8 to 10 minutes in a moderate oven (375 degrees).

Lace Cookies[1]

½ cupful of sugar	½ cupful of oatmeal, uncooked
1 egg	½ cupful of coconut
1 teaspoonful of melted shortening	½ cupful of nutmeats
¼ teaspoonful of salt	1 teaspoonful of vanilla

Beat the egg without separating, and add the sugar and mix thoroughly. Add the other ingredients in the order named. Drop onto a cooky pan, leaving plenty of room between each cooky so that they can spread out. Bake in a moderate oven (375 degrees)—Mrs. H. R. H., Texas.

Lebkuchen (Honey Cake)[3]

1 pint honey	2 coarsely cut lemon peels
2¾ pounds of flour	2 ounces of cinnamon
1⅛ pounds of sugar	¼ ounce of cloves
7 ounces of almonds	2 teaspoonfuls mace
7 ounces of orange peel	Baking powder
7 ounces of citron	1 glassful cherry cordial or Arrac

The honey should be at least a year old. Put the honey and sugar on the stove. When mass begins to raise put in almonds and let them roast for some time. Then take the pan from the fire, add the spices and, when cool, the cherry cordial, and last the flour and baking powder. While the dough is warm, roll it ¼ inch thick. Cut into oblong pieces and lay in a pan dusted with flour and set aside overnight. Then bake in a moderate oven (375 degrees). While still hot, cut with a knife and when cold break apart. For an icing, boil sugar until it threads and spread the cakes with it.

Mertizan Cookies[1]

1 pound of sweet almonds	1¼ pounds of powdered sugar
¼ pound of almond paste	2 egg whites

Blanch the almonds and dry overnight. Next morning, grind them very fine and mix in the almond paste. Sift the powdered sugar over them. Mix and knead to a stiff paste with the egg whites, unbeaten. Roll with the hand on a board which has been sprinkled with powdered sugar, and cut in pieces the size of a walnut. Roll ½ inch thick and bake for 20 minutes in a moderate oven (325 degrees).

Sprengerle[3]

(These are the very hard cakes with designs on top, strongly flavored with anise)

1 pound flour sifted	Butter size of walnut
1 pound sugar	Baking powder
4 eggs	Anise seed

The sugar, butter and eggs are stirred a quarter hour and made into a dough with flour and baking powder, setting aside a little of the flour. Put dough on the board, knead, roll to thickness of half a finger, dust with flour and with a cutter stamp out desired figures. After that lay on a board and sprinkle with anise. Leave overnight in a dry place. Next day wax a pan and put cakes in it. Bake in a moderate oven to light brown color.

STORY OF THE PRETZEL

The old calendar sign for the Winter solstice was a circle with a dot in the center; it represented the wheel of the sun. A symbolical cracker was made at this season, called a Bretzel or Pretzel. The original form was a circle of dough with a cross in the center to represent the four seasons. The present form, is, therefore, a variation caused by making the cracker of one piece of dough.

GREECE

Interesting remarks on Grecian bread are found on page 240.

HOLLAND AND BELGIUM

Holland and Belgium have their special forms of cakes and sweetmeats for the St. Nicholas season.* In Holland these are the flat hard cakes called *Klaasjes*, once made exclusively in the form of a bishop and his horse in honor of the Bishop St. Nicholas, but now made in forms of every conceivable kind of beast, bird, or fish. In certain places on the Rhine the figure of the saint himself, the *Klasmann*, is baked in dough with currant eyes, or an especially palatable little horse is formed of honey cake dough and the *Klas* is inlaid

*Hough, P. M., *Dutch Life in Town and Country*, G. P. Putnam's Sons.

on the horse. Then there is the *Letterbanket* made in the form of letters so that one may order his name in cake, and the *Marsepein*, now made in a great variety of forms, but formerly made only in heart-shaped sweets ornamented with little turtle doves made of pink sugar or with a flaming heart on a little altar. The *Marsepein* was formerly used as a device in wooing. The young man sent a boy figure *Marsepein* to the young lady of his heart, and if she accepted, he knew his cause was won.

There are also various accounts of the way the cakes are made. In Vorarlberg if, on the morning of St. Nicholas Day, mist is seen to rise, one tells the children that St. Nicholas is baking his cakes, called *Zelten* or *Klösse*. All the different figures found on the *Zelten* have been made by St. Nicholas' ass stepping on them with his shoes. Another explanation of the origin of the cakes has more direct relation with the life story of the saint. The story is told that the three maidens rescued from shame by St. Nicholas at their marriage, out of gratitude, baked triple kneaded rolls and distributed them among poor children.

HUNGARY

Cakes cooked in the shape of horseshoes and filled with poppy seeds or walnuts are one of the main attractions on the Christmas table of Hungarian-American families. Natives of Hungary also make a fudge-like candy called *Szalon Cukor* which they serve at the Christmas season.—*Folk-News*.

ITALY

Christmas is indeed a time of feasting among the Italians, both in Italy and in America. From earliest times it was their custom to bake Magi Cakes. These took the place of visiting cards and were exchanged between friends. The larger the cake, the greater is the appreciation shown. The Prince of Borghese received a Magi Cake adorned with his coat of arms which was six meters long.

Previous to Christmas Eve the Catholic Italians have been fasting so that they are ready for an excellent feast. The Italians are very fond of their *Capitoni*, which is made from fried eels. Italians do not buy dead eels, so that the fish markets have huge tanks filled with living eels. One may see windows of New York butcher shops with these eels swimming gayly around.

They also like dried cod and squid, which they call *Calamai*.

Melons which resemble our casaba are also served. They serve sparkling wine such as Burgundy at Christmastime, and then the feast starts.

First comes chicken broth, then *Capitelli*. The *Capitelli* is served on a plate and resembles little dunce caps. The white meat of chicken and pork is chopped and mixed with eggs, and spices. This is encased in an inch-high dunce cap made of noodle dough. A whole plate of these little caps and sauce is served. It is given a dressing known as *Moutarde de Cremona*. If you were to ask an Italian what this is, he would answer "This is a mustard which is not." It has the tingle of mustard but it does not bite. It is made of fruits, mustard, and spices.

After the *Capitelli* comes a fowl, after which we are ready to return to Burgundy, but this time there are walnuts floating in it. They will tell you that the wine helps digest the nuts, and the nuts help the wine. After the dinner comes nougats.*

JUGO-SLAVIA

The foods of Christmas are described in a story on page 249.

LITHUANIA

A Poppy Loaf is made for Christmas Eve. The tiny loaves are made of bread dough and baked hard in bread pans. Poppy seeds are ground in an iron kettle using an ax handle. To them water and sugar are added and the loaves

*Mainly derived from a newspaper clipping, source unknown.

are dipped in the solution. The Poppy seed water is also used as a beverage.

On Christmas night a twelve-course dinner is served. It includes mushrooms, fish, a paste of chopped mushrooms and oil. Wine and everything sweet is in order. Chicken and goose are often prepared.

NORWAY

Instead of traditional turkey, we have Christmas porridge, codfish steeped in lye, roast ribs of pork, pickled pork, sometimes a barbecued young pig on the table, with an apple in its mouth, and paper frills upon its ears. We have our own special homemade cakes and cookies in the shape of people, animals, hearts, and the like. Here are a few cakes that are baked all over Norway at Christmastime: *Fattigmannsbakkelse* (poor man's cookies); *Hjotetakk* (stag's antlers); *Peppernotter* (peppernuts or gingerbread).

As the Christmas porridge was served in earlier times, one of the persons in the room fired a gun as a sort of salutation, and to drive away the evil gnomes and sprites that wished to seize upon the beloved porridge.—Tang, Sigrid. *The American Home*, December, 1932.

See also "A Norwegian Rural Christmas," page 256, and Dr. Ousdal's remarks on page 260.

Mrs. C. F. Isley, of North Platte, Nebraska, says that sausages made for Christmas in Norway present striking designs when sliced. Stars and other symbols are formed with different sorts of meat.

POLAND

A popular Polish dish is *Golumpi* made of chopped meat, rolled in cabbage, stewed in the oven and served with vegetables and sour cream.

On the night before Christmas, pickerel and cod are favorite fish. Poppy seed is ground fine and mixed with honey, and the paste is used to stuff cakes and doughnuts.

A Polish Christmas card shows us the typical family on the night before Christmas as they eat their cod

PORTO RICO

Sweets and foods are described on page 269.

RUMANIA

Thin dry wafers are baked which represent the swaddling clothes of the Christ Child. Because they are flavorless, they are eaten with honey and syrup.

A special dish is stuffed pig's stomach.

See also page 270.

RUSSIA

Before the regime of the Soviets it was customary to have a buffet decked with numerous *Zakuskas* or *Hors d'oeuvres*, also flasks of *Vodka*. The company ate and drank heavily and when gayly stimulated they would sit down to a ten-course dinner. Well-to-do families had no less than thirty *Zakuskas*—herrings, sturgeon, cod, salmon, and such. The main dinner dish is roast suckling pig stuffed with mushrooms, buckwheat grain (*Kasha*), and served with horse-radish.

A pudding is filled with stewed pears, apples, oranges, grapes, and cherries cooked with honey and served cold.

Additional facts about the old Russia are found on page 272.

SWEDEN

Someone has written: "It is by no means disparaging to the Swedish people to say that Christmas Eve is spent by a great many in slumber at the very table from which they have dined." This is due to the favored *Julglogg* made from brandy, port wine, spiced with eight or nine condiments, as well as almonds and raisins.

Besides the recipes below, the reader will enjoy the story of Swedish foods on page 279.

Edith Barber* writes:

According to my Swedish friends, Christmas Eve is the time for special feasting. There is of course the Smorgasbord, that unique collection of relishes and appetizers that precedes every good Swedish dinner and which is even more elaborate at Christmastime, with special kinds of cheese, anchovies, salads, herring, spiced fish, and caviar.

Then comes the traditional *lut-fisk*. (Author's Note: Some prepare this dried cod by burying it for days in wood-ashes before it is boiled in a cloth. It is served with a milk gravy.)

The dessert (*Julgrot*) is a special kind of rice pudding to which a few almonds are added. The first unmarried person to find an almond, so the legend goes, will be the next to be married.

On Christmas Day the main dish at dinner is roast pig served with a bright red apple in its mouth, or goose, or sometimes both. There are jolly parties all of Christmas week, and then the many delicious cakes, with which every household must be stocked, are brought out.

*Barber, Edith, *Christmas Comes But Once a Year*, *Better Homes and Gardens*, December, 1930.

Then she gives this recipe for

Swedish Cookies

½ cupful of butter	1 egg white
1 cupful of sugar	4 tablespoonfuls of sugar
1 egg	1 teaspoonful of cinnamon
1¾ cupfuls of flour	Blanched almonds
2 teaspoonfuls of baking powder	

Cream the butter, add the cupful of sugar gradually, and the egg, well beaten. Then add the flour, sifted with the baking powder. Chill, roll ⅛ inch thick. Cut in rounds or stars and brush over with the white of an egg and sprinkle with sugar mixed with cinnamon. Split the almonds, arrange 3 halves on each cooky at equal distances, and bake 12 to 15 minutes in a slow oven (300 degrees).

SYRIA

Sweetmeats and foods are described on page 286.

UKRAINIA

During a thirty-nine day fast no meat is eaten until Christmas Eve, when a twelve course dinner is served, one course for each apostle. Served at this dinner are buckwheat and mushroom soup, prunes, pancakes in flax, cabbage, fish, bread, and nuts.

Miles* tells us an interesting custom of serving honey and porridge on Christmas Eve. It is called *Koutia*. The dish is said to represent the Holy Crib. First the porridge is put in, as straw in the manger. Then each one helps himself to honey and fruit, symbolizing the Babe. Honey represents the spirit or blood.

*Miles, Clement A. *Christmas in Ritual and Tradition, Christian and Pagan.*

CHRISTMAS AROUND THE WORLD

NO ONE who travels widely or reads extensively can help but be impressed by the diversity of Christmas customs; nevertheless, beneath them all one discerns a similar thread of observance so that the customs of one country overlap those of the next.

The reader from a foreign shore will surely say that the custom here described does not do justice to his country. He will perhaps blame the writer for presenting a false view, but the intention in each case is to record a custom which may or may not now be in practice, yet which has a basis of authenticity. May I illustrate: In writing of Finland, the writer consulted Dr. Alfred Pearson, former ambassador to Finland. He read the discussion of the Finnish bath to Dr. Pearson, who replied, "Please do not get the impression that all the Finnish people take their baths in a small shed. The modern bath in the cities is as up-to-date as we have in the United States." I can only reply, "Naturally, that would be true. However, the old Finnish bath is more interesting to me, and, no doubt, to you." I desire at all times to present these stories in the light of history or news and I do hope that through it the reader will refrain from believing that I have anything but a friendly, unprejudiced feeling toward these people of other lands. I shall record superstitions but the reader must not assume that all intelligent people in these countries hold similar, benighted beliefs. Because a resident of New York City trembles when a black cat crosses the road in front of his car does not mean that 122,000,000 other Americans believe it an omen of bad luck.

CHRISTMAS IN ARGENTINA*

Christmas dawned as Midsummer days do in San Juan, hot and dry, with a stifling *zonda* wind blowing from the north. I can hear the measured tones of the bell in the belfry of the cathedral which called the faithful to early mass. Passing through a crowd of worshippers kneeling on the stone floor, with some difficulty I reached the high altar. Within its enclosure the birth of Our Saviour was rudely represented for the figures were disproportionate.

Christmas dinner was served in a garden. A single grapevine, said to be 80 years old, was the size of an ordinary tree. It was trained to form a shelter over a trellis that ran along the side of the house and shaded a stone walk forming a sort of veranda. The table was laid under the shade of the grapevine and was decorated with Rose buds and Jessamine. In the center a suckling pig was placed.

A soup was served—a rich bouillon, each plate containing an unbroken egg yolk floating about to be deftly and noiselessly mixed with the clear bouillon by the guest with his spoon.

The entree was *niños envueltos* (children wrapped up) consisting of pieces of steak, 3 inches square, rolled and stuffed with minced meat seasoned with olives, hard-boiled eggs, and spices.

The *pièce de résistance* was a roasted peacock, a dainty dish and of more delicate flavor, but not as satisfactory as turkey.

ARMENIAN OBSERVANCES IN PERSIA AND INDIA†

One week before the holiday of Christmas all the villages, without exception, fast by not eating animal food, and on the last day eat no food at all. On Christmas Eve they take

*Clara G. de Bischoff, *The South American*, Dec., 1915.

†The main facts of this story, written by Azam Yezemian, are derived from the Armenian *Gotchrug* of New York City, dated December 31, 1922. This information was supplied by the National Institute of Immigrant Welfare.

communion. All are present at the church and the Book of Daniel is read by the children. After the evening service the people return to their homes immediately. The women light all the lights in the house, and the members of the household break their fast. *Pilav*, a rice food, is eaten for the evening meal. As soon as the meal is finished the children, in groups, go to the housetops, hang their handkerchiefs over the roofs and sing:

> Rejoice and be glad,
> Open your bag
> And fill our handkerchiefs.
> Hallelujah !   Hallelujah !

The people in the houses fill their handkerchiefs with raisins or fried wheat, or tie some money into them.

That evening the priest visits the homes of mourning in his parish and repeats a prayer for the souls of the dead and words of comfort to the living.

On Christmas Eve engaged young men present to their fiancees a tray on which are twelve pieces of cake, a candle (*Kata*), nine eggs, some raisins, a plate of *Halva* (a kind of sweet meat), and a box of *Hina* (something sweet smelling used to paint the hair and hands).

Early the next morning church services are held and all the villagers hasten to be present. The ceremony of pouring out the Holy Oil of Baptism (*Meron*) then takes place. Glasses are dipped into the blessed water, which is partaken of with the greatest earnestness. Some take the water home to mix with the pure earth, called *Meronhogh* (Earth of the Holy Oil), and it is kept in a special vessel and used for purifying purposes. For example, if a mouse or any other such thing falls in a vessel, thus making the utensil unclean, the same is washed with *Meronhogh* to make it pure again.

During Christmas week young men and women visiting, greet each other with "Happy blessing-of-the-water to you. May you live to see the Holy Resurrection." And the proper

answer is, "With you together let the blessing of the Holy
Oil of Baptism be on your house." The priest all through the
week visits and blesses the homes of his flock.

There is a lovely poem recited at Christmastime, which
reads as follows:

The lips of the Christ Child are like to twin leaves;
They let roses fall when He smiles tenderly.
The tears of the Christ Child are pearls when He grieves;
The eyes of the Christ Child are deep as the sea.
Like pomegranate grains are the dimples He hath,
And clustering lilies spring up in His path !

Louis A. Boettiger* tells us that on Christmas Eve everyone takes a bath, and at the evening meal after the church
service they eat fried fish, lettuce, and boiled spinach, for
it is believed that spinach was the food that Mary ate on
the Eve of Christ's birth.

In the preceding story we have told how the people go
to the church fasting, and Mr. Boettiger assures us that the
abstinence from food for one week, with the little snack on
Christmas Eve, often results in persons fainting with hunger
at the church service. The people start to church an hour
before dawn and the service is not over until 10:30.

The churches are bowers of flowers. Every available
space is filled with glorious blossoms.

The Christmas observance lasts three days, during which
all shops are closed. The third day is Ladies Day, on which
they give and receive calls.

New Years

The New Year is called the entrance of the year. Early
in the morning the women make dough and call it "Kneading
the New Year." From this dough certain cakes are made,
which are round and thick and full of raisins and almonds.

*Boettiger, Louis A., *Armenian Legends and Festivals*. **Research
Publication 14,** University of Minnesota.

In one cake a piece of money is placed. Whoever receives it is called the Lord of the Year and he is said to be lucky.

The priest performs the mass in the morning, after which one by one they kiss the priest's hand, saying, "Bless the Lord, a Happy New Year to You." The young men go in groups to the house of the priest to bid him a Happy New Year once more. The priest blesses them, returns their greetings, giving them something to eat. Then, accompanied by the priest, the young men go to the homes of other church officers and are similarly entertained. The entire day is spent visiting from one house to the other. The women also spend the day visiting but go by themselves, not with the men. On this day newly married bridegrooms visit their parents-in-law and kiss their hands. The mother-in-law is presented some money and in return a pair of stockings or some other article of wearing apparel is received.

ST. NICHOLAS DAY IN BELGIUM*

St. Nicholas Day celebration, December 6, was introduced from Germany. This is a great day of happiness for the children. They set up a tree and expect St. Nicholas to make a preliminary visit to their homes the night before. He is depicted as being dressed in a bishop's robes with a pastoral staff and mitre. He gives praise or punishment to the children and promises to return the next morning with presents. As soon as he leaves the house, children place their shoes, baskets, and plates around the room. Then they put out water, hay, carrots, and a potato for St. Nicholas's gray horse or white ass. When the children rise the next morning, they find that the chairs are tipped over and the room is in general disorder, which shows that St. Nicholas has been there. The bad children find rods left but the good ones enjoy sweet meats and playthings.

Christmas day is mainly a religious holiday.

*Quoted by George H. McKnight from O. von Reinberg-Düringsfeld *Traditions et Legendes de la Belgique*, p. 323.

CHRISTMAS IN BETHLEHEM

JANE CARROLL BYRD, Santa Barbara Community Christmas Committee

In December, 1928, I was in the Holy Land. As Christmas approached, I asked the *concierge* at my hotel about the Christmas ceremonies.

"Which Christmas do you mean ?" he asked.

I looked at him nonplussed. To me there was only one Christmas and I had crossed three continents and one ocean to spend that one at Bethlehem.

Various Christmas Observances

"Oh," he said, "in Palestine we celebrate three Christmases. The Roman Catholics observe December 25, the Greek Orthodox, Syrians, and Abyssinians, January 6, which is the western Feast of the Epiphany; and the Armenians, January 18, which is January 6, old style."

Then I remembered that while Europe and her colonies and the Americas use the Roman calendar, the Greek church still uses the Julian.

Author's Note: Originally all the East celebrated Christmas on January 6 until late in the fourth century, when they adopted December 25, which had been previously observed in the West. Only the Armenians cling to the

"O little town of Bethlehem, how still we see thee lie"

original Eastern custom. For a more complete explanation, see page 16.

In Jerusalem there had been little evidence of the approach of Christmas as we celebrate the season; but this ceases to astonish when we realize that the majority of the population is of the Moslem and the Jewish faith, considerably less than one-sixth being professed Christians. Of this small Christian population the largest is the Roman Catholic group which includes those of the Armenian rite, the Latin rite, and those who acknowledge spiritual allegiance to the See of Rome; the next largest is the Greek Orthodox which gives its allegiance to the Greek Patriarch of Jerusalem. Smaller groups of native Christians are the Independent Armenians and the Copts, the latter descendants of an early sect in Egypt. There is also an evergrowing Protestant colony; of which, since the English Protectorate, the church of England is the largest denomination.

An understanding of this diversity in creeds is necessary to any real conception of Christmas in the Holy Land.

In Bethlehem the people are almost entirely Christian. I was struck at once by their superiority over the people of Jerusalem. The men are manly, robust, and well clad; the women comely and graceful.

The Holy Procession

Here, today, were people from all over the world, drawn to Bethlehem on Christmas Eve. They were gathered on the square before the Church of the Nativity awaiting the entry of the Patriarch of Jerusalem—Cardinal of the Holy Land— who each year brings in state to Bethlehem, an ancient effigy of the Holy Child to lay in the manger in the cave where Christ was born—an age old custom of Palestine.

The whole place was ablaze with flags and decorations. Men and women crowded the windows and doors to the utmost, and watched from the square, flat housetops as was done of old.

Suddenly the watcher from the highest point gave the signal and we knew that the procession was at hand.

Dramatically heralded by a flying horseman holding aloft a streaming banner, it came: a corps of native police mounted upon fiery Arabian horses, that pranced and curveted to the music of bands; a single horseman standing upon a coal-black steed and carrying the cross on high; the Patriarch in his cardinal and ermine; mitred bishops in their purple and lace; clergy in embroidered vestments of cloth of gold; the jeweled pavilion of the Holy Child, preceded by white robed acolytes with swinging golden censers. Then followed the magnificent cortege of the native government; the dignified body of the British protectorate in full dress parade; the foreign embassies in panoply of orders with their respective retinues, bands and gay outriders dressed as Crusaders with banners floating from their lance heads. Finally, an interesting mingling of native two-wheeled carriages with picturesque oriental Jehus and automobiles of American make followed.

The Cave of the Nativity

The processional entered the church and dignitaries were installed in their proper stations; but the placing of the effigy could not be witnessed by the public, as that part of the Church of the Nativity above the Cave of the Nativity is under the jurisdiction of the Greek Orthodox Church.

A dark, narrow stairway, cut into the stone, leads down from the church into the grotto—a small cavern hewn from the face of the rock. We were obliged to descend single file; and at this congested time to pass along rapidly.

There is nothing here to suggest a stable as we know the term, but in Biblical times houses were built against a hill and chambers were hewn out of the rock for men and beasts. It was a common thing for Judaean travelers to be housed thus with the beasts under the same roof for warmth.

In the Cave of the Nativity on a low shelf a silver star has been inlayed in the rock that indicates the actual spot where Christ was born. Opposite on a higher ledge is the place of the manger in which He was laid. I could wish that it could have been left in its native state; but the pious zeal of ages has ordered otherwise. The entire space is ornamented with rich mosaics, costly hangings, and precious jewels.

Hundreds of worshippers of every Christian sect pass silently and reverently before the sacred place. Some kneel, some sob, some fall on their faces—to be aroused and prodden on by the Greek monks and native soldiers on guard. Even the Arabs bow their heads in prayer; Jesus to them is a prophet, second only to Mahomet.

Midnight Mass in the Church of the Nativity

We went away but returned at eight o'clock to be sure to secure places for midnight mass in the Church of the Nativity, and found ourselves present at the Christmas Eve celebration of the Protestant Mission on the Bethlehem Square. Members of all denominations have assembled to sing carols above the birthplace of the Holy Child. It certainly warmed our hearts to hear the good old Christmas hymns in the English tongue. I watched the singers longingly out of sight—just a wee bit homesick.

My friend and I remained for midnight mass and together made a last pilgrimage to the Cave of the Nativity where we read the "old, old story" from the Gospel of St. Luke and could now without hindrance spend the time in prayer and contemplation.

Silently we left the grotto. It was one of those perfect nights in the Holy Land when Nature seems a living, throbbing thing. The low-hung velvet sky was luminous with stars; across the rocky slopes came the half-human cry of the jackal; near at hand the Arab dogs barked, disturbed at our passing; from the hills came the tinkle of the bells of a train of camels with their mysterious burdens disappearing into the night.

On such a night over nineteen hundred years ago, Christ was born in Bethlehem !

BRAZILIAN CHRISTMAS IN SUMMER

MARCHANT, ANNIE D'ARMOND, *Bulletin of the Pan American Union*, December, 1936

The Christmas season in Brazil begins on Christmas Eve (*Vespera de Natal*) and ends with the Feast of Epiphany on January 6. This is the Day of the Three Wise Men, also called the Three Kings—hence Kings' Day (*Dia de Reis*). Christmas Day itself (*Dia de Natal*) does not stand out as a day of merrymaking so definitely as among Anglo-Saxons, yet nevertheless holds a distinctive place among the three feast days.

It's Midsummer

The very fact that the Christmas season falls in Midsummer instead of Midwinter is a profoundly modifying factor, endowing the occasion with all the varied and alluring characteristics of Summertime festivals, such as fireworks, picnics, open air "festas," boating excursions, and other diversions.

And then, too, Christmas at this time of the year is doubly welcome to the young folks because it comes directly after the excitement of examinations, school festivals, and closing exercises, and ushers in the long school holidays with their promise of homecoming, travel, rest, and relaxation throughout the Midsummer months.

Christmas Eve Mass

The festival is a composite affair, partaking of the nature of several sets of customs superimposed one upon the other. First and foremost, naturally, are the ceremonies and traditions brought over from Portugal, the mother country. Impressive processions on Christmas Eve and Christmas Day are a colorful part of the church festival. In many homes late Christmas Eve supper is a traditional custom and provides a delightful occasion for family and friends to gather around

the festive board. After this comes midnight mass, or *Missa
do Gallo*, so called, no doubt, owing to its being celebrated at
the hour of the crowing of the cock. The *Missa do Gallo* is
celebrated all over the country with greater or lesser pomp
in the large cities and small hamlets, and in some places in
the open air.

Country people sometimes travel long distances to attend
this first mass of Christmas Day. Thus a great many persons
stay up the best part of the night of Christmas Eve. And,
indeed, the balmy, fragrant air is an invitation to young and
old alike to wander forth on Holy Night and hark to the
midnight bells proclaiming that Christ is born.

Presepios

A characteristic feature of this traditional manner of
celebrating Christmas, as in other Catholic countries, is the
preparation in many churches and homes of *presepios* (see
page 50).

National Holidays

In many cities both religious and civic organizations celebrate open-air festivals for the distribution of gifts to under-
privileged children. These affairs are usually attended by a
vast concourse of people of all classes in an atmosphere of
music, flags, and flowers. Christmas Day is known in Brazil
as the day of spiritual union among the Christian churches,
and New Years as the day of universal brotherhood, both
being respectively so designated in the official list of national
holidays.

New Year's Day

New Years Day (*Dia de Anno Bom*) is a great occasion
for celebrating, feasting, friendly intercourse, and the exchange of greetings. It is the day *par excellence* for joyful
visiting, enthusiastic greeting, and effusive well-wishing on
the part of all.

King's Day

Dia de Reis vies with Christmas in the distribution of gifts, especially to children, in symbolization of the gifts of the Wise Men to the Child Jesus, the youngsters placing a shoe outside the door upon going to bed, with the same implicit faith in the miraculous held by their northern cousins in the hanging of the Christmas stocking.

Brazil is a vast country, and throughout the years, in addition to the customs brought over from Portugal, the Christmas festival has gathered about itself many features and traditions, characteristic of each respective locality. These have endowed it with a particular local charm and enriched it with many quaint and interesting ceremonies, folk songs and folk dances. On Christmas Eve, among the people, open air dancing and carols often occupy the time leading up to the Christmas Eve supper, which precedes midnight mass. An interesting feature of King's Day in some places is a sort of poetry contest between two parties, who challenge each other by improvising verses which they sing to the accompaniment of the *viola* (a four-stringed guitar). In the homes of the well-to-do, balls, banquets, and other entertainments hold sway throughout the season.

Miracle Plays

In olden times miracle plays (*autos*) used to be performed in adoration of the Holy Child, the occasion taking on all the dramatic fervor of a religious performance together with the gracious hospitality of a social function.

These were often in the form of dances elaborately gotten up and meticulously performed to the music of an orchestra. Out of a great variety of miracle plays, all on different themes, the dance of the Four Parts of the World, which appears in *Festas e Tradicos Populares do Brazil*, by the Brazilian writer Mello Moraes Filho, serve as a good example. The roles were performed by girls dressed for the part.

In succession, Europe, Asia, Africa, and America declaim, finally getting into a discussion regarding their respective rights to make oblation before the Child of Bethlehem, the dispute finally being settled by Father Time, who appears at the crucial moment.

The scene is at once solemn and fantastic, the brilliant accessories of the participants, feathers, spangles, jewels, and what not, waving, shimmering, and sparkling in a luxurious setting of tropical foliage and flowers.

European Influences

These old customs still prevail in many places, though Brazilians often deplore the fact that the good old Christmas traditions of yore are dying out and being replaced by a modern Christmas.

True, in the course of time, through foreign influence and intercourse, another set of Christmas traditions was introduced and took root in Brazil, not displacing the established customs, however, but jogging sociably along with them. For jolly old Santa Claus (*São Nicolau*, more often referred to as *Papae Noel*) with his ruddy face and beaming smile, went riding down to Brazil, drawn by his valiant reindeer and carrying in his wake his Christmas tree, Christmas stockings, Christmas cheer, and the rest of his paraphernalia, so that today, in the larger cities, a distinctly cosmopolitan Christmas spirit pervades the air.

Grandpapa Indian

Years ago there was a mild movement on foot to dethrone this superimposed wintry personage and have his role taken over by an Indian to be known as *Vovô Indo* (Grandpapa Indian), but old Santa merely chuckled, knowing full well that the idea would not take root and that his place was secure.

The traditional chimney, however, had to be dropped, there being practically no homes equipped with such things.

So it enters not at all into the Christmas experience of Brazilian youngsters who, if they stay up on Christmas Eve, do so with a view to taking part in the festivities and supper with their elders and perchance accompanying them to midnight mass, and not to spy on Santa's doings.

Greeting Cards

In greeting cards there is not so much emphasis placed on Christmas as among Anglo-Saxons. Those sent before Christmas usually include in their good wishes New Year's Day and a great many of them King's Day as well. A vast number of New Year's cards are sent after Christmas and continue to be received right on up to January 15, and this in their own right without any implication of making up for omissions at Christmas.

However, the usual greeting is that which corresponds to the whole Christmas season, and so to you, dear reader, *"Boas Festas e Feliz Anno Novo !"*

BULGARIA—GIFTS, CHRISTMAS LOG, NEW YEARS*

On Christmas Day, December 25, or old style, January 6, the children of Bulgaria received gifts from Grandpa Koleda, an ancient Winter god. Before breakfast, corn was put into a stocking and a portion sprinkled on the doorstep of the head of the house, who says, "Christ is born indeed." Sparks are struck from the Christmas log, with a wish to each blow—health to the farm and a plenteous crop. The ashes of the log are gathered and a coin is hidden in them.

New Years Day

On New Years Day, January 1, old style January 14, the real children's holiday is held. The children, dressed in their best, bring little things to their elders, kiss their hands, and receive gifts of money in return. When the children in the rural district visit their neighbors on New Years they sing:

*From Gladys Spicer Fraser, Foreign-Born, 12–20, p. 27.

Happy, happy New Year
Till next year—till eternity!
Red apples in your garden,
Golden grain in your wheat field,
Health to your family.
Happy, happy New Year.

They gently switch the householder with cornel rods and greet him with the word *Surva*. They expect to be served with food at each home but sometimes the food is exhausted. Even so, the children accept this with a good natured smile.

At midnight on New Years Eve a cannon is fired and each wishes his neighbor a Happy New Year. The government allows everyone to gamble on this night.

On the Feast of the Epiphany, January 6, old style January 18, a procession goes to the river, where the priest breaks a hole in the ice and casts a cross into the water. This ceremony is also performed in Greece and Rumania.

CHRISTMAS IN ANDACOLLO, CHILE

Forty miles from La Serena, Chile, at Andacollo, Ruth Sedgwick* witnessed an unusual Christmas celebration. Enroute to this little town they joined a swarm of people, many of whom were walking over rocky passages, either from necessity or as a *manda*, which they penitently perform. On the streets of Andacollo there were stalls selling dolls, trinkets, handkerchiefs and hot *empanada* (individual meat pies), and *chicha* (a fermented drink).

Andacollo is famous for streams of gold that float out of the river bed. This gold became the exclusive property of the emperor under Inca domination. The story goes that an Indian woodcutter, named Collo, had a vision in which a celestial figure appeared saying, "Go, Collo, to the hills, for wealth and happiness await you." He went out and one day his hatchet struck something strange. He dug up the statue

*Sedgwick, Ruth, *Bulletin of Pan American Union*, December, 1935.

of a Virgin three feet high. He placed it upon an altar in his hut. Soon many came to worship her and Collo became her guardian. Years have passed, and now at the Christmas *fiesta*, as many as 30,000 visitors come to see her.

There are numerous dancers in white, red, blue, and green; then the Virgin is brought, in a carved wooden frame of massed Roses. The Virgin is dressed in a white robe embroidered in gold. She has a gold cane in her hand, a gold chain and a red sash around her embroidered waist. Her gold crown, as well as that of the Christ Child, are studded with emeralds and precious stones. This is only one of the many costly robes given to her by wealthy admirers. She is known as the *Virgin del Rosario*.

CHINA AND THE TREE OF LIGHT

In China the Christmas festival* is known as *Sheng Dan Jieh*, the Holy Birth Festival. This celebration has gradually penetrated inland. Various paper decorations and evergreens adorn the churches and homes. Paper chains are made of green, red, yellow, and blue, and are suspended in interlocking festoons from the ceiling. On the white walls large posters are hung. On them are elaborate characters meaning peace and joy. The Chinese call the Christmas tree the Tree of Light. No candles are used but the tree is decorated with paper flowers, colored paper chains, and cotton snow flakes. There is usually an early service. The church is dark except for lanterns carried by the worshippers. Carolers wend their way along the road before dawn, singing the Chinese words to such melodies as "Hark, the Herald Angels Sing." The service consists of reading the Christmas message from the Bible, music, dramatization of the manger scene, and an offering for the poor. Gifts are distributed to children. The packages contain such things as tangerines, peanuts, pretty picture cards (sometimes used cards sent from America), candy, and western lead pencils.

*Wernecke, Herbert. *Carols, Customs, and Costumes.*

COSTA RICAN PRESEPIOS AND SANTA CLAUS

Crede Haskins Calhoun* tells us that in Costa Rica they have an interesting variation of the presepio known as the *Portal*. Sometimes a whole room of a house is filled with a replica of a Holy Scene and at Christmastime one goes from house to house to see each interesting one. Some reproduce mountains, lakes, and forests, and the inhabitants are very much interested in devising hundreds of such holy and secular figures. At midnight mass the Holy Child is carried in a long procession on a pillow of embroidered silk.

Since earliest times the Christ Child has been accepted as the giver of the gifts, but due to the influence of Europe and the United States, the shops have changed to Santa Claus.

St. Nicholas conducted to earth by a white-clad angel. St. Nicholas descends from heaven on a golden cord according to Czechoslovakian legend

Mr. Calhoun writes, "Once I saw a wax model of one of those simpering young women generally used to display the latest models from Paris, who was given a beard and the rest of the regulation equipment of the jolly old fellow."

Mr. Calhoun's remarks on food will be found on page 180.

CZECHOSLOVAKIAN CHRISTMAS FROLICS

While driving through Czechoslovakia last summer we picked up two hitch-hiking lads, Otta Mizera and Zdenek Mika, from Prag, who told us much of Christmas. They said the celebrations start on *Svaty Mikulas* Day, Dec. 6, and end with the visit of the *Tri Kralu* (Three Kings), Jan. 6.

*Calhoun, Crede Haskins. *Panama Times*, Dec. 26, 1925.

Svaty Mikulas, the patron saint of the children, is supposed to descend from heaven on a golden cord. He is conducted to earth by a white-clad angel, and leads an evil spirit, *Cert*, in a black hood.

Some friend of the family dresses up like *Svaty Mikulas* and another plays the part of the angel, while a third carries a whip and is attached to *Svaty Mikulas* with a rattling chain. As soon as the children hear *Svaty Mikulas* coming they rush to the table and start saying their prayers. If they know the prayers well, the angel is charged to distribute little gifts among them, whereas the evil spirit lurks in the background ready to whip any naughty child who does not know his prayers. Quite often it is the village schoolmaster who is asked to dress up as *Svaty Mikulas*, for he knows the children best.

Christmas in Domazlice*

In the old city of Domazlice, the stronghold of the valiant race of the Chods, a group of night watchers, strong, imposing men, stood in the city square and sang the following song:

> Glory to the Heavenly Father,
> And to His Beloved Son,
> And also to the Holy Ghost.
> The midnight hour is striking.
> Ave Maria !

As soon as the clock strikes twelve the men separate, each walking to another part of the sleeping city, singing the song alternately, one after the other. The keeper of the church tower waits for the song of the night watchers and repeats the two verses after each of the group. The night watchers sing four times, once in each quarter of the city. Then the keeper of the tower sings the song four times, each

*Extracts from a paper by Pavla Molnarova in the files of the *National Institute of Immigrant Welfare*.

time from another side of the tower. The solemn tune and words thus repeated eight times by different voices and from different places, from below and from above, mellowed by the night wind, sound as if an aerial garland of melodious bells were ringing through the quiet darkness.

Mrs. Jan Matulka tells us that everyone has been fasting during the day before Christmas. The children are urged to abstain from food till evening so that they may see the Golden Pig and if they ask for anything to eat, they are told they will not see the Golden Pig on the wall. In the evening when the table is set the best dishes and table linen in the house are used. The Christmas Eve supper consists of seven courses and what is left over—and there must be some—is fed to the pigs.

As soon as the candles are lighted the Golden Pigs appear on the walls and ceiling, for the lighted candles cause this illusion. This fills the children with delight because the table is laden with delicious food and then after the meal there are so many delightful games and divinations to play.

On Christmas Day the churches are decorated with evergreens and Christmas trees. There is always the manger scene, called the *Jeslicky*, which is also found in every home. Around it young and old sing the sweet old Christmas carols, first of all being the beloved "*Norodil ze Kristus Pan, veseme se*" ("Christ the Lord is born, let us rejoice!"). This song dates back to the time of John Hus, the great Bohemian religious reformer. This melodious tune and those joyous words echo and vibrate in our hearts, filling them with fresh hopes that go forth radiantly to meet the new year.

The Christmas celebration lasts three days, Christmas day being one of feasting in the homes and the second day groups of children go caroling from house to house.

Divinations of Bohemia

Beside the divinations discussed on pages 173, 174 and 175 Mrs. Matulka gives a number of other interesting ones:

When an apple is cut across, if the star is perfect and the seeds plump, the persons will be happy and healthy. If, however, the seeds are shriveled and the star poor, the person will have misfortune or illness.

Grown-ups crack nuts and if the nut is spoiled the opener dies during the year.

Candles are placed in nutshells and floated on a basin of water. If the shells float toward the center, the person will go on a long journey from home that year. The girl whose candle burns longest will get the best husband and live the longest.

Young girls go to the top of the stairs and throw their slippers down. They count the number of steps touched before the slipper stops. Each step represents a year before her marriage.

Girls cut holes in the ice at midnight and look into the dark water to read the future. Whatever they see is their destiny.

On St. Barbara's Day, December 4, girls cut cherry branches and force them to bloom for Christmas. They wear them to Christmas mass in their bodices. The lad who steals such a branch will be the future husband.

Parychta and Bruna

After the Twelfth Night a season of revelry and masquerading sets in. A villager known as the *Parychta* is dressed like a monster with a mare's head, frightening the children and threatening the spinning girls if they spin on days when they should not. *Bruna*, another terrifying masquerader, is adorned with fantastic horns, reminding one vaguely of a giraffe, a camel, or a goat. This animal sometimes walks alone and is often accompanied by a train of grotesque attendants, persons disguised in every possible way. The frolicsome cortège haunts the whole community, intruding on every house, playing tricks on the children, teasing the maids, and at the end distributing little gifts.

DENMARK

Happy Memories of Christmas in Copenhagen

By Ingeborg Praetorius. Supplied by Miss Pearl Chase,
Santa Barbara Community Christmas Committee

How well I remember that festive season in my dear old country—and old indeed it is. Denmark is the very oldest kingdom in all the world. My last Christmas in my native city of Copenhagen was some years ago but customs were not changed since my childhood days.

Preparations began weeks before when all girls started their various bits of hand embroidery and when the dough for certain cookies was made—and indeed there was need of many, as it is the custom that no one who enters a house during the Christmas season must leave without first partaking of a glass of wine and some cookies; otherwise, they would "carry away the Christmas" and that would never do.

Christmas Dinner

Christmas Eve is the festive time. We do not hang up our stockings as they do in countries where Christmas Day is the time of celebration. And the Danish have no Santa Claus as we know and love him here in America, but we have Julenissen—a similar and most generous bewhiskered person who leaves his bag of toys for well behaved children. Christmas dinner is generally about six or seven o'clock and the menu is always rice in which is cooked a whole almond. As a special inducement for everyone, young and old, to eat this wholesome food, a prize is given to the one in whose portion of rice the almond is found. The lucky one (and this is important) must not make known that he has found the almond because if he did the excitement would cease and the rice might not be eaten.

Then comes the roasted goose, stuffed with prunes and apples, sugar browned potatoes, red cabbage, currant jelly. When all are served the head of the house gives a toast in delicious claret for a merry Christmas. The dessert is apple cake covered with whipped cream, all kinds of fruit and nuts. Immediately after this happy dinner someone opens the living room, the doors of which have been locked for days. The family marches in—and oh, the beauty of it all. Electric lights may be far safer but they will never be quite so enchanting as the flickering, wee candles. We take each others hands and dance around the tree singing one or two carols. Every member of the household joins the family—and there the gayly wrapped packages are distributed, beginning with the youngest members, probably because by this time their patience is fairly well exhausted.

Later in the evening, tea, sandwiches, and Christmas cakes, and all those delicious cookies are served—and so the most joyous day of the year is ended.

Christmas Day is a "home day." Many callers come and genuine hospitality is shown. The second day following is also a holiday and the evening is generally spent at the theater.

JACOB RIIS AND JULE-NISSEN

By JACOB A. RIIS, " *Yuletide in the Old Town*," *Century Magazine*, December, 1908

I do not know how the forty years I have been away have dealt with Jule-nissen, the Christmas elf of my childhood in far-off Denmark. He was pretty old then, gray and bent, and there were signs that his time was nearly over. When I was a boy we never sat down to our Christmas Eve dinner until a bowl of rice and milk had been taken to the attic, where he lived with the martin and its young, and kept an eye upon the house—saw that everything ran smoothly. I never met him myself, but I know the house cat must have done so. No doubt they were well acquainted, for when in the morning I went in for the bowl, there it was, quite dry and licked clean, and the cat purring in the corner. So, being there all night, she must have seen and likely talked with him.

I suspect, as I said that they have not treated my Nisse fairly in these matter-of-fact days, not altogether for our own good, I fear . . . However, if they have gone back on him, I know where to find him yet. Only last Christmas when I talked of him to the tenement house mothers in my Henry Street Neighborhood House, New York, I saw their eyes light up with the glad smile of recognition, and half a dozen cried out excitedly:

Jule-nissen of Denmark lives in the attic and is a great friend of the cat

"The little people ! The leprecawn, ye mean. We know him well."

And they were not more pleased than I that we had an old friend in common.

For the Nisse, or the leprecawn—call him what you like— was a friend indeed to those who loved kindness and peace.

If there was a house in which contention ruled, either he would have nothing to do with it, or else he paid the tenants back in their own coin, playing all sorts of tricks upon them and making it very uncomfortable.

The Nisse was of the family, as you see—and certainly not to be classed with the cattle. Yet they were his special concern; he kept them quiet, saw to it, when the stableman forgot, that they were properly bedded and cleaned and fed. He was very well known to the hands about the farm, and they said that he looked just like a little old man, all in gray and with a pointed red night-cap.

Wandering-Jew*

A legend associated with the Wandering-Jew and Christmas Eve also comes from Denmark. As you recall, the Wandering-Jew is the legendary person at whose door Christ stopped to rest on his way to Golgotha. The Jew bade him go on, to go faster. Jesus turned and looked at him. "I will go," he said, "but thou shalt tarry until I return." So the Jew has been driven by fear and remorse to wander from place to place and has never yet been able to find a grave.

On Christmas Eve, according to the Danish legends, he wanders over the white fields from farm to farm looking for a plow and harrow. If, on this night he can find some tool used in honest toil, over which the cross has not been made, his wanderings will be at an end, and the curse will depart from him, to flee henceforth to the luckless farmer. Therefore, the farmers go over their fields, blessing their plows and harrows, and as midnight strikes the travelers may hear the Jew's sorrowful wail as he flees over the heath and vanishes.

Klapper-bock

In the *Chautauquan* we read of the Klapper-bock, or the Yul-bock, a steed made of a long pole covered with a goat's skin and bearing an animal's head. He goes about bucking the children who are ill behaved.

Dashing Crockery

A curious New Years Eve custom prevails in Denmark. Throughout the year each household saves its old broken crockery, and when New Year comes this crockery is tossed against the door of your favorite friends. You dash it against their door and run, but you do not want to run too far, as you desire to be invited in for doughnuts, and when New Years morning arrives, the most loved citizen in the community is he who has the most broken crockery before his door.

*Supplied by the *National Institute of Immigrant Welfare*.

MERRY ENGLAND AT CHRISTMASTIME

By Dr. Helen Sexton, courtesy of the Santa Barbara Community
Christmas Committee

A busy time is the English Christmas. The keynote of the
jollity and unfeigned happiness is that everyone loves his
neighbor more than himself. Peace and good will is the
British Christmas slogan. The atmosphere is so redolent of
the golden rule that if "Mrs. Vere-de-Vere" of the "upper
ten," meets Mrs. O'Toole who takes in washing, they both
greet each other with "Merry Christmas," though the next
day Mrs. Vere-de-Vere passes Mrs. O'Toole by with a dignified bow, which is returned in like manner by Mrs. O'Toole,
who "knows her place."

Kitchen Preparations

The Christmas spirit starts at least a week before the
actual day. Young folks, girls and their swains, take possession of the kitchen in the evenings and occupy themselves
for at least two hours, getting ready the plum puddings to be
distributed among their poorer brothers and sisters.

The girls stone the raisins and pick over the currants, but
don't think they allow the boys to be idle—oh, no, they have
to chop the suet and cut into thin slices the tough citron peel.
Occasionally one or other bursts out into caroling. Then, at
about 10 p.m. the Queen of the Kitchen (the cook) arrives
and takes possession, whilst the young people wash their
sticky hands.

The cook in England is such an absolute monarch that
at her word all scatter away. The night's work is completed
by serving steaming hot chocolate. Next evening, after
preparation for the puddings are complete, the boys beat the
eggs and are given the work of stirring the contents. Each
of the party has to give a stir, for that brings luck to the
stirrers. Then comes the long evening, when these precious
puddings are put in their respective cloths, looking like huge

puff-balls before they are dropped into the copper of boiling water. You ask "What is copper?" It is a huge concrete receptacle only to be found in old English houses and is for the same purpose as the American wash boiler, only they are stationary and there is a small furnace under it. The puddings are each weighed carefully before being robed in their boiling cloths. Why? Well, you see, if "Mrs. Brown" got a pudding which weighed one-half ounce less than that of "Mrs. Jones," "Mrs. Brown" would bear it in mind for months. Even the cloths are torn into the same size squares. The boys take turns as stokers, for there is no convenient gas stove under the copper. The Christmas songs and carols are sung, stories are told until Kitchen Queen announces that the puddings "have biled long enough and it's time you young ladies and gents got out of MY kitchen."

Before Christmas Eve arrives the morning is spent beautifying the churches. Holly berries are under foot, the young men doing the ladder work, with the girls beneath saying in anxious tones, "Oh, do be careful, you might fall." And the old rector below, wondering if they would be as anxious if he were on the top.

Then Christmas evening—the mystery of it! Parcels are done up with their bright wrappings and ribbons. The tree in the dining room is decorated and the hallway beautified with Holly and Mistletoe. The sly chaps are hanging a sprig of mistletoe over each doorway, so that the girls will have no chance to escape the kiss—even if they wanted to.

At 11 p.m. the call comes to prepare for church and the young folks calm down, for England's religious life is taken seriously, and any frivolity at that time would place a black mark against the culprit's future welcome. There are carols and Christmas hymns, joined in by all, young and old, sweet young voices and voices that are old and quavery, and the whole atmosphere is filled with the homage paid to the memory of the wonderful Babe. A gradual hush at midnight approaches, as the words, "O, Come let us adore Him," sink gradually into silence and the communion service begins. After that, as the worshippers pass out of the church, the bells ring out all over the towns and merry greetings begin.

The Waits

Many companies of waits (carol singers) are met with, both before the service and after the young people and old folks get home. Parties of carol singers come to the front of the houses with a wagon drawn by a stalwart horse. On the wagon is always an ancient harmonium, or American organ, and someone plays for the others to sing. When the house-holders are beloved there is the lovely song, "God bless the master of this house." A silver offering exchanges hands and in many houses hot coffee is ready and cake in goodly quantity, to "warm their whistles," as they express it. Before the household settles down and the guests depart, a huge pitcher of "Tom and Jerry" goes the round. About 3 a.m. the house is hushed in slumber.

Christmas Morning

At 8 o'clock Christmas morning there is a meeting of the younger members of the family and their friends, all clad in a miscellaneous and motley lot of dressing gowns, and amidst giggles they creep to the door of the hosts of the house. After sundry false starts, owing to pitching the notes too high or too low, they burst forth into "Hark, the herald angels sing," after which they creep mysteriously away, so when the door is opened to show appreciation, no one is visible and the master and mistress of the house are supposed to stretch their imaginations to think it really was the "angels."

Next they all meet in the dining room, and seem astonished to find it decorated and a Christmas tree there in all its beauty covered and banked up with presents. No one is forgotten, for the retainers all come in for their gifts too. Breakfast over, the mother calls them to get the baskets to deliver the plum puddings, the father puts an envelope with each pudding, containing a bright new shilling. When the puddings are delivered there is a hearty welcome for the young ladies and their beaux. The kiddies are made to show their appreciation. "Now, Mary, make your curtsy to the ladies," or, "Tommy, hain't you got no manners to show the quality?" And Tommy, murmuring something which might be a curse or a blessing, steps out and, pulling his forelock retires. Of course, there is generally a baby with a moist nose but it is Christmas so the girls kiss it on the dryest spots. Then home to find awaiting them a big tray of "Tom and Jerry"—redolent of the cup that cheers.

The Day of Feasting

Lunch and afterwards, the old folks take a rest whilst the young ones go for a brisk walk or, if there is ice, they enjoy skating. Home again, and such appetites, hardly time to dress for dinner but they get in just in time for the short blessing asked by the head of the house. Not much left of the turkey but there is another for the kitchen. A hearty greeting comes from all as the plum pudding is brought in alight with spirits which have no relation to spookdom. The pudding contains a ring, a thimble, a button, and a bright shilling—all done up in paper so they can be seen and not swallowed. A yell of delight as some pretty girls holds up the wedding ring, with its happy omen; a groan from some bachelor who has found the button; and a funny look comes over the face of the girl who has discovered the thimble. "I don't want to be married," she says, but no one believes her and she and the "button man" sympathize with each other for the rest of the evening. There's a shout of delight when another finds the shilling for that augurs the millionaire. Then comes dessert and the servants come in (they would not like to be called "help") and all the glasses are filled with bubbling champagne; each makes his toast, but the one that is most heartily received, yet with a feeling of reverence, is "Absent Friends."

Then they adjourn, young and old, to a room which is prepared for a frolic and all join in games that are never unappropriate for Christmas, but who would not play Blindman's Buff, or Family Post, or Musical Chair, any other day in all the three hundred and sixty-five! Grandfather and grandmother and the tiny tots forget their is a discrepancy in their ages. And when the sandman arrives and the small kiddies disappear carrying to bed a newly acquired doll or Teddy Bear, the games go on just the same but perhaps more roughly.

About midnight the guests depart and the home is again wrapped in peace for it has truly been a time of "peace on earth and good will toward men."

Christmas Mummers

Since the earliest days in England it has been a custom to stage mystery plays at the Christmas season. These plays were given by Mummers, which is another name for a masker. Men and women interchanged clothes and went to their neighbors. It seemed a part of the common desire to be someone else for awhile. Out of the practice of masquerading grew much evil. Murders and robbery were particularly rife when the responsibility could not be easily placed. In the

Characters of the Mummers Plays. Reading from left to right: The Turk, the King, the Dragon, St. George, the Doctor

reign of Henry VIII a proclamation was made prohibiting the wearing of masks on the streets. So that, instead of everyone taking part in the masquerading, the custom was transferred to the enacting of Christmas plays.

In each neighborhood we have a different type of play, but they generally are based on the story of St. George and the dragon. The Mummers' play is a half-magical presentation of Nature's annual death and renewal. A victim is slain as Winter and brought back to life again as Spring. A doctor is introduced into the play, who tries to save the victim's life, but he generally fails, so that a clown is often present, who has magical powers and brings the victim back to life. A king and queen are often introduced to supply a human parallel in this Nature fertility drama.

In the giving of these plays they have been handed down from one generation to another and much of the language is so old that it is difficult for the audience to understand. For example, in one such play where the doctor places the bottle to his patient's lips, he says: "Tak soom o'mah niff naff dahn thy tiff taff."

The Hodening Horse clanks his teeth and scares the children

Hodening

The holiday season of the British Isles has always suggested strange miracle plays and in these there was generally a character which rode on a hobby horse. In many parts of rural England years ago it was common to carve from wood the head of an animal. This head was made as grotesque as possible and painted. It was usually represented as having dug-out eyes and a large, awe-inspiring jaw, with hob-nail teeth. Two boys beneath a sheet formed the horse under a horse blanket and manipulated strings that made the teeth clank. The horse and his followers went to the windows of the houses and frightened the inmates almost out of their wits. Sometimes a lighted candle was placed in the hollow of the head and the mouth seemed to belch forth flames. After giving the good family a scare, they expected to be invited in for a treat of cakes and cider.

In Wales it was a custom for the Hodening horse to recite long, extemporaneous poems, whereupon the host returned other extemporaneous poems, and if the disguised horse could outwit the host he gained admittance.

It was the custom in some parts of the British Isles for unknown Hodening Horses to attack wealthy citizens, and these in turn were not released until they had paid a fine.

Are You a Good First Footer?

"First footing," shouts the first person to enter your home on Christmas morning. It is quite important who first comes through your doorway, and woe be unto the household if you enter a certain home without bringing something with you, even a piece of coal for the fire, for without some object to bestow upon the homestead you bring them unhappiness. A dark haired person is preferred as are men and boys, rather than women or girls.

James Napier* tells us that in western Scotland nothing was permitted to be taken out of the house that day except presents. Servants and members of the family who left the house also brought something back with them. Every piece of coal, stick of wood or garden stuff brought good luck to the household, and to omit these courtesies was tantamount to wishing a curse on the family. A flat-footed person (or a plain soul, as he was called) was an unlucky first footer, as was also a pious, sanctimonious person, whereas a hearty,

*Napier, James, *Folklore in West of Scotland.*

ranting, merry fellow was considered the best sort of first footer.

It was necessary for luck that that which was poured by the first footer (whiskey or other drink) must be drunk to the dregs and others must do the same by theirs.

In Macedonia it was customary for each visitor to bring a rock which was desposited at the side of the fireplace.

Boxing Day

In England, December 26 is known as Boxing Day. Its origin antedates Christmas, being traced to a Roman custom of giving and receiving presents during the Saturnalia.*

During those centuries when the trade guilds were at the height of their influence, apprentices and journeymen were in the habit of levying contributions upon their master's customers. The tradespeople, in turn, added to the bills they rendered, in order to complete the cycle of compensation payments for expected gratuities.

The modern householder, who deals with a chain store rather than with a separate butcher, baker and candlestick maker, still "remembers" the postman at Christmas time, as well as the milkman, the paper boy and perhaps others. The presentation of bonuses to the staffs of large business houses, reintroduced this year after long non-observance, is really today's equivalent of the old custom of gift-giving, in cash or in kind, by master to employe, and it was on St. Stephen's, or Boxing Day, that the Christmas boxes were collected. In England the day is now distinguished in most of the large cities by the opening of the Christmas panto-mime.

A box was taken aboard every vessel that sailed out of port near Christmas. Contributions were dropped into this box according to whether the day had been propitious or otherwise. The box was not opened until the ship reached the home port. It was generally used as a contribution to

*New York Times, December 20, 1936.

some needy person, who paid for a mass to be said for all mariners.

English Christmas food is discussed at length on page 182 and the story of a mediaeval dinner is found on page 104.

FINLAND—THE BATH, FOODS, FESTIVITIES, AND CHURCH

In Finland there is much to be done in preparation for Christmas, for when Christmas day arrives all the work must be finished by noon. The whole house must be washed and the floors covered with clean straw, on which the children sleep, reminiscent of the Christ Child. Then, just before Christmas Eve, the whole family must take a Finnish bath (*Sauna*). The Finnish bath usually consists of a hut of three rooms—one for steaming, one for rubbing, and one for dressing. A stone oven is heated for hours before the bath house is entered. The men bathe first, followed by the women and children. After the bath birch twigs are used to strike the body to increase circulation, after which one is supposed to take a roll in the snow.

When everyone has bathed it is time to have a bite to eat, and the usual food is barley porridge, in which have been mixed almonds, cream, and sugar. Some of the poor eat rice instead. Then there are prune tarts and stockfish to be enjoyed.

Several superstitions are connected with the meal. If one fasts for a day previous, during this meal he will see the person he will marry stand before him unseen by the others. If you step to the window and look out you may see a headless person. This signifies the death of the person just seen.

After the meal the men match their strength on the straw covered floor, and the girls steal away to blacken their faces, don men's work clothes, and then incognito they visit other homes to see Christmas. They never speak nor accept food but go from house to house merely watching the festivities.

The Heaven

A common feature of the dining room is a "heaven" suspended from the ceiling. A framework of cord is covered with straw, and decorated with paper cut in the shape of stars and other designs. Lit from below by the fire and candlelight, it gives a mysterious effect and is greatly enjoyed by the children. Evergreens are never used in the home or church because they are the symbols of mourning.

Early to Church

On Christmas morning everyone rises before daybreak, for they must be present at the 6 o'clock church service. The best horses are hitched to the sleds which are covered with bright rugs. As many bells as possible are attached to the sleigh, for they must make the merriest of sounds on the way to church. Every window in the house is filled with candles, and in former days a torch bearer stood at the back of the sled.

The church is filled with candles everywhere. The windows are full and so is the altar. It shines like a brilliant lantern when seen from without. The horses are tied outside and their breath makes clouds of white vapor. But the congregation is often so sleepy that one man is kept busy rapping the knuckles and tapping the nodding heads of those who are too far gone to mind.

As soon as the service is over there is a race to the sleds, and then a race home. The horses strain abreast along the roads and across the frozen lakes. Arriving home, there is the meal of Christmas ham and other seasonable food, and then a rest. For Christmas day is not devoted to play. At intervals carols are sung and the Bible is read.

St. Stephen's Day

St. Stephen's Day follows. On this day fortunes are told and the days from then until New Years are devoted to calling on friends. A popular feature of all the parties is to practice divinations by melting lead and pouring it into water to see what form it takes. This is held up to cast a shadow on the wall and from this one's fate is determined.

Wainamoinen and Ukko

In some sections of Finland gifts are presented to the children by Wainamoinen, the Kalevala hero, or from Ukko, the gift-giver, impersonated by an old man with long, white moustache, a white cap with blue bands, and a red coat. Generally, the gifts exchanged are food, wines, and useful wearing apparel. Wainamoinen was the original of our familiar Hiawatha story. In fact, Longfellow even uses a meter so similar to the Kalevala that one could not be sure whether he is reading one or the other.

My story is based on the following references:
Reade, Arthur, *Finland and the Finns*.
Apuli, Heleni and Kunsisto, Mrs. Interviews from the *National Institute of Immigrant Welfare*.
Pearson, Alfred. Conversations with Dr. Pearson, former Ambassador to Finland.

FRANCE—THE REVEILLON AND THE FEAST OF THE KINGS

In France, particularly in Paris, Christmas Eve is a fete. The cafes are crowded and are open all night for the Christmas *Reveillon* or supper after midnight. Flora Macdonald Thompson (source unknown), writing of Christmas in France, says that Christmas began at a midnight mass in an ancient church. The altar was beautifully decorated in greens and flowers, and resplendent with light. Following the mass, nearly all in attendance were bidden to a hospitable French home. Here in a long room was a table bright with candles and loaded with brown, baked ham, roast chickens, salads, cake, fruit, bonbons, and wine. At each plate was an original menu card and a dainty gift. Host and hostess sat side by side at the head of the table. While the gay party was supping the *bonne* continually appeared with gifts for Monsieur and Madame, which various guests had confided to her keeping.

Foundling Hospital

At Lyons the first infant* received at the Foundling Hospital on Christmas day is welcomed with great honor. A handsome cradle is in readiness. The softest clothing is provided, and the kindest solicitude is evinced. It marks the contrast between the lot of the Saviour and one of the most helpless and forlorn of His creatures at the beginning of the great renunciation, a lesson in charity not soon forgotten.

Twelfth Night

In France a great celebration takes place on the *Fête des Rois*, the Feast of the Kings, or Twelfth Night. In Paris an elaborate dinner is staged either in a restaurant or at home but most people prefer to go out for this meal.

The principal food is a cake, in which a China bean (*la Fève*) is hidden. The cake is cut into as many pieces as there are persons in the party. When a man finds the China bean, he shouts "The king drinks ! " And all join in the toast, and he is made automatically king of the Twelfth Night. He proceeds immediately to choose a queen.

Should a woman find the bean, all in the room salute her and she exclaims, "The queen drinks!" She looks about the room and chooses her king.

The king and queen of Twelfth Night then direct each member of the party to follow their ridiculous wishes.

Home Coming at Epiphany

Epiphany is a purely family holiday and in many French provinces it is customary for everyone to return home for this one night. It is impossible to keep a servant on the farms for that night. They would rather lose their positions than be absent from the family reunion. At this period

*Notes and Queries, Dec. 25, 1858.

servant girls expect an extra month of pay and clerks in stores also anticipate a bonus. Tradespeople expect a Christmas box and shops set up large trees, around which patrons contribute heaps of gifts for the poor and hospitals.

THE HOME CHRISTMAS IN GERMANY

The Advent Wreath

Christmas in Germany is a personal and family affair. Preparations for it begin weeks ahead. Emmanuel Poppen* tells us that a large Advent wreath with a red candle is hung on the first Sunday in Advent, four weeks before Christmas. Each Sunday another red candle is added and a paper star is placed each day. Bible passages are written on the stars, an Old Testament verse on one side, a New Testament on the other. The verses are memorized by the children.

Beginning with December 6, St. Nicholas Day, a *Christmarkt*, or Fair, starts. The streets are filled with Christmas spirit. Booths are built for the sale of cookies, candies, trees, and toys.

A story and recipes for Christmas cookies is found on page 189.

The day before Christmas little work is done in Germany. Even the restaurants are closed because the servants must all go home to be with their families.

Christmas Eve

On Christmas Eve most families go to church. As soon as they arrive home mother retires to the parlor, in which she has set up the Christmas tree and from the attic she has brought out all the old ornaments with which she has decorated the tree since perhaps she was a little girl. Then there are the many objects with which the *Krippe* (the Christmas Crib) can be built. Perhaps there is a musical holder for the Christmas tree.

*Poppen, Emmanuel, *Christmas*, Augsburg Publishing House, 1931.

There must be individual tables for each member of the family. Mother becomes extremely busy on this evening. In fact, everyone in the house is industrious, as each member of the family has been making things for those they love. Perhaps a soap rose, an artificial flower, a bit of lace, a sofa cushion, or an embroidered table spread.

Julkapp

And all of these presents must be wrapped, not just in tissue paper, with a baby ribbon about it. No, the Germans do it differently. They frequently wrap the presents in various papers called a *Julkapp*, each with a different person's name on it, until when the last package is opened, it bears the right name, and sometimes after all of this unwrapping and cutting of strings, there is no present inside, merely directions for finding the gift. Sometimes there are several cards which may re-direct the receiver to still another place.

Soon the room is ready and from within we hear mother starting to play the piano. With one accord the family rushes into the room, where all join hands and sing "*O Tannenbaum.*"

Soon everyone is receiving presents which are heaped beneath the tree and tied to it. Besides the German manufactured ornaments for the tree, there are many apples, gilded nuts, and paper ornaments which mother has devised for this occasion.

Christkind

Before the time of Luther the character of St. Nicholas was becoming too prominent so that Luther began preaching against the introduction of such an outsider to the neglect of the central idea of Christmas which was the birth of Jesus. So Nicholas was replaced by *Christkind* (krist'-kint), which name has been modified into Kriss Kringle. In Germany, the children are taught that the *Christkind* brings them their presents, although it is not the Infant Jesus himself but his messenger who comes to earth at Christmastime (see page 37). The *Christkind* is generally represented by a child dressed in white robes, wearing a golden crown, and having big, golden wings. Candles are placed in the window to light the *Christkind* on his way.

You will enjoy reading the story told to all German children at Christmas. It is called "The Little Stranger," and will be found on page 158.

Sometimes the *Christkind* was accompanied by Knecht Ruprecht or by St. Nicholas, both of whom question the children and the parents about the children's behavior. Another character called Hans Trapp is sometimes introduced. He is generally a gruesome individual who would scare the children very badly were it not for the *Christkind*, who interferes and excuses the children for their minor misdemeanors.

In Schleswig-Holstein the children are taught that the *Christkind* lives in the mountains, on a church steeple, or even in the loft of the house.

In some parts of Germany we have what is known as the *Pelznickle*, who is perhaps the same as the Knecht Ruprecht. Literally translated, this means Nicholas dressed in fur. This character is well known among the Pennsylvania-Germans in the neighborhood of Reading.

The Christmann*

In some places there is a mixture of heathen and Christian customs. In Ruppin a Christmas procession is lead by a rider on a white horse (the fabulous horse of the god Wotan). Then follows Father Christmas (*Christmann*) clad in white. He wears a hat decorated with flowers and ribbons and his coat has immense pockets filled with candy and fruit. There is a band. The young men blacken their faces and are dressed in women's clothes as "fairies." The procession goes from house to house. The rider enters, jumps over a chair, and

*Translated from *Mississippi Blaetter*, St. Louis, December 19, 1920.

Father Christmas follows, but the "fairies" are not allowed to enter. The men and women servants are assembled and sing a Christmas carol. The rider dances with one of the girls of the family, while Father Christmas asks each child to say a verse, and if it is good, he receives a present. Then Father Christmas dances and the "fairies" are admitted, after which there is great festivity.

Habersack

In the Harz Mountains there is a youth known as a *Habersack*.* He carries a forked stick, with an old broom between the forks, surmounted by an old hat. He covers himself with a long cloak and appears as a monster with horns, scaring the children. The elders try to guess his identity, for he is generally one of the neighbor boys.

GREECE—THE CHRISTMAS LOAF, DIVINATIONS, AND THE KARKANTZARI

In Greek homes special loaves of bread are baked for Christmas. Each loaf is marked with a cross on the top and a silver coin is concealed within. The housewife fumigates everything in the house with frankincense, after which the father and mother seize the special loaf of bread and break it into small pieces. The first section goes to St. Basil, to the Holy Virgin, or the patron saint whose icon is in the house. The second piece is for the house itself. A third portion goes to the domestic animals. A fourth is for inanimate property. The remainder of the loaf is divided among the members of the family according to age. Each portion is dipped in wine with the words spoken as eaten, "This is for our Grandfather, St. Basil." He who finds the coin is considered to be lucky and prosperous through the year. The money is always used to purchase a candle for the church.

Even in New York City, the Phlophos (Friends of the Poor Society) invites everyone from consul to the very poor

*Nash, Elizabeth, *Chautauquan*, Vol. 32, page 242.

to partake of a meal. The bread contains a five-dollar gold piece and is cut in the customary way.

The table is not cleared after the evening meal but is left, hoping that St. Basil may partake of the remains. After dinner games and divination follow.

Around the Christmas Log

Two olive leaves are placed on the hot cinders. Each is designated by the name of a boy and girl lover. If they curl toward each other, this, of course, means that they love one another. And if they curl away the reverse is true. If they are consumed immediately without drying or curling, this is best of all for it shows that they are exceedingly fond of each other and will have a long life of happiness.

The Christmas log is kept burning all night and the Christmas fire burns brightly all through the holiday season up until the Epiphany, for at this time the *Karkantzari* are expected.

The Karkantzari

The *Karkantzari** are mysterious beings known and dreaded for their deeds which make a peasant's life nearly unbearable. They are believed to wander about Macedonia from Christmas until Twelfth Day. They set upon men in their sleep and beat them. The best way to get rid of them is to wait until an orthodox Greek priest comes around with his copper vessel of Holy Water. He carries a cross entwined with sprigs of Basil. The priest dips the cross into the water and sprinkles each room. With this the *Karkantzari* disappears and is not expected to return until next year. Old shoes are kept throughout the year so that they may be burned at the holiday season, for the odor of burning leather is said to be very offensive to them. The *Karkantzari* are inclined to appear when folks fall asleep after an unusually heavy meal of rich foods.

*Abbott, G. F., *Macedonian Folklore*.

Twelfth Day

On Twelfth Day, at the end of the mass, the priests and congregation go to the nearest pool or river. The priest casts into the water a wooden or metal cross, symbolical of the baptism of Christ. Young men dive into the water for it. The one who gets it is the hero of the day. This same practice is carried on at Tarpon Springs, Florida, by the Greeks, and by the Bulgarians at Steelton, Pennsylvania—and, of course, in their own homeland.

A NOISY CHRISTMAS IN HAWAII

LADY LAWFORD, *The Queen*, November 19, 1936

Lady Lawford says that she once spent Christmas in Honolulu, Hawaii, and that she sat down to an elaborate dinner at 5 p.m. From then on till morning the air was rent with the noise of fireworks, millions of firecrackers, and horns that made the night hideous. If you don't put out your lights and lock your doors, your home will be invaded by hordes of strangers, all of whom expect food and drink and this would cost you plenty.

The trees used at Christmas are painted white to simulate snow, although one-fourth of the inhabitants have seen ice only as it is frozen in a refrigerator. Inexpensive Christmas presents are exchanged. Even the servants in the hotels expect a present.

HOLLAND, THE SINT NIKLASS LAND

It is on St. Nicholas Eve, Sint Niklass Avond, December 5, that the principal celebration takes place in Holland. So delightfully has this Dutch festival been described by P. M. Hough that I am taking the privilege of quoting several pages from his book, *Dutch Life in Town and Country*

The sixth of December is the day dedicated to St. Nicholas, and its vigil is one of the most characteristic of Dutch festivals. It is an evening for family reunions, and is filled

When St. Nicholas' white horse eats the hay, it is replaced with
goodies for the Dutch children

with old recollections for the elders and new delights for the
younger people and children.

Just as English people give presents at Christmas, so
do the Dutch on St. Nicholas Day, only in a different way, for
St. Nicholas presents must be hidden and disguised as much
as possible, and be accompanied by rhymes explaining what
the gift is and for whom St. Nicholas intends it. Sometimes a
parcel addressed to one person will finally turn out to
be for quite a different member of the family than the one
who first received it, for the address on each wrapper in the
various stages of unpacking makes it necessary for the
parcel to change hands as many times as there are papers to
undo. The tiniest things are sent in immense packing cases,
and sometimes the gifts are baked in a loaf of bread or hidden
in a turf, and the longer it takes before the present is found
the more successful is the "surprise."

The greatest delight to the giver of the parcel is to remain
unknown as long as possible, and even if the present is sent
from one member of the family to another living in the same
house, the door bell is always rung by the servant before
she brings the parcel in, to make believe that it has come from
some outsider, and if a parcel has to be taken to a friend's
house, it is very often entrusted to a passerby with the
request to leave it at the door and ring the bell.

St. Nicholas

In houses where there are many children, some of the
elders dress up in full episcopal vestments as the good

Bishop St. Nicholas and his black servant. The children are always very much impressed by the knowledge that St. Nicholas knows of all their shortcomings, for he usually reminds them of their little failings, and gives them each an appropriate lecture. Sometimes he makes them repeat a verse to him or asks them about their lessons, all of which tends to make the moment of his arrival looked forward to with much excitement and some trembling, for St. Nicholas generally announces at what time he is to be expected, so that all may be in readiness for his reception.

When the presents have all been distributed, and St. Nicholas has made his adieus, promising to come back the following year, and the children are packed to bed to dream of all the fun they have had, the older people begin to enjoy themselves. First they sit round the table which stands in the middle of the room under the lamp, and partake of tea and *speculaas* (hard cookies), until their own "surprises" begin to arrive. At ten o'clock the room is cleared, and all the papers and shavings, boxes, and baskets that contained presents are removed from the floor; the table is spread with a white tablecloth; *letterbanket* (chocolate or cakes made in the form of an initial) and hot punch or milk chocolate are provided for the guests; and when all have taken their seats a dish of boiled chestnuts, steaming hot, is brought in and eaten with butter and salt.

Preparatory to the St. Nicholas celebration, figures of St. Nicholas, life size, are placed before the windows of shopkeepers, and, like in America, sometimes men are hired to stand in front of business establishments dressed like the good saint. Other times he rides around the city on a white horse, followed by a cart laden with parcels which have been ordered and are left in this way at different houses. St. Nicholas is always followed by a crowd of children, singing, and howling, and clapping their hands.

Some legends say that St. Nicholas comes in a boat from Spain, accompanied by his servant, a little Moor named

Black Pete. The children place their wooden shoes filled with hay and a dish of water for St. Nicholas' horse, in front of the fireplace; this is a sign to St. Nicholas that the children are safe in bed.

Christmas Day in Holland is generally devoted to church and to social visiting.

CHRISTMAS IN INDIA

Lady Lawford* relates an interesting incident of Christmas in India. Her servants had heard about Christmas and how the British decorate at that time of the year, so they decorated her dogs and horses with ribbons, Marigolds, and Roses, and all the claws of the pets were painted with gold. The whole thing cost her over a hundred rupees in *backsheesh*. As a special treat they baked her a sugar cake containing Rose leaves.

HUNTING THE WREN IN IRELAND

The Danes were sleeping soundly after an arduous day's march. The Irish were creeping up on them ever so quietly. A drummer boy had just finished eating and as soon as he dozed off, down came a wren who had spied some crumbs left on the drum head. The boy was awakened by the pecking on the drum and beat the alarm; thereby the Danes were able to protect themselves and the Irish troops were defeated. Since then the poor wren is hunted and killed on Christmas morning. A branch of Holly or Ivy gayly adorned with bright ribbon is attached to his body and it is carried from door to door by the Wren Boys, who sing songs and collect a little money. I think the modern-day Irish are a little ashamed of this practice, for the wren is indeed a bird which they now welcome to their homes. At any rate, perhaps it was not a wren; it may have been a starling or a sparrow.

*Lawford, Lady, *The Queen*, November 19, 1936.

CHURCH AND FEASTS OF ITALY

During Advent, the Calabrian shepherds, or *Pifferari*, enter Rome and salute the shrine of the Virgin with their wild bagpipe music. They stop at all carpenters in honor of St. Joseph. Their pipes are somewhat similar to the Scottish bagpipes in form and sound. It is generally the custom of the pipers to visit the various homes, and if they are welcome, they leave a wooden spoon. Later they return with their instruments to play. For payment they receive wine, dried figs, and money.

The Christmas season in Italy* lasts for three weeks, from the Novena (eight days before Christmas) until the Twelfth Night. During the Novena the children go from place to place reciting Christmas poems and expect coins in return. These they use to purchase delicacies. For twenty-four hours before Christmas Eve everyone fasts and then an elaborate banquet is served.

We have discussed the food of Italy on page 195.

At sunset in Rome a cannon is fired from the Castle of San Angelo proclaiming the opening of the Holy Season. By 9 o'clock everyone is in church to behold a procession of beautifully robed church officials, after which an elaborate Christmas mass is celebrated. Many of the congregation attend church in evening dress. The streets are often flood-lighted so that in Rome and other cities the famous fountains and historic squares are thrown into sharp relief.

Instead of evergreens, bright flowers are used in the home and church. Christmas itself is not the time for gift giving. That is reserved for the Epiphany.

Epiphany Eve

It is on Epiphany Eve that Befana brings the children their presents. See page 27 for the interesting story of the ancient dame who hesitated to follow the Star and the Wise Men and now shows her repentance by bringing gifts to children.

*Wernecke, Herbert H., *Carols, Customs and Costumes*.

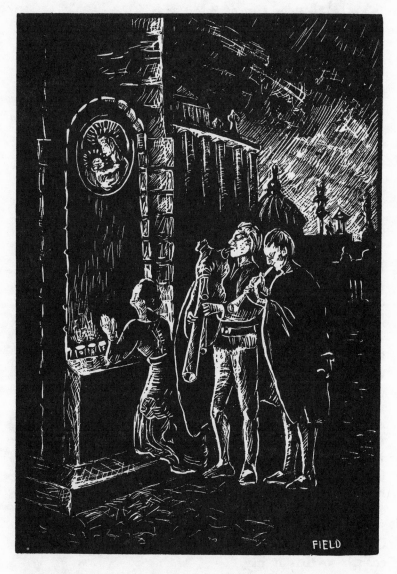

The Italian bagpipers descend from the Calabrian Hills to play before the shrines. (Suggested from Hone's *Every-day Book*, 1826)

Urn of Fate

The Urn of Fate, from which Italian children obtain some of their gifts

On this evening most Italian homes have a large bowl, the Urn of Fate. It is filled with many wrapped presents. Each member of the family draws from this bowl and many draw blanks before getting a real present.

Marionette shows, as in many other European countries, have always been very popular in Italy, and at the holiday season they become particularly numerous.

The Ceppo

In the Fourteenth Century Boccaccio described the burning of the *Ceppo* for a Christmas log. He tells how in Florence the family gathered about the hearth and a libation was poured from a cup of wine upon the glowing wood, after which all drank from this cup. Later writers tell how the Christmas log was always beaten and at each blow one made a wish. The Italians always like the Christmas log to be large enough so that it may burn for many days. Gradually the Christmas log was greatly trans-

The characteristic Ceppo, an early Italian equivalent of the Christmas tree

From *A Florentine Christmas of a Century Ago*, by E. A. Tribe

formed and became a highly decorated and fantastic object, such as we show on page 248. Mr. Field has made a drawing which is a reproduction of a sketch appearing in *A Florentine Christmas of a Century Ago*, by E. A. Tribe. Recently the *Ceppo* has been replaced by the more conventional illuminated Christmas tree.

The pyramidal shape of the *Ceppo* may have been suggested by the flames rising from a burning log, or it may have been partly modeled from the *Praesepe*, which was sometimes represented as a sort of room ending in a pointed vault. In some families there is a *Ceppo* for every child.

Signor Tribe describes the construction as follows: These curious pyramidal constructions of cardboard were made on a framework of three or four laths, or canes, from 1½ to 3 feet high. These were crossed with transverse shelves of wood or cardboard rising to three or four stories, according to size, and the whole covered with colored paper with fringes and tufts and tassels, and ornamented with little gilt Pine cones symmetrically arranged. At the top of the pyramid was placed a much larger gilt Pine cone or a puppet, and along the sides of the pyramid were lighted wax tapers and little flags of many colors. The shelves on which the smaller presents were placed were covered with moss, or with colored paper. The lowest story often contained in the center the cradle with the Infant Jesus in wax or plaster, surrounded by shepherds, saints, and angels. The *Ceppi* were sold already ornamented, but without presents; these were left to the choice and generosity of the parents and friends, who secretly brought to the house their contributions of toys, sweets, and fruits.

AT THE HOME OF MILOSH IN JUGO-SLAVIA

A heavy snow had fallen and the last rays of the sun were touching the marketplace when Milosh Gengish left the inn (*mehana*) crowded with sheepskin wrapped peasants. It is

Badnjak Eve (Christmas Eve) and he must hurry home for there is much happiness in store for Milosh and his family.

Mother has filled all the drawers in the living room with clean shirts, richly embroidered vests, linen tunics, and family heirlooms. She has given the animals extra food. The stables have been thoroughly cleaned, and, much of the furniture from the house has been moved out to make space for the festivities. The younger members of the family may sleep out in the stable.

Yes, it is *Badnjak* Eve and mother is wondering where Milosh has tarried so long. He must bring in a huge armful of clean straw.

Soon Milosh enters laden with countless packages which he hastens to hand to mother who reminds him of the straw which is needed immediately.

When Milosh has gathered a huge bundle of straw he attempts to enter but the armful is so large that he cannot get through the door. The children are eager to help him. Soon they are all spreading straw thickly over the floor, for this represents the manger. After mother has spread the tablecloth over the straw, she lights candles and incense. Then all kneel in prayer.

Angels and the Springs

It is on this Eve that the angels are said to pass over all springs, touching them with their wings and making them pure. At dawn virgins will take their pitchers to the stone-top fountains and throw basil and corn into the water to typify cleanliness and a plentiful harvest. There is great ceremony attached to the drawing of water to be used at Christmastime.

Badniak Log

Milosh and his two sons go out next morning to hew the Christmas tree from which he will cut the *Badnjak* Log. He stands with bared head as he faces the East and bows in prayer. He feels confident that luck will attend his family throughout the year as the log falls straight and the tree touches no other in falling. As Milosh brings in the log, he is greeted with song and the sons shoot off several guns.

The small branches are cut from the *Badnjak* Log and are used to sweep the chimney, while the big log is placed in the fireplace and soon it is burning brightly on the hearth. As it burns Milosh throws grain and a cup of wine over it. He then chants an ancient greeting to the Little God (Christ), a peasant like himself. He makes a sign of the cross over the heads of his children and embraces each one, saying: "May Christ's perpetual light shine upon us through ages eternal."

He makes a wish that the grain and wine may be plentiful through the year and speaks kindly of the love which all Nature has for its young—the sheep for its lambs, the cows for its calves, and the love of human beings for each other. As he utters these words he throws a coin, some corn, salt, and honey on the fire, and casts a few walnuts to the four corners of the room, representing the four corners of the earth from which Christmas comes.

At the far end of the room his youngest grandson is holding up a copper dish filled with incense. He looks at the boy and asks, "Is it the devil thou wilt hunt from amongst us ? If so, your task is a sore one." And smilingly he continues, "It takes more than children's prayers and spices to drive evil out of our home and country."

Welcome to the Polaznik

On Christmas morning a *Polaznik* is invited to join the family. The *Polaznik* is usually a young man greatly admired by the family. He is invited to come very early, for no one, neither king nor priest, may enter before him. As he arrives he throws a handful of wheat over the members of the family and wishes them all a Merry Christmas. He is the guest of the day and must taste all the holiday dainties. When he leaves that night he is given a gift for bringing good luck to the family.

Mother's Ceremony

Mother also has her little ceremony to perform. She takes some branches from the holiday log and carries them through the house. She is followed by her children, each holding to the one in front of him, as chicks follow a hen, and as the children trail after their mother they peep like chickens.

Christmas Dinner

A whole pig is placed to roast over the log, but at 10 o'clock everyone goes to church. As soon as the people enter their homes again they kiss each other, saying, "The peace of God be among us today. Christ is born, truly He is born, let us bow before our Christ."

Soon dinner is ready and as each one takes his place at the table, he is given a lighted candle, which he holds in his hands while the father prays. Mother has prepared much. There is *Chorba*, a thick soup. There is the *Chestnitea*, the Christmas cake. This cake is cut into as many pieces as there are persons present, and a silver coin hidden therein is supposed to bring much good luck to the one who finds it in his piece.

Sometimes when there are girls in the family various trinkets, representing the various vocations, are hidden in the cake, and the object which the maiden finds portends the occupation of her future husband.

In the afternoon the young men in their gayest clothes ride their finest horses up and down the streets firing pistols to express their happiness. There is much singing to the accompaniment of the *gusla*, *tamburica*, and the *gajda*. The older persons go to vespers.

When night comes two tapers are lighted, one on each side of the open door. Candles are also placed in all the windows of the house to guide the departed spirits as wailing for light they wander forth all over the face of the earth on the birth night of Jesus.

The day after Christmas the straw is gathered and the father scatters the *Badnjak* Log ashes at the roots of the fruit trees, meanwhile exhorting them to be fruitful.

On the Epiphany the worshippers at the church form a procession led by the priest who blesses the waters of the rivers and the people are sprinkled with it. Each one has provided himself with a container and takes some of this holy water home for future use.*

MALTA

The festival of Christmas is heralded in Maltese villages by the appearance of *tambour* or *Zakk* players.†   A *Zakk* is a wind instrument of inflated dogskin played to represent shepherds of Bethlehem. See Italy for similar bagpipe players.

MEXICO, THE LAND OF POSADAS

Every Mexican home must be decorated and ready to receive guests by December 16, for the next nine nights there will be great festivity. Each home is made gay with decorations of white Lilies, Spanish Moss, evergreens and colored paper lanterns. Every home erects an altar, with a *pesebra*, a representation of the Nativity. All this is in preparation for the *Posada*. The word "posada" means a resting place and commemorates the journey of Mary and Joseph and their attempt to find lodging for the memorable night. Families go to each others homes, and as the guests arrive, the merrymakers are divided into two groups—the Cruel Hearted Innkeepers and the Holy Pilgrims. Each of the Pilgrims is provided with a lighted candle. The party forms a procession with an angel at the head guiding the way for Mary, Joseph, and the Pilgrims to follow. The procession marches round

*The atmosphere of my story is derived from one in the *New York Evening Telegram*, December 26, 1922, but the details of the observance were obtained from a story in the *Serbian Independent Herald*, January 1, 1922, also from a story by Gladys Spicer Fraser, supplied by the *National Institute of Immigrant Welfare*.

†Folklore, 1903, p. 80.

and round the corridors of the house, singing the Litany of Loretto.

Soon several members of the party slip into a room and close the door. They become the Cruel Hearted Innkeepers. Joseph who stands without begs entrance and in mourning tones entreats:

> "In heaven's name I beg for shelter
> My wife tonight can go no farther"

Those inside reply in angry male voices:

> "No inn is this, begone from hence,
> Ye may be thieves, I trust ye not"

After some coaxing and explanation of just how fatigued Mary is and how much she needs shelter, the Pilgrims enter and go to an improvised altar decorated with toys of all sorts. The party kneels and prayers are said.

Soon the religious part is over and the evening is spent in jollification.

The last night is the most lavish of all and everyone hopes to be invited to the home of some rich man who can entertain best. On this last night the altar is beautifully decorated with tinsel and flowers, and the Infant Jesus is found in a moss-lined crib. The whole party sings many more songs— almost a whole book of them—and continues with an elaborate repast of liquors and food. Everyone dances until finally it is time to go to the cathedral for midnight mass.*

The Piñata

A feature of the jollification which follows the *Posada* consists of breaking the *Piñata* (pronounced pin-yah´-tah) Instead of a Christmas tree the Mexicans use a fragile earthen jar (*olla*), which they elaborately disguise and decorate with

*These notes have been derived mainly from an interesting bulletin by Jose Tercero, *Christmas in Mexico. Pan American Union Bulletin 65,* December, 1931.

Following the Posadas a Mexican Piñata is broken on each of the
nine nights preceding Christmas

tissue paper and tinsel. It often takes the form of a doll's face,
a bull fighter, or some entire figure. It is filled with nuts,
candies, and goodies. The children are blindfolded and given
a club. Each child is given three chances to break the *Piñata*.
Inasmuch as these earthen jars are made so fragile, they are
easily shattered, causing a shower of fruits, gifts, and candy
so that the entire party makes a wild scramble and obtains
a share.

On the Epiphany children put their shoes in the window.
The next morning they are filled with presents.

A NORWEGIAN RURAL CHRISTMAS

My friend Mrs. Kristi Wick Schrader has frequently told
me of her pleasant memory as a child on an island, Daa Im

Quien, Norway, 50 years ago. She writes me that although her father and mother came from widely different places, the celebration was carried on the same and her cousins still in Norway assure her that it is the same old Christmas except that the electric lights have done away with the candles. Here is the way she tells the story.

Clothing and Shoes Home-made

To us children Christmas war the great feast and holiday season of the year. It sounds overdrawn but preparations for Christmas started six months before December 24. Everything we used, such as clothing, house furnishings, and food were prepared in the house. Leather for shoes was tanned from hides raised on the place. Cloth for all clothes from the skin out was woven on hand looms, from wool cut from our own sheep. All foods were prepared from our garden produce and it took a great deal of time. All of us, young and old, had to have new shoes for Christmas. Early in the year the master cobbler and his apprentices came to our house, measured our feet, and made our shoes from leather which we had made ready for him. Also the tailor and his helpers and the dressmaker came and made the clothing for the entire family from cloth woven in our house. Yes, we wove the material for our underwear, our dresses, the men's suits, and even the overcoats. It took the entire year to prepare this material, so that surely by Fall the preparations for clothes and shoes needed to be finished. The tailors, cobblers, and dressmakers could not be in all places at once.

Foods for the Year

The butchering was done in October or November. Meat for the whole year was cured. There were several different kinds of sausages to be made. There was mutton to dry, and beef to salt—all in preparation for the Christmas holidays. When the butchering was finished the suet was melted for use in making the candles. Of course, we used lamps too,

The birds' Christmas tree, a feature of
all Scandinavian Christmas celebrations

but candles were used extensively and were hand dipped. We children always prepared the small ones for the Christmas tree. One candle usually had three prongs—at times five. It was placed at the top of the tree and represented the Three Wise Men.

The women made a year's supply of baked goods, all of which would be good and fresh even over a long period of time. There was *Flat Bröd*, Waffles, and *Lefse*. Also at this time dozens of different kinds of cheese were made and the choicest put away for Christmas. *Flat Bröd* was a thin bread made from Oat flour (not oatmeal as we have here) to which was added water and salt. It was rolled very thin with a large rolling pin. It was baked on a large flat griddle set in the huge fireplace. The griddle had short legs and was set on a slow peat fire so that the *Flat Bröd* was always dried more than baked. We made vast quantities of this bread. It was piled in stacks in mouse-proof rooms and served at each meal all the year round but prepared for the whole year at Christmas. *Lefse* was made of mashed potatoes, salt, cream, and flour, rolled thin like a pie crust and baked on a griddle. It was served buttered with syrup.

After the grain was harvested with sickles in the Fall the children gleaned the fields and made bundles of straw, which were kept until Christmas Eve, when they were set up on poles in the yard. We called them the birds' Christmas trees.

Many currants and other berries grew near where we lived, and mother bottled much juice from these.

Cleaning and Decorating

House cleaning began in early December. It started in the attic and ended in the cellar, if there was one. Everything was washed—walls, floors, furniture, windows, furnishings, and bedding. Our house was torn up for weeks. Everything was given a new coat of paint. The rugs were thoroughly clean. Old pieces of furniture were recovered, and we children felt that the house smelled like a bit of heaven.

Evergreens were used freely in decoration, as well as many branches with red Mountain-ash fruits and blue Juniper berries. The Mountain-ash was cut in the Fall and stored in the cool cellar. Everything we could gather from the woods was used to add a touch of beauty.

Finally, though it seemed it would never come, December 24 dragged itself around. It was a wonderful day. Everyone was busy putting up and decorating the tree. Packages were smuggled from one room to the next; odors came from the kitchen where a huge beef roast was being prepared. Then there was the delicious *Rome Grod*, a rice mush made with cream. Other native foods had to be served.

Dinner at Six

At 6 o'clock dinner was served in courses to the whole household, after which we all retired to the room where the Christmas tree was located. Father lighted the candles and gave a short talk, retelling the story of the birth of the Christ Child. Then we all joined in with the singing "Glaedelig Yul, Helige Yul" ("Silent Night"). Then father offered prayer, and at the close the presents were passed out. These consisted mainly of something to wear. Each one was also given an apple and some rock candy.

To Church in a Boat

On Christmas morning father and mother passed currant juice, or chocolate and some cookies, or *Lefse* to everyone in the house. It was a pre-breakfast treat, a special Christmas morning favor, brought to our rooms before we rose. Later we had breakfast and then, weather permitting, we all went to church. However, in order to attend our church it was necessary to go 14 English miles in an open boat on the North Atlantic, so that this trip was seldom made in Winter. Instead, father held services in the house.

Second Day of Christmas

December 26 was called the second day of Christmas. Had it been possible we also would have attended church, for this was a holy day. Much food had been prepared for Christmas and it was not necessary for mother to do more than serve the food, to which it was often necessary only to make a fresh roast, for we served five meals a day.

Every member of the household wore new clothes from skin out. Shoes and clothing had been put away through the months passed.

The third day, December 27, was also a holiday. Spinning, knitting, weaving, and cooking were reduced to the bare necessities. Even the men laid off their work until New Year's Eve.

New Year's

On New Year's Eve all the manor houses invited their tenants and families for dinner. They came about 7 o'clock in the evening and were served a huge meal composed of roast beef, fresh fish, baked potatoes, *Rome Grod*, *Lefse*, Waffles, *Kringler*, and many other Norwegian dishes. *Kringler* were made of yeast dough twisted, frosted with brown sugar and flavored with Cardamon seed. After we had eaten, the tree was again lighted, and the head of the household made a speech, after which gifts of books and toys were passed to the children. Each family was given some choice bit of food-stuff. They stayed all night and had a fine breakfast. Then they went home, facing the new year with a friendly glow of good cheer toward the landlord and the whole world in general.

Even now the Christmas holidays were not ended. Until January 13 the families visited and the servants rested or did fancy work for themselves. Some went home to spend a few days with their folks. The Christmas holidays were indeed a time of leisure, visiting, feasting, and fun.

As children, we were not taught about *Jule-nissen, Jule-buken,* nor the "little men" but sometimes we went to the servant's quarters and heard some talk about these things, but they were generally hushed up when we came. When we asked mother about the strange creatures, she told us in such a wonderful way that these persons were fisher folk, that they had many superstitions and did not know the Christ Child story, and that their minds were darkened and they often believed things which were not so.

The peace which Christmas brought seemed to surround all that was done. It stimulated good will between land-holders and their tenants, and labor troubles were unknown.

Christmas in Tonstad*

Five o'clock on Christmas Eve in the little Norwegian hamlet of Tonstad and the church bells are beginning to ring in the holiday season. For an hour they will chime out in the slowly fading twilight, for although the sun started to set at midafternoon, the light lingers on, held by the long, snowy stretches of the upland valley. And as the long northern night closes down on each home, the family is gathered to-gether, for the ties of blood, always close, seem drawn tighter at this happy season.

*As told by Dr. A. P. Ousdal to Ruth Stansifer for the Community Christmas Committee, Santa Barbara, California.

What bustling in the kitchen for the Yule pig is almost finished roasting! And in the cellar the bread has been baking at the huge oven which opens into a fireplace so large that a grown man can stand upright in it. Three hundred loaves of bread, but they will not last long with all the Christmas entertaining.

Dinner and the richly browned pig has the place of honor, but it is flanked by pickled pig's head and broiled mutton and veal. The special keg of Christmas beer is broached and the Yule dram drunk. It is the custom, handed down from the Viking days, that with the drinking of this dram, vows shall be made of the next year's accomplishments. The after dinner speeches consist of a renouncing of any grudge that one member of the family may have against another. And the father reads the story of the Nativity from the Bible as well as the famous Christmas sermon of the pastor Melanchthon, who, with Martin Luther, founded the Lutheran Church.

The Tree

The first ceremonies over, the children are eager for the tree. During the weeks before Christmas it has been locked in a room that only the mother can enter. Now the big brothers bring it in. The tree is decorated with lighted candle and cookies cut in all animal shapes. On the very top is a triangle of burning candles—the three points of flame making a star. Around the tree the family dances, old and young alike, and they carol as they go "Glaedelig Yul, Helige Yul" —Silent Night, Holy Night.

Jule-nissen

How honored the child feels who is chosen to distribute the presents! He calls the youngest to help him and together they deliver the gifts. But the best is yet to come—wait for *Jule-nissen!* To keep them awake until midnight there is the *Lefse*—unleavened bread that is as thin as writing paper—

and with it beer and pickled herring. But is it not almost time?

"As the Jule-buken capers, we are not supposed to recognize him as the pet, and of course, that is not big brother dressed as the elf"

Midnight and the small children are all eyes and ears; they even forget their pride in the toys, and the older ones stop fingering the satin surface of the new skiis or watching the reflection on the skates. A commotion outside the door, into the room he comes— *Jule-nissen* astride the *Jule-buken* — a red clad figure with pointed cap and long white whiskers.

All the year he has lived in the manger in the stable but now he is visible—the naughty elf that has played so many tricks! Around the room the goat capers, and grown-ups are not supposed to recognize him as the pet that had been trained and, of course, that is not big brother dressed as the elf! All the small ones are breathless. Who will be bumped by the goat? Certainly none of them for only bad children are bumped. But he leaps out of the door and all is well.

Before bed there is the Yule porridge. It has been bubbling on the stone in a 50 litre (quart) copper—rich milk and rice and cinnamon. How delicious it tastes—And now to bed.

Good Things to Eat

Christmas day with the greeting "He is born" and the answer "Gud Signe" (God's blessing) and after a breakfast of coffee, bread and cheese the Yule table must be fixed. In the living room a long trestle is loaded with all varieties of good things, not for the regular meals, but for the many friends that will be in and out. Breakfast of eggs, meats, and hot cakes and at eleven o'clock to church for the bell has been tolling for an hour. After church there is the fish dinner—fish soup and all the varieties of baked, fried and broiled fish that one can imagine.

The neighbors are calling and the Yule table is raided for a basket for the servants or the poor widow's family. Tea time with sandwiches and sugar cakes and then dinner. The roast dinner, prefaced by a fruit soup, includes the special Christmas sausage that has been frozen since its mixing. Before bed there is the last of the Christmas porridge and good-bye to that delicacy for another year.

But though the "day" is over, the holiday festivities last for twelve more days. There are all manner of Winter sports and with all the children home, how gay it all is! And there is always entertaining and visiting; no people are more hospitable than the Norwegians and, after all, it is Christmas.

Christmas in Hoyanger Sogne, Near Bergen, Norway

H. O. Hjetland tells this story: I lived on the farm in Norway between the valleys of the mountains in one of the fjords which was a branch coming in from the North Sea.

At 6 o'clock someone in the neighborhood would fire a gun announcing that it was Christmas and a bundle of oats was placed in the trees for the birds. There was a legend that *Jule-buken*, a ram or goat, would come rolling down from the mountains in a barrel all on fire, but I never saw that. Another was that if we carried a bucket of water from the river at 12 midnight and used certain signs, the water would be turned to wine. I did that, even walking five or six miles to a place where the water was a little different than it was near home, but was never successful.

Julafred

Sigrid Tang, in *The American Home*, December, 1932, tells us that from time immemorial Christmas in Norway has been the time of peace and charity. During that period all quarrels have to cease, and men met unarmed at the sacrificial festival. Nor must any door be locked, for no thief dares to harm at Christmastime. The punishment is thrice as severe as usual, and the spirits of the deceased and the kindly disposed gnomes must be able to enter the home and taste the Christmas food if they wish. Even the wild beasts and the mischievous mice were left at peace during the holy Christmastime.

Christmas lasted for three weeks. Work had to be reduced to a minimum, for it was believed that the spirits of the deceased did not like to be disturbed with noise when leaving their tombs during Christmas. This period was known as the *Julafred*, or the Peace of Christmas.

In Norway wheels must not turn at this season, for this shows impatience with the sun, which also is conceived of as a wheel which is turning toward Springtime. As a part of the *Julafred*, neither bird, beast, nor fish is trapped, shot, or netted for two weeks.

In most households a light burns in the window on Christmas night, and Wernicke tells us that this is the sign of welcome for any traveler who may need food and shelter.

Blessing Silverware

Crippen tells us that all the family silverware and pewter is put out on the table Christmas Eve so that the candlelight may shine upon it. It is like a benediction for the household.

Christmas gifts are frequently wrapped in layer after layer of straw, some lovers even hiding precious gifts in 17 or 18 layers.

Superstitions

There is an old superstition that on Christmas night men may change into wolves, which become more ferocious than the usual wolves. They attack horses, enter homes, and destroy storehouses. Special prayers may keep them away.

Blessing silverware on Christmas Eve under the candle's glow

Anyone who comes to the spot where these wolf men were transformed dies within a year.

Sigrid Tang* says that there is also a belief that if anyone dares steal away into the darkness on Christmas night and gaze through the windows, he will be able to see the persons who are going to die during the whole year to come, sitting headless in their chairs.   There is, however, great danger in being out of doors on this night, for one might be seized and carried away by the *Oskereien*. All through the Christmastime this horrible and sinister cavalcade of unblessed spirits and ogres are believed to tear past at a dizzy speed, trying to catch people and carry them away through the air.

But there are also plenty of kindly supernatural beings. First and foremost there are the household spirit or *Nissen* who must have his share of the Christmas porridge on the

*Tang, Sigrid. *American-Home*, December, 1932.

barn bridge. Then there is the holy tree in the courtyard
with the spirits of the ancestors living within it, that must
have beer poured on its roots. In a valley called Setesdal, the
people even as late as 1850 were worshipping a sort of patron-
deity, made of carved wood and with large eyes of brass and
a hole in his hat. On Christmas Eve the *Faxe* was seated in
the High Seat at table, and got beer in his hollow hat, while
different sorts of food were set before him, after which he was
left in private for a while, that he might get peace at his meal.
If by any chance the parish minister happened to call in, the
Faxe was hidden in a hurry. And this less than 100 years ago!

The Star Boys

On New Years Eve* or at Epiphany there formerly was
a large procession of poor urchins, called The Star Boys,
who used to walk about the towns from house to house with
a star on a pole, and they would perform a sort of versified
biblical drama with alternating songs. The last Christmas
rite was called "sweeping out Christmas," or sweeping out
all the spirits and gnomes with a broom.

YULETIDE IN OLD LIMA, PERU

Christmas is observed in Lima as a church holiday. There
is also the great bull fight of the year and this is followed by
an elaborate religious procession, at the head of which a
statue of the Virgin is carried. When this is ended the people
enjoy themselves as they desire.

On Christmas Eve the streets and squares are crowded
with vasses laden with fruits and liquors. Great masses of
branches are brought down from the mountains. The ice
stalls are crowded with perspiring pleasure seekers, as this
night is usually very sultry and hot. Most of the merrymakers are masked. One hears guitars, gourds, and castanets
everywhere. Everyone is welcome, and jollification enters
and leaves each home. In the patio of each home the drama

*Tang, Sigrid, *American-Home* December, 1932.

of the Nativity is presented. Soon the midnight bell strikes and all is quiet.

In a Lima newspaper clipping* we read:

At midnight mass the boys carry whistles and rattles and display their skill in zoological phonetics by imitating the crowing of cocks, the braying of donkeys and the bellowing of bulls.

The Indians are masters in fashioning the figures of the Christmas Crib. The Virgin, Child and Wise Men are made from rags, colored wool, and paper. Indians travel many miles to make these shrines for their patrons. Wild dancing is carried on in front of the Cribs, sometimes on the street corners, but generally in the churches.

FESTIVAL OF THE STAR IN POLAND

On Christmas Eve, called the Festival of the Star, a Shepherds' Mass, or *Pasterka*, is celebrated at midnight both in Europe and in the United States. The churches are decorated with Christmas trees and are brilliantly lighted. Each church stages an elaborate Christmas Crib, which is allowed to remain until the Day of the Three Kings.

Before Christmas each child writes a letter telling what he wants for Christmas and this is placed on the windowsill or by the fireplace where the Wise Men can get it easily.

December 24 is a fast day, until the evening meal. Baskets of food are either taken to the church during the day for a blessing, or in the small towns the priest comes to the home and blesses the food that will be consumed that evening.

As soon as the first star appears on Christmas Eve, the feasting begins. Among other things eaten on Christmas Eve, there is always a supply of small round wafers made from flour and water which have been stamped with sacred figures and blessed by the priest. Straw is scattered under the table and one chair is left vacant for the Holy Child. Before touch-

*Anonymous, *New West Coast Leader*. Lima, December 19, 1933.

ing the other food, all at the table break and eat the wafers, exchanging good wishes. Then follow fish, rye mush, currants and almonds. Near each plate is some modest present— a small sugar heart, a gingerbread figure, or a piece of money.

After supper, the children are taken to a parlor where the Star Man (often the parish priest in disguise) examines them in the catechism, reproving those who give the wrong answer and rewarding the good. Gifts are brought by three young lads representing Wise Men who carry an illuminated star and sing carols. They are followed closely by young people dressed as wild animals, or as characters of the Nativity. The animals represent those which worshipped the Christ Child in the stable. They go through the streets and knock at the cottage doors and wish all a good year, singing traditional songs as they go. Sometimes they carry portable stages on which marionette shows, portraying biblical scenes, are given. One of the most popular scenes depicts Herod's slaughtering of the children of Bethlehem. This is sometimes practiced in the cities and towns of Pennsylvania and the Middlewest.

St. Sylvester's Eve

December 31 is St. Sylvester's Eve. On this night one does anything one wishes from 12 to 1. No law obtains. Everyone is his own master. Those who wish to engage in less riotous activities practice the various divinations and have a general good time at home.

TWO CHRISTMASES IN PORTO RICO

Previous to the acquisition of Porto Rico in 1898 by the United States, Christmas day was celebrated as a solemn religious holiday. Due to the Americanizing process, however, Santa Claus has been accepted and the children have seized upon him as their particular friend, to the end that indulging parents find themselves helpless before this new tradition. Christmas trees are shipped from New England to many points. Santa Claus customs are in greater demand each year.

The old celebration of Christmas was on Three Kings Day, January 6. I am indebted to Señorita Comas for an account of Christmas as it was celebrated in her girlhood in Porto Rico. The Three Kings go from house to house in the country, dressed in elaborate costumes. They bring presents, principally fruits. The children gather grass at the river banks and fill paper boxes with it, for the Wise Men's camels, and when the children ask how the Wise Men may enter the homes to distribute gifts they are told that the Three Kings become ants so they may easily enter the house.

Every Porto Rican home holds open house for three days, January 6, 7, 8. The men go from place to place on their horses playing guitars. Real early in the morning callers begin to arrive and the hostess must greet them with a *Copla*. This is an impromptu song composed to suit each visitor.

In each house a *Velorios* or altar is constructed. A sheet is placed on the wall, in front of which is placed a cross and an image; also many flowers and plants are arranged, and up to it leads a staircase of boxes. Combined with the worship and singing there is a great deal of eating and drinking. For Christmas we made a *Batea*, or large tub, which we filled with a huge chunk of candy made from rice, cocoanut, raisins, sugar and cinnamon. We called this *Arocco con dulce*. We also served chocolate and coffee.

RUMANIAN HOLIDAYS

It was a raw, cold evening when I was invited into the study of the Rev. Ambrose Neder, pastor of the Rumanian community in New York City. I had told him that I should very much like to have him tell me about Christmas in Rumania, so he had kindly called in his good friend Aristotle Mucenu.

On the *Nosterea Domnului Isus* (Christmas Eve) everyone eats a special cake called a *Turta*. It is made of many layers of thinly rolled dough, filled with melted sugar or honey, ground walnuts, or hemp seed. The dough is prepared the night before and is taken into the garden, where a tree ceremony is enacted by husband and wife to insure the fruitfulness of the trees. The head of the house goes from tree to tree, threatening to cut each one down. The wife in each case tries to prevent him from touching the tree, saying, "Spare this tree, for next year it will be as heavy with fruit as my fingers are with dough."

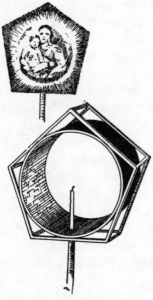

The *Turta* with its thin coats of rolled dough represents the swaddling clothes of the Christ Child.

Starting on Christmas night, boys go from house to house singing carols, reciting poetry, and legends for a fortnight. They carry with them a *Steaua*, wooden star covered with gilt paper, or colored paper, adorned with bells and frills of paper. A picture of the Holy Family is painted or pasted in the center. A candle is placed inside.

The diagram on this page shows how they are commonly constructed. With a cheese box as a basis, a 5- or 6-pointed star is constructed, using material about 1 inch by 1 inch. This is fastened to a stout pole or broom handle, and could easily be reproduced without much ingenuity by any person.

Rumanian star made of paper and a cheese-box (See text)

Special Christmas cakes are made which contain nuts and raisins, and the Christmas supper is generally sauerkraut and pork.

Priestly Visitations

On the Epiphany, January 6 (which is also the celebration of Christ's baptism, or in the Rumanian tongue known as the *Boboteaza* or *Bobezul Domnului*), a priest goes to the home of each of his parishioners to bless it. He dips a bunch of basil in the Holy Water, and with this he sprinkles the house. He carries with him a kettle in which the householder drops a coin and presents him with a bunch of hemp, a ham, or tongue, and some grain. With the hemp the native priests in Rumania can weave their own cloth, and from the food which they receive at this season they can support themselves.

Rev. Nader laughingly said that at each home one is invited to eat and drink some wine and that the poor priest would be ill fitted for his duties if he were to accept all these well-meant invitations. He then spoke of the practice of the priest throwing a cross into the water, to be rescued by the young men of the church. This has been described as a custom in several other countries, notably in Bulgaria and Greece. See pages 215 and 242.

A Few Superstitions

Superstitious people ask the priest to sit on their beds, believing that the brooding hen will not neglect her eggs if he does so.

It is also the practice for the housewife to place grain under the mattress to increase the supply of eggs.

Some of the hemp is begged from the priest to be used to tie a bunch of Sweet Basil to the fish nets, which is supposed to bring luck to the fishermen.

When a maiden begs a bit of Sweet Basil used by the priest she places it under her pillow in order that she may dream of her sweetheart.

New Year's Day

New Year's Day has an interesting legend connected with it. It is said that the heavens open and that lucky persons catch a glimpse of it and make wishes. Beasts speak on this day and if you overhear them you may die. F. Vexler related an interesting story to the National Institute of Immigrant Welfare, saying that the young men go from house to house, cracking whips, singing, and exchanging greetings. This is called *Plugusor*, named from the original custom of carrying a little wooden plow which has been replaced by a special hemp whip for each caroler and a bell for the leader.

The gypsies in Rumania carry a hog's head (*Vasilca*) which is dressed and ornamented.

CHRISTMAS IN OLD RUSSIA

Since the revolution little of the traditional Russian observance of Christmas remains. Nevertheless, it will be interesting to read of Christmas in former days.

Processions went through the city singing carols (*Kolyada*).* These were old sacrificial songs surviving from heathen days and dealt with the gods and goddesses which have been endowed with Christian characteristics so that they seem to be sacred Yuletide songs. The processions visited the resident noblemen and higher church dignitaries begging for money or presents (*Kolenda*). Armed with their gifts, they returned to their homes and masqueraded in imitation of cows, pigs, and goats in remembrance of the Holy Nativity manger animals.

As soon as the evening star appeared a supper (*Colatzia*) was served. The table was covered with straw, with a cloth over this. A samovar was placed on the table with fish and cakes. The feast began by dividing the blessed wafer, of which all partook. When the feast was over, the peasants visited a noblemen's home for an elaborate Christmas tree, from which presents were distributed and small coins were given to the peasants.

*Walsh, William S., *Curiosities of Popular Customs*, J. B. Lippincott.

The Christmas Captain and Madam Kedrina Remember*

The day before Christmas is a fast day, no food being tasted until the evening star appears. It is common for the priest to visit the homes of his communicants, accompanied by boys carrying a vessel of Holy Water. He sprinkles a little of the water in each room and blesses the house.

At midnight almost everyone goes to church services. The children are impatient for the service to end so they can hasten home through the snow to light the tree. We always had real candles and real trees. In Russia only close relatives and friends exchange gifts, which are always personally delivered.

The Christmas dinner is a special meal. There is no meat but we had cold vegetable soup with mushrooms in it and little rice cakes that resembled pies, which also have mushrooms in them. Sometimes we had cold fish.

Divinations

Because our Christmas customs go back to the times before Christianity, we still practice various interesting forms of divination. The superstitious old women of the neighborhood can suggest many interesting interpretations from the form that wax takes when it is melted and dropped into cold water. We also melted lead and dropped it into the snow to harden.

Perhaps the most fun was another form of divination: Five piles of grain are placed on the kitchen floor. Each pile is given a name, such as Hope, Ring, Money, Charcoal, and Thread. We girls went to the henhouse and roused a drowsy hen. She is allowed to walk around the kitchen and choose a pile of grain. If she chooses Hope it means a long journey or the fulfillment of a great wish. The Ring, of course, means marriage; Money is wealth; Charcoal portends death in the family; and Thread means a life of toil. How the conversation

*The main facts were contained in some material supplied by Pearl Chase of the Santa Barbara Community Christmas Committee.

"Which pile will the drowsy hen choose?"

flows when these divinations are played. Old songs were sung, and the old women and country girls could devise entire stories from the action of the hen.

Sooner or later each of the girls would slip outdoors, and standing just inside the gate, but with her back to it, she would kick her slipper high over her head into the road behind her. Then she would run to see in which direction it pointed, for that is the way from which a lover will come or the way she will go to be married. And, alas, if the slipper points toward the gate she will not be married that year.

Some girls sit in a room alone with the doors closed. Two candles are lighted and two mirrors are used so that one reflects the candlelight into the other. The point is to find the seventh reflection and to look until one's future is seen.

A wedding ring is dropped into a glass of water. If one gazes intently at the circle formed by the ring, one's future will be revealed.

A glass of water is placed before the image of a saint. The yolk of an egg is dropped in. The next morning the yolk will tell the future, for it will become discolored and reveal many things to the imaginative mind. The precaution is usually taken to turn the saint to the wall so he will not hinder the result.

Ukrainian Christmas*

When the 39-day fast begins before Christmas the people prepare for the Nativity. On Christmas Eve the house is spick and span and the housewife is preparing a sumptuous 12-course dinner, a course in memory of each of the Twelve Apostles. As in other parts of Russia, no food is eaten until the first star appears in the sky. During the supper everyone must speak in a low, gentle voice, for if there is peace and order, love and affection on this Eve, then it will bless the household until the Christmas which follows.

Among Ukrainians Christmas extends over three days. Each day the singers (*Kolyadniky*) go from house to house singing folk songs.

THE NOCHE-BUENA OF SPAIN

Gone was the characteristic Christmas celebration of Spain when the civil war began in 1936. But in former years the Good Night, or as the Spaniards call it *Noche-buena*, was a time of great activity. The streets in many of the cities were brilliantly lighted. Plump turkeys, quacking ducks, and cooing pigeons crowded the marketplace. There were delicious fruits, quaint pigskins of wine, booths of toys, shops exhibiting sweets and fancy goods. All these were a festive part of the season.

*Information derived from the *International Institute Y.W.C.A.* by Miss Lola de Grill.

The Charity Fair, or lottery, was one of the most popular forms of Christmas entertainment. Cards were repeatedly collected and thrown into a swiftly turning glass jar and the lucky numbers were whirled out. Each lucky number won a present.

As the stars appeared in the heavens, tiny oil lamps were lighted in each home and among the devout Roman Catholics the image of the Virgin was illuminated with a taper. On the streets the air was filled with a spirit of unrest and gayety until the hour of midnight, when the church bells called to mass. It was far into the morning before the crowd turned homeward, for the wee hours were spent in singing and dancing. So writes Herbert H. Wernecke in his *Carols, Customs and Costumes Around the World.*

The *Courrier Des Etats-Unis* (New York) tells us that in Spain the Christmas dinner is often eaten in church and songs are sung which do not bear a strictly religious character.

The Nacimiento

In every home a *Nacimiento* is staged. This, of course, is the Christmas Crib of other countries. See page 50. The children dance around it to the music of tambourines and joyously sing the Nativity songs.

After the mid-day breakfast on Christmas morning, the people either seek outdoor pleasures or join in family groups. Song, dance, and laughter are characteristic features of Yuletide and the festivities continue until Twelfth Day.

Urn of Fate

In Roman days it was common to have an Urn of Fate and from this ancient custom, the Spanish place the names of all their friends in a large bowl. From this the names are drawn and fate decides who shall be devoted friends for the year; they become almost lovers to each other. Sometimes this is a great disappointment but everyone tries to be philosophical about it.

Going to Meet The Wise Men

According to a well loved Spanish folk tale, the Wise Men go each year to Bethlehem to pay homage to the Infant Christ. As they pass through Spain they leave gifts of sweetmeats and playthings for all good children. On the Eve of Epiphany the children fill their shoes with straw for the Wise Men's horses and place them on the window ledges or balconies and retire early. In the morning the straw is gone and the shoes are laden with presents. Wealthy citizens distribute presents on the window sills of the poorer sections of their towns.

In Madrid it has long been the custom for men and boys bearing torches, bells and tin cans to go out to the city gates to meet the Magi. One of the group carries a ladder upon which he climbs from time to time to see if the train is approaching.

Frederic Mistral* gives a charming account of going forth as a child to greet the Kings, who came each Epiphany Eve to Maillane to worship the Holy Child. With joyous hearts and eyes full of visions, the children of the countryside sallied out on the road to Arles to meet the distinguished guests. In their hands they carried offerings of cakes for the Kings, figs for the pages, and hay for the camels. In the last rays of the setting sun their childish eyes seemed to see a vision of the splendor of the Magi with their blazing torches and gem-set crowns.

"We stood there entranced," writes Mistral. "But instead of approaching us, little by little the glory and splendor of the vision seemed to melt away before our eyes with the sinking sun, extinguished in the shadows. Crestfallen, we stood there, gaping to find ourselves alone on the darkening highway.

"Which way did the Kings go ?' 'They passed behind the mountain,' the white owl hooted. Fear seized us, and

*Memoirs of Mistral, translated by C. E. Maud, London, Arnold 1907, chapter 3.

huddling together we turned homeward, munching the cakes we had brought for the Kings."

Later in the evening the children beheld the Kings in church, paying homage at the Christ Child's Crib and heard the townsfolk sing, "This morn I met the train of the Three Great Kings of the East. This morn I met the train of the Kings on the wide high road."

SWEDEN—A HAPPY CHRISTMAS LAND

By Mrs. Ernst Beckman, Santa Barbara Community Christmas Committee

Before the Christmas festival, there comes a time of cleaning and scouring and washing in Swedish homes— hated by all men who generally put cozy quiet first—but Swedish housewives consider this absolutely necessary. Some-one has said that dirt is like sinful thoughts and cannot be tolerated at the Holy Festival.

The fresh white curtains, the brilliant shining big copper cooking vessels which belong to all good kitchens in Sweden, and the sense of absolute cleanliness everywhere are, to say the least, very cheerful. Of course, gifts have been devised in secret and the midnight oil has often been spent over surprises for members of the family.

Handiwork

In the schools of Sweden, a great deal is made of handiwork and carpentering for boys, and sewing and mending for girls are well taught. This kind of work is adapted to Christmas presents during the Autumn term: the children are proud to come home with a well made bookshelf for father, a carved paper knife for mother, or a pair of neatly sewn pillow cases with embroidered initial, or a nice apron, all made by their own hands. These are secreted with care.*

*In *Sweden*, Rev. and Mrs. Liddle say that girls sit up through one whole night to sew. They invite a few friends and have a real party.

Swedish Foods

The days before Christmas are especially busy with preparing the Christmas food. Pork plays a great role at Christmas time in Swedish homes. On Christmas day a little pig roasted whole with a red apple in its mouth is the equivalent to turkey here. On Christmas Eve one of the given courses is rice porridge cooked for hours in milk—and more milk, then served with powdered cinnamon sifted on it in patterns. But the most interesting part of the rice course is the almond which is put in the porridge just before serving. Whoever finds the almond in his or her portion is *sure* to be married within the year.

There are piles of pretty brown loaves made of rye flour somewhat sweetened, and a special taste given them from a kind of malt from a brewery.

Then the deft fingers of the Swedish housewife makes ginger snaps, ginger cake, Siamese twins and goats for the children, almond rings, currant cookies, macaroons—yes *all* kinds of tempting small cakes. A Swedish hostess at Christmas time expects to offer, with coffee, at least six different kinds of attractive cakes, besides a round, braided loaf of especially good, sweet white bread colored strongly yellow with saffron and made with raisins and citron in it and ornamented with sugar.

Instead of mince pies there are little patties of puff paste made in the form of conch-shells, filled with preserves often made of a berry which grows only within the Arctic Circle. The taste of this berry may be said to be between a raspberry and a strawberry—quite a subtle and delicious flavor.

Julafton

But now to the real festival, Christmas Eve, or *Julafton*! Of course, the biggest Christmas tree, the *Julgran*, has been procured—either a Norway Spruce or a Hemlock—and the decorating of this treasure is done within closed doors, where

the home permits it.   Meanwhile, the other members of the
family are wrapping their gifts for each other.

Every gift, however small, is well wrapped in paper and
neatly sealed with red sealing wax. (The very *smell* of sealing
wax to Swedes means Christmas, all their lives.)   Do you
think the parcels are ready ? Oh no! The donor writes the
name of the one he is giving the package to and then a dedication in the form of something about the gift or its uses,
generally in doggerel—or poetry, if he can. This is known as
the *Jul-klappan*.

The recipient is to guess from whom it comes. In the late
afternoon when the tree has all its candles placed securely,
its red apples and gingerbread twins and goats hung, its
chains of silver frost work and its sparkling cotton-snow
put among the branches, then in another room the coffee
and Christmas cakes are served to the impatient waiting
ones—if there are children—and after this the door is thrown
open and the always lovely sight of a lighted Christmas tree is
unfolded in all its mystic charm.*

The family's Christmas gifts are placed in a basket by the
tree, and if there chance to be such large ones that do not
have room there, they are shrouded in sheets or cloaks, so
no one can guess the contents. Now the mother or older
sister takes her place at the piano or organ and the first
Christmas carol is sung by all the family in unison.

The father seated by the tree then reads the story of the
birth of Christ from the Gospel, and afterwards, in a few
short words, calls down the blessing of God on those present
and the members of the family absent. Another carol is sung
and then—the gifts are the center of attention! The head of
the family takes up one parcel after another, reads the name
of the lucky owner and the verse.

When the family group is a large one the youngest children serve as messengers to and fro. If there are maids em-

*The national flag often waves on top with various other flags
scattered over the tree.

ployed in the family, they are always invited in to enjoy the Christmas tree, their gifts mixed in with all the others. When this part is over, there is a great deal of thanking done on all sides, and all take part in singing another Christmas carol and afterwards join hands in a ring and to music dance around the tree, thus ending one Christmas Eve's celebration.

Then Comes Christmas Morning

Let us imagine ourselves in the country, with deep snow everywhere, the pine forests decorated with frost crystals and

> "Every pine and fir, and hemlock
> Wore ermine too dear for an earl,
> And the poorest twig on the elm-tree
> Was ridged inch deep with pearl."

The service at the country church is at half past six in the morning, and it is five miles away from where we are staying.

The house is astir early; several sleighs are waiting to take us to church. Each sleigh is accompanied by a man standing on a little high platform behind and between the runners and driving the horse, the reins running on a forked support on the dashboard.

One of the occupants of the sleigh holds a big torch in his hand which is quite necessary for it is still pitch dark.

As we draw nearer the church the roads all seem to converge to it, and countless torches flame up and enliven the scene. Every house we have passed has lighted candles in all the windows, welcoming Christmas and the church folk. At a short distance from the church all the torches are thrown together and make a fine bonfire watched over carefully that no harm may come.

On entering the edifice light streams from hundreds of candles, rows of them in all the windows, at the ends of all the pews outlining the capitals of the pillars, and in the chancel they are concentrated in a big star. This is the Christian form which the northern heathen Feast of Light has taken at this time of the year when the turning point has been passed, and light is here the symbol of our Saviour—"The light which lighteth every man that cometh into the world."

Birds' Christmas Tree

The Swedish birds made happy with a sheaf of wheat surmounted by a tiny evergreen tree

In all Scandinavian countries it is common to give the birds a Christmas tree, but let's ask the Honorable W. W. Thomas, Jr., formerly minister to Sweden, tell us about it. "One winter day at Yuletide I had been skating on a pretty lake, Daljen, three miles from Gothenburg. On my way home I noticed that at every farmer's house was erected, in the middle of the dooryard, a pole, to the top of which was bound a large sheaf of grain. 'What is that?' I asked my companion. 'Oh, that is for the birds, the little wild birds. They must have Christmas, too, you know.' There is not a peasant in all Sweden who will sit down with his children for Christmas until he has first raised aloft a Christmas dinner for the little birds that live in the snow."

Tomte

The Good Spirit of the house, *Tomte*, is given special offerings. *Tomte* is a miniature of the good St. Nicholas and keeps watch through the year, protecting the house, the cattle, and the crops. The housemother fixes his dish and puts it in the corner where no one can see it. Later this dwarf will come in and quietly eat his meal after which he disappears. While the whole family is making merry with singing and dancing, *Tomte* is expected to enjoy all this while he sits

Lucy goes through the house very early Christmas morning
and awakens all sleepers

unobserved in his corner. This, of course, is merely a variation
of *Jule-nissen* of Denmark.

Lucy

On December 13, St. Lucy's Day, the prettiest girl in the
house impersonates Lucy. She is dressed in white with
a red sash and wears a wire crown on her head covered
with Bilberry twigs. (This is much like our Cranberry.) In
this crown are fixed nine candles. Lucy goes through the
house very early Christmas, even at 3 or 4 o'clock, and awak-

JUL-DOCKA ROMANCE*

From Sweden there came a swain and a dame,
They arrived just at Christmas and were part of a game.
The man was of straw and the maiden the same,
For the romance that followed, the wind was to blame.

The maiden was fair with long yellow hair.
She stood on the table top right over there,
And turned her back coldly not seeming to care
For the man, with a hat, with a brim, with a flare.

The angel watched with her twinkling eye.
His straw chest puff out with a passionate sigh,
As he stretched out his arms and declared he will die,
And the chicken's low cluck sounds much like, "My, my."

A window was opened, the maid blew away
To the arms of her lover and there she did stay.
The angel declared they'd be married on May-day,
But the chicken knew better, right now was their hey-day.

*A common feature of the Christmas celebration in Sweden was the
Jul-docka, or straw doll, made in many forms—boy, girl and chicken

ens all sleepers, giving each one a cup of coffee or a sweet drink. This story is related by Crippen.*

Perhaps you would be interested in knowing who St. Lucy was. Just as Lucy was about to be married, she received her dowry, and instead of turning it over to her sweetheart, she gave it all to the Christians because she admired their courage so much. When her fiance heard of this he informed against her. She was condemned to be burned, but when the fire was around her, she remained unharmed and did not die until thrust through with a sword.

SWITZERLAND

There is an interesting Christmas custom in Switzerland dealing with Lucy and Father Christmas. Father Christmas is depicted as having a jovial red face, white beard, and long, fur-trimmed robe. He marches around the village with his wife Lucy. Lucy wears a round cap over her long braids of hair, a laced bodice, and a silk apron. She distributes gifts to girls, while her companion, Father Christmas, looks after the boys.

St. Lucy's Day is December 13. The story goes that she was martyred and that her rejected suitor betrayed her Christian allegiance to the authorities.

THE FASCINATING HOLIDAYS AND FOLKTALES OF SYRIA

The holiday season in Syria is characterized by a most fascinating series of observances and the folklore differs from that of any other country. Even the Syrians in New York carry on religiously the customs of their forefathers. As one man, a father of eight, said, "Have not our fathers talked

*Crippen, T. G., *Christmas and Christmas Lore.* Blackie and Son, Ltd., London, 1928, and by Liddle, Rev. William, *Peeps at Many Lands—Sweden.*

with those to whom these things were revealed ? Have they not seen the place ? Have we not received the benefactions of the good St. Barbara ? Has the Holy Oil not increased in our own cruses ? Must we neglect the lessons of our fathers ?"

St. Barbara's Day, December 4

The Syrian Christmas begins on December 4, St. Barbara's Day, and continues until Epiphany, January 6. The Syrian father continued: "Each year we observe the feast in honor of St. Barbara. St. Barbara was a good girl; her faith and love toward God made her an example to the children. We arrange a table of sweetmeats prepared from nuts, sugar, honey, and wheat, the latter in memory of the dead and significant of the resurrection of the soul."

On St. Barbara's Eve the little Syrian children are taught lessons of unselfishness and thoughtfulness for others less fortunate than themselves. A prosperous family will look after a number of households, where either sorrow or poverty makes the usual celebration impossible. To homes where loved ones have passed away, sweetmeats are sent, and to the houses of the poor the children carry their little cakes saying, "May God bless you and bring you happiness every year. Father and mother beg you to accept these gifts from us."

Another custom of the Eve is for the boys, masked and dressed in fantastic robes, to go singing from door to door, demanding a blessing wherever they go. They are given such trifles as coins, eggs, and candies.

When the neighbors, relatives, and friends meet to celebrate the feast, all kinds of pastry such as *Buklawa, Burma*, and *Bkhout*, as well as many kinds of candy sweets, are prepared. Enough wheat is placed on the fire to serve all the guests. The cooking of the wheat is in remembrance of the event in the life of St. Barbara which is being commemorated, for as the wheat cooks the host tells the story of St. Barbara to his guests, which translated is as follows:

Barbara, the Saint, was elected of God,
She gave her bread to the poor,
Her miserly father rebuked her
And threatened her with his sword,
When he caught her with the bread in her lap
She cried unto God in her fear.
God turned the sword in her father's hand
Into a crochet needle.
When her father demanded to see
What she concealed in her lap
She cried unto God for help
And the bread in her lap turned to Roses.

A social hour takes place in which they dance and sing and play games during the cooking of the wheat. Then the hostess removes it from the fire and mixes sugar, rose water, and candy into it. Each of the girls in the party, as a sign that they have learned the lesson of the good Saint Barbara, come one by one to an old woman who anoints their eyes with an eye salve.

St. Nicholas Thaumaturgus, the Wonder Worker

On December 6 a special mass is said in the churches for St. Nicholas Thaumaturgus, the Wonder Worker. We have recounted the story of St. Nicholas on page 32, but the Syrians tell it a little differently. They say that when shipwrecked he sailed safely over the stormy seas in his hat. They tell how he went to a certain council meeting and performed the miracle of restoring life to his donkey which had been decapitated by robbers. Obviously, this St. Nicholas is another version of our modern Santa Claus.

Christmas Eve

On Christmas Eve pilgrims from Jerusalem and adjacent villages go to Bethlehem to attend services in Shepherds Fields. After prayer and song they proceed to the Church of the Nativity, there to kiss the silver star marking the spot where Christ was born. For a more complete discussion of the observance, see page 207.

In each Syrian church on Christmas Eve a bonfire of vine stems is made in the middle of the church in honor of the Magi who were cold from their journey. In the home on Christmas Eve the father tells the story of the Christ Child and all join in singing Christmas hymns.

Christmas Day

Christmas Day itself is observed very quietly. On that day and the next all shops and places of business are closed and no unnecessary work is done. The principal feature of the day is the holiday dinner, at which is served such delicacies as chicken, oranges, nuts, and Turkish Delight. The Syrian Christmas is not a period of merrymaking and exchanging of gifts but a season of prayer and quiet rejoicing. Children are taught to save their pennies for the Christ Child. One of the well-to-do ladies in the town usually sets up in her home what is known as the Bethlehem cave, another name for the Christmas Crib. The children bring their offerings, which are used for the relief of poor children.

The Day of Circumcision

January 1 is the Day of the Circumcision. With the Syrians this is a time of peculiar rejoicing. All work is laid aside, special mass is said, presents and good wishes are exchanged, and children go from door to door with New Years greetings, receiving candy and money in return. As on Christmas Day, the men visit from neighbor to neighbor, staying no longer than a half hour at any one home. The wives remain home to serve the guests with Turkish coffee and sweetmeats. On January 2 is the women's visiting day. The Syrians are particularly hospitable people and believe in sharing all good will and rejoicings with their friends.

The Night of Destiny

The ceremonies of Epiphany Eve are especially characteristic of Syrian holiday ideals. *Lilat-al-kadr* or the Night of Destiny is considered by the Latin Church as the time when the Magi presented their gifts to Christ, and by the Greek as the anniversary of His baptism. Regarding the Eve of January 6, many beliefs are held, differing according to locality. Only one tradition is universally accepted, the bowing of the trees; for it is thought that just at midnight on the eventful Eve, every tree bends its trunk and inclines its branches in homage to the Christ Child. Each tree offers its own peculiar gifts: fruit, nuts, or blossoms. This superstition was doubtless adapted from the Mohammedan which claims that Al Koran came from heaven on that night, and hence all trees (and according to some versions, all animals, too) bow in recognition of the divine revelation. Some say the trees, bending in reverence before the Magi who had worshipped the Infant Lord, revealed to them the "other way" by which they returned to their own country. The same story is told of how the trees directed the Holy Family as it fled into Egypt. To this day, the inhabitants of Cairo claim that a tree of rare healing powers marks the spot where Joseph, Mary, and the Child rested after their flight.

The Magic Mule

Many and varied are the tales connected with the bowing trees. Most interesting of all, however, is the Lebanon legend giving the origin of the Magic Mule, which in Syria corresponds to our Santa Claus.

Once, on the blessed Epiphany Eve, a certain man was traveling through the country on his mule. Stopping about midnight, he fastened his animal under a tree and went away on an important errand. When he returned later, he looked about for his beast until finally glacing upward, he saw it lifted high above his head in the topmost branches of the tree. This proved that just at the hour of midnight the tree had bent down in honor of the Christ Child, and, in its rebound, had caught up the animal. Since then the mule has been considered a blessed creature.

"When we were boys" smiled a Syrian, reminiscently, "I well remember waiting for the Magic Mule. We used to leave the doors wide open hoping that he would enter with blessings and gifts. We sprinkled grass from the threshold to the bed. We propped open our eyelids with our fingers in a vain attempt to keep awake, for the Mule could be seen only at the hour of twelve."

The Gentle Camel of Jesus

In southern Syria mules are less common, so the Gentle Camel of Jesus travels over the desert with presents for the children.   Legend says that this was the youngest camel of those which brought the Wise Men to the Christ Child. Exhausted by the journey, it lay moaning until Christ blessed it with immortality.   So the children sent out water and wheat.   The Camel loves all good children and gives them presents, but it makes a black mark on the wrists of those who are bad.

In many parts of southern Syria brightly burning candles placed in the windows, light the Christ Child on His way as He walks abroad over the Judaean hills.   Perhaps the original desire, as in other lands, was to show the eagerness of all to welcome Him into their homes.

The Blessed Leaven

A universal custom on Epiphany Eve is the making of the Blessed Leaven.   Every good housewife prepares dough, places a silver coin in the middle, and, wrapping all in a cloth, hangs it in the branches of a tree. Turpentine pods and sage, both giving forth a sweet odor like incense, are hung with the dough; oftentimes also, other objects are included upon which a special blessing is desired. At midnight, so it is said, the dough becomes leaven.   At dawn of the Baptism Day the dough is taken from the trees. Boys and girls carry it to the streams and fountains where they immerse it three times in the water, according to the Greek Orthodox form of baptism. By this means the blessing is completed. As the rite is being performed, the children sing: "John the Baptist is the Baptiser and Mary was his Godmother." The Syrian housewives keep the lump of risen dough throughout the year and use it as yeast until the next Epiphany season. One old Syrian woman says regarding the custom of making leaven, "Oh, but I have tried it in your land and nothing happened. Therefore our country must be peculiarly hallowed."

The Wonder Night

As the Epiphany Eve is considered the Wonder Night of all the year, many strange things are said to happen to the very devout. No unconfessed sin may be upon the soul, and no vow left unfulfilled; no surprise or haste must be shown; and there can be no greed; else the miracle will not occur. But if the heart is pure, special blessing will be shown. The women say, for example:

If you bathe on this night, your body will become strong and beautiful.

If you comb your hair, holy sparks will fly and it will grow long and shining.

If you draw water from the well just at midnight, it will turn to gold.

If you make any wish and have faith in its fulfillment, it will come to pass.

But woe to the faithless and to the greedy! Take for instance the story of the woman with the red cap. On this night of miracles she placed a tub of water beneath a tree and seated herself inside it saying, "I'll sit here until midnight and see for myself if this tree bends and if the water in this tub turns to gold." Now God in His wisdom caused the woman to sleep soundly until dawn. When she awoke and looked overhead, she beheld the red cap she had worn hanging in the upper branches. Thus it was proved to her that the tree had bowed at midnight, but because of her lack of faith, the tub still contained water instead of gold.

In some sections of Syria, on the Baptism Night, men,
women, and children bathe in the streams and pools. To
the sinless the waters are warm but to others they remain
icy cold.

The Miracle of Increase

On Epiphany Eve the Night of Increase occurs to the
very holy. The old women still have faith in this miracle
which did, they declare, occur many times to their grand-
mothers in their native land. For instance, here is a story
told about a great grandmother, a woman who was nearly one
hundred years old and was accounted very blessed. One
year, desiring to give Epiphany cakes to many poor people,
she put all her store of nuts, honey, and fruits into a bowl
and prayerfully began stirring the ingredients. The mixture
increased and was poured into a larger vessel which it soon
overflowed. Finally in surprise and dismay, she cried aloud,
"Oh, what shall I do with it all?" The change in her spirit
caused the immediate cessation of the miracle.

On the Night of Increase it is customary for every old
woman to go to the cellar and shake her jars of wheat, oil,
and wine. If her faith is strong, the stores will multiply as
did the cruse of oil and handful of meal
of Zarephath's widow in the days of
Elijah. Many Syrian women have assured me of the truth of this miracle.
A woman living in Washington Street,
New York, told me how her grandmother
once entered her storeroom on Epiphany
Eve and noticed that the oil was gushing
forth as if every jar were broken. More
jars were brought and the oil became a
source of great profit to the family who
saved every drop of it.

Syrian cruses for
the holy oil on the
Night of Increase

The material found in this article is derived from notes gathered
by Dorothy G. Spicer of National Institute of Immigrant Welfare and
gleaned directly from Syrians living in Washington Street, New York,

and in the vicinity of Atlantic Avenue, Clinton, and Pacific Streets, Brooklyn, N. Y. Besides this, the following were consulted:

Van Slyke, L. B., *In the Country Where Babe Jesus Was Born.* Delineator, 1911, Vol. 78, p. 509.

Rihbany, A. M., *Syrian Christ.*   Boston, Houghton, 1916, p. 383–387.

Additional information on the subject of Syrian customs, traditions, and superstitions may be obtained from the following publications:

Huxley, H. M., *Syrian Songs, Proverbs and Stories, Journal of American Oriental Society,* 1902. Vol. 23, pt. 2, p. 12–228.

Rouse, W. H. D., *Notes from Syria. Folklore Society,* 1895. Vol. 36, p. 172–175.

Wilson, H. B. *Notes of Syrian Folklore Collected in Boston. Journal of American Folklore,* 1903. Vol. 16, p. 133–147.

CHRISTMAS IN THE WORLD WAR TRENCHES

Even the discipline of the German army was not strong enough to keep the spirit of Christmas out of the trenches. In *A German Deserter's War Experience* (B. W. Huebsch), the author, an anti-government Socialist, tells of a Christmas celebration on the Argonne front.

"Christmas in the trenches! It was bitterly cold. We had procured a Pine tree and decorated it with candles and cookies.

"Christmas trees were burning everywhere in the trenches, and at midnight all the trees were lifted on to the parapet with their burning candles, and along the whole line German soldiers began to sing Christmas songs in chorus. 'O du froeliche, O du selige, gnaden bringende Weihnachtszeit' ('O thou blissful, O thou joyous, mercy-bringing Christmas-time!')—hundreds of men were singing the song in that fearful wood.

"The French left their trenches and stood on the parapet without any fear. There they stood, quite overpowered by emotion, and all of them with cap in hand. We, too, had issued from our trenches. We exchanged gifts with the French —chocolate, cigarettes, etc. They were all laughing, and so were we; why, we did not know. Then everybody went back to his trench, and incessantly the carol resounded, ever more solemnly, ever more longingly—'O thou blissful—'.

"All around silence reigned; even the murdered trees seemed to listen. The charm continued, and one scarcely dared to speak. Why could it not always be as peaceful ? We thought and thought, we were as dreamers, and had forgotten everything about us. Suddenly a shot rang out, then another one was fired somewhere. The spell was broken. All rushed to their rifles. Our Christmas was over."

THESE UNITED STATES OF AMERICA

Our United States are scattered across a vast territory inhabited by the peoples from all sections of Europe. Christmas comes to each of us with different traditions. Could we be in all places at once on Christmas Eve we would surely stop suddenly to say that this is not our country after all.

Each evening for a week last year the writer attended a different New York Christmas celebration. Going from the International Institute, the International Y. M. C. A., International House to the homes of the people, I saw quaint Swedish folk dances, British Mummer plays and also the party of the ever-so-serious German Youth Movement where no one applauded the splendid speeches, solos, zither selections, and food.

But to adequately describe Christmas in New York, we would need to enter millions of homes each with their own traditions. We would find the Dutch, for instance, celebrating on December 5, for that is St. Nicholas Day—when gifts are distributed. Then we would have a continuous round of Christmas festivity until January 6, Twelfth Night, when many of the Eastern nations are presenting their gifts following the belief that it was on this night that the Wise Men brought their gifts to the Christ Child.

We would find that some of foreign citizens think of Christmas as a strict, religious holiday—no gifts, no feast, but midnight mass. We would enter the churches to find the Lutherans and Catholics have elaborate Christmas Cribs.

We might attend the vesper services at the Church of the Intercession and join the lantern-lighted procession across busy Broadway to the grave of Dr. Clement Moore, author of the favorite Christmas poem, "The Visit of St. Nicholas." (See page 41.)

If, on the other hand, we could visit the South we would find the day not only warm but the night air would be filled with fireworks and sound of cannon crackers. If we visited Yosemite we could attend the dinner staged to simulate the days of Washington Irving where a feast is held in the Ahwahnee Hotel, much like that described on page 104.

If we visited Bethlehem, Pennsylvania, we would see the old customs of the Pennsylvania-Dutch surviving with the elaborate construction of the Putz, an adaptation of the Christmas Crib (see page 50) but including a whole landscape of sheep, camels, buildings, with a tree quite subordinated.*

A few celebrations associated with various sections and periods of America follow but many of the customs are found elsewhere in this book.

Christmas in Colonial Times

Of Christmas in Colonial times little is recorded in the histories, because history is more often concerned with wars and politics. Naturally, the colonists in Virginia, Maryland, and Georgia brought over the English customs, whereas in New York, New Jersey, Pennsylvania, and Delaware, the customs came from Holland, Sweden, and Germany. The Moravian Germans observed Christmas as purely religious. The Quakers near Philadelphia were not given to observing holidays, and in New England the whole idea of Christmas was frowned upon.

The Puritans were bitterly opposed to it, and such Episcopalians as there were celebrated it, but being in the minor-

*Hark, Ann. *Country Gentleman*, December, 1936. This is a splendid source of material on Christmas in Bethlehem, Pennsylvania.

ity, their practices were not liked by their fellow citizens.

In Massachusetts, in 1659, a law was passed which read: "Whosoever shall be found observing any such day as Christmas, or the like, either by forebearing of labor, feasting in any other way, shall be fined 5 shillings." This was a law for 22 years, and Christmas was not a legal holiday until late in the first half of the XIX Century.*

Governor Bradford rebuked boys for playing a game on Christmas Day. They replied that it was against their conscience to work, and he retorted that it was against his conscience that they should play through the day, which was meant for labor. "Work or go to jail," was his edict. The Puritans were impressed only with the excesses of the season, and struck it from their calendar as a season of frivolous excitement.

Our early ancestors did not seem to lack good food at Christmastime and here are some of the things that were available for the Christmas feast: beef, pork, mutton, turkey, wild duck, rabbit, and squirrel, together with codfish, mackerel, and oysters. Among vegetables there were pumpkins, potatoes, beans, parsnips, turnips, and carrots. Of fruits there were apples, pears, and quinces, together with a plentiful supply of such preserves as blueberry, raspberry, blackberry, strawberry, and grapes. For sweetening and for the making of various confections there were honey, maple syrup, molasses candy, and sugar.

Beacon Hill Carols

So charming is the custom of singing carols in the old Beacon Hill district of Boston that the writer must pass on to you at least a brief excerpt of the story as told by Warren Ordway† and by Annie Bryant.‡

*Geyer, Ellen and James, Dr. Alfred, from *Pittsburgh Radio Publication 43*, University of Pittsburgh, 1928.

†Ordway, Warren. *Carols and Candles on Christmas Eve*, Lincoln and Smith Press, 516 Atlantic Avenue, Boston, Mass.

‡Bryant, Annie. *Christmas at Beacon Hill*. Dennison Manufacturing Co. An interesting addition to the material here used.

"Noel, Noel," sing the carolers on Beacon Hill, and in reply myriads of candles flickering in small-paned windows return a bright "Merry Christmas ! "

There is nothing quite like Christmas Eve on Beacon Hill. The hush that falls when motors are gone seems more than silence—it is time itself turning back the centuries until we live in a land of imagination, where automobiles are a fantastic dream. "Peace on Earth," for a few hours, here, becomes a reality.

It seems strange that such a colorful custom as candle lighting and singing carols should have started in very Boston, where about 230 years ago, an act was passed by the early settlers of the Colony, forbidding the observance of the "Festival of Christmas and kindred ones, superstitiously kept."

To come for the first time into Louisburg Square, bright with Christmas candles, is to enjoy an unforgettable experience. The whole scene makes it seem more like a bit of Dickens' London than staid Boston! One expects to see rotund Mr. Pickwick emerging from some friendly doorway!

Then, to join the good natured jostling crowds and wander through the narrow streets and queer little squares and courts is a delight. Everywhere, the old paneled doorways with their brass knockers are bright with Holly and Laurel. Through the candle-lit windows we can glimpse Christmas trees, and the gleam of old Sheffield silver, the rich brown of Chippendale and Sheraton sideboards, and the beauty of old family portraits.

Among the pleasantest things to see are the Christmas decorations in the windows, which reflect the taste and hobbies of the householders. There are simple baskets of fruit and little Christmas trees, as well as more elaborate arrangements, using such beautiful things as jewel-like bits of stained glass or rich embroidered altar cloths and vestments from ancient churches. Most of these have foreign figures, some of them are rare pieces of old Italian wood-carving, before which boys and girls knelt years before their countryman discovered America.

Of course, carols have been sung for years, but in 1910, Mrs. Ralph Adams Cram persuaded a few friends to light their windows and join her in singing a few carols. The next year more friends were induced to join her and the circle widened until there were enough to form "The Chestnut Street Christmas Association," which was largely responsible for the universal acceptance of the custom on the Hill.

Virginia—Negro Christmas Custom

"Well, yes sir," said he, "we Negroes have a little different Christmas custom in Virginia than I have observed in the Northern states.

"Early Christmas Eve our Mammy spread a big sheet over the dining room table with a box here and there to make the sheet stand above the table level. We then wrote our names on slips of paper and pinned them on the cloth. During the night we sneaked in with our gifts and placed them under each person's name.

"When morning came the youngest children could hardly wait, for the presents were not revealed until all the family was up. Then Grandmammy and Uncle Joe grasped the corners of the sheet and lifted it to reveal all the presents hidden beneath.

"Eggnog was served and soon breakfast was ready—such a breakfast that we never cared much for Christmas dinner. Folks just dropped in and we ate when they came. Just pieced all day, I'd call it."

Los Pastores

In San Antonio, Texas, each year a hybrid Spanish-Indian play, Los Pastores* is given. It has no definite time for beginning, for the actors must come when work is finished.

*Goldschmidt, Thea, Bulletin 66 of the Pan American Union, 1932. Another account may be read in Junior League Magazine, December, 1931, a story by Mary Aubrey Keating.

It secretly takes place in someone's back yard—no curtains, no properties. It is desired that none shall see the miracle play who comes for idle curiosity rather than for its spirituality. It was introduced to Mexico by Spanish monks. It is given from Christmas to Candlemas by an amateur group who go by invitation from house to house.

At one end of the yard is an altar—of rude wood, covered with black sateen, which becomes the background for *nacimiento*, manger scene. On the steps the family places the various objects from their homes which are to them choice and beautiful—Christmas cards, tinsel, pincushions, patron saints. Streamers of crepe paper decked with roses hang from above. In the center of the lowest step the Christ Child (a life sized doll) is placed on a platter of gaudy Christmas candies. Near this may be small plaster donkeys, shepherds—in sizes disproportionate to each other and the Christ Child.

Opposite the *nacimiento*, at the other end of the yard, is a tent with lurid volcanoes, devils, fire, and brimstone. The emergence of live devils and the fact that a bonfire is burning give evidence that it is meant to be hell.

Finally, the play begins. Perhaps a shy girl dressed as an angel comes out and walks back and forth reciting. Then come shepherds, dressed in pink coats with tinsel and silver braid, a beaded satchel over the shoulder, suspended by broad red ribbon. Each carries a highly ornamental staff. They drone a seemingly endless song. Behind them comes Ermitano, a hermit, the comic relief who wears a long grey robe festooned with moss, and carries a wooden cross or a rosary of spools, and wears the mask of an old man with white beard. He also represents the good in the world—the soul on its earthly journey. He is often accompanied by the Archangel Gabriel, a boy dressed in white with large paper wings, a crown of silver and a sword.

Then follow seven devils, six in dead black with sequins and the masks of animals, and then Lucifer in brilliant red, with a forked tail. Each wears a sparkler in his cap.

It is a never-ending performance. The devils are finally vanquished, and the shepherds kiss the Child.

A wild Indian enters and there is a combat with him. He is finally subdued, and kisses the Child. Then all in attendance solemnly and as slowly as possible, approach the altar to pay respects to the Babe. Candy and food are given to the troop.

Only the initiated can find this Los Pastores for it is in out-of-the-way places. The Mexican never tires of seeing it again and again.

INDEX